1938. England *v* Scotland at Twickenham. The Scottish captain, R. W. Shaw, after a brilliant solo run, beats the England full-back on the touch line to score the first of his two tries, to make the score 12–9 at half-time. Just before 'no-side' he scored a second individual try which made the final score 21–16 in Scotland's favour.

THE SCOTTISH RUGBY UNION

Official History

THE
SCOTTISH RUGBY UNION

Official History

A. M. C. THORBURN

Published by the
SCOTTISH RUGBY UNION
in association with
COLLINS PUBLISHERS

© Plates and Text 1985
The Scottish Rugby Union
Murrayfield, Edinburgh

Published by
William Collins
    Sons and Company Limited

British Library Cataloguing
    in Publication Data
Scottish Rugby Union
The Scottish Rugby Union: official history.
1. Scottish Rugby Union—History
I. Title
796.33'3'060411   GV9448
ISBN 0 00 435697 7

CONTENTS

Set in Linoterm Melior
by Speedspools, Edinburgh

Text printing and binding:
Clark Constable Ltd, Edinburgh

Printing of illustrations and jacket:
Ivanhoe Printing Co., Musselburgh

Process work:
Kings Town Engraving & Co. Ltd, Hull

Text paper:
Wm. Sommerville & Son, Penicuik

Paper for illustrations and jacket:
Donald Murray (Paper) Ltd

Design and Production:
John McI. Davidson (Royal High RFC)

Jacket design:
Adam Robson (Past President, SRU)

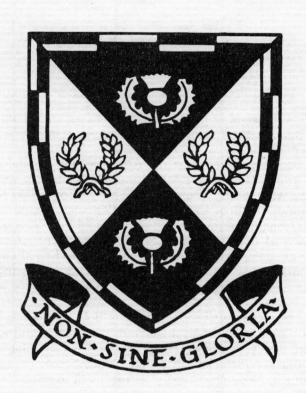

·NON·SINE·GLORIA·

FOREWORD

IT gives me the greatest possible pleasure to be writing the foreword
to this official history. The writing of the book is in itself an interesting piece of history.

The research was begun at the request of the Committee of the
Scottish Rugby Union in 1969 by the late R.Ironside and A.M.C.
Thorburn, who jointly produced the very appropriate booklet to
commemorate the Scotland v England Centenary match in 1971. In
1975 Bob Ironside retired from the project having done much commendable work in developing it. Sandy Thorburn then rewrote much
of the original material, in which he was aided by the additional
information he had compiled when preparing his own book *The
History of Scottish Rugby*, a valuable source of reference which was
published in 1980.

A Book Sub-Committee, convened by Bob Munro and including
Adam Robson (President in the Grand Slam year) and Jock Steven,
along with Sandy Thorburn (Honorary Historian and Librarian of the
Union), John Davidson and Bill Hogg (Union Secretary), took up the
manuscript in November 1983. The results of the Sub-Committee's
efforts are now contained within this publication. I would pay a
special tribute to the parts played by John Davidson, who has given
great assistance with the text and appendices and in the selection of
photographs, and by Bruce Stenhouse, who has collaborated in the
text and the yearly summaries.

May I close by wishing you the greatest of pleasure in reading this
book, which I am sure will do much to place on record and give a full
understanding of matters in Scottish Rugby over the last 110 years
and finishing with the best of all possible closing chapters, that on a
Triple Crown and Grand Slam.

J. W. Y. KEMP
President, SRU, 1984—85

1. J. W. Y. KEMP
President, 1984-85

2. PAST PRESIDENTS AND OFFICE-BEARERS, 27.2.1909

Standing: A. B. Flett 1907-08 (Edin. Univ.), J. W. Simpson 1904-05 (RHSFP), R. C. Greig 1903-04 (Glas. Acads.), D. S. Morton 1892-93 (WOS), B. Hall Blyth 1875-76 (Merchistonians), W. H. Kidston 1876-77 (WOS), R. S. Davidson 1902-03 (RHSFP), T. Ainslie 1891-92 (Edin. Inst. FP), G. T. Neilson 1901-02 (WOS). *Seated*: J. A. Smith, Hon. Secretary 1890-1914 (RHSFP), J. D. Boswell 1898-99 (WOS), M. Cross 1884-85 (Glas. Acads.), D. G. Findlay 1896-97 (WOS), A. Harvey 1874-75 (Glas. Acads.), D. Y. Cassels, President 1908-09 (WOS), A. Buchanan 1879-80 (RHSFP), L. M. Balfour-Melville 1893-34 (Edin. Acads.), R. D. Rainie 1897-98 (Edin. Wrs.), I. McIntyre 1899-1900 (Fet.-Lor.), A. S. Blair, Vice-President 1908-09 (Fet.-Lor.).

3. PAST PRESIDENTS AND OFFICE-BEARERS, JANUARY 1928

Standing: J. D. Dallas 1912-13 (Watsonians), A. B. Flett 1907-08 (Edin. Univ.), R. T. Neilson 1923-24 (WOS), J. M. Dykes 1920-22 (Glas. HSFP), I. McIntyre 1899-1900 (Fet.-Lor.), T. Scott 1914-15 and 1919-20 (Langholm), R. C. Greig 1903-04 (Glas. Acads.), R. Welsh 1925-26 (Watsonians), C. J. N. Fleming 1910-11 (Fet.-Lor.), G. T. Neilson 1901-02 (WOS), J. D. Boswell 1898-99 (Fet.-Lor.). *Seated:* A. S. Blair 1909-10 (Fet.-Lor.), D. S. Morton 1892-93 (WOS), Sir R. C. Mackenzie 1924-25 (Glas. Acads.), J. Aikman Smith 1926-27 (RHSFP), M. M. Duncan, President 1927-28 (Fet.-Lor.), Sir D. McCowan, Vice-President 1927-28 (WOS), L. M. Balfour-Melville 1893-94 (Edin. Acads.), R. S. Davidson 1902-03 (RHSFP), R. D. Rainie 1897-98 (Edin. Wrs.). *In front:* J. T. Tulloch 1906-07 (Kelvinside Acads.), J. R. C. Greenlees 1913-14 (Fet.-Lor.).

4. A. ROBSON
President, 1983-84

INTRODUCTION

ALL rugby-playing nations owe something to William Webb Ellis. He can justifiably be rated a great legendary figure in the annals of sport, such is the mutual acceptance of the likelihood that he was the catalyst in the evolution of the game of rugby. It was over sixteen decades ago at Rugby School since reputedly he caught the ball and under the existing rules he should have remained stationary or retreated—his opponents were not allowed to pursue him—but he chose to run forward with the ball in his hands. His very unorthodox reaction proved to have astonishing repercussions in the long term and was, of course, the distinctive feature of the handling game which was to develop. Curiosity about the origins of this fascinating ball-carrying phenomenon led the former pupils of Rugby School to investigate the origins of rugby, and in 1895 they concluded that in 1820 the fashionable form of football at the school was more akin to the Association code; that at some date between 1820 and around 1830 running with the ball in the hand was introduced; that in all probability William Webb Ellis was the instigator of that wonderfully creative touch in 1823.

There are claimants who aver that Ellis was of English origin. They theorise that he was born in Manchester. Undeniably he did attend Rugby School. No question. There are also those who imply that Ellis first saw the light of day in the Irish county of Tipperary. Certainly the Irish could maintain that he had enough sense in him to be Irish! Probably the Welsh would confirm that he was good enough to justify Welsh nationality. And the Scots would hardly demur—for William Webb Ellis is universal to the eternal brotherhood and fraternity of world rugby. Any man who had the spontaneous vision which must have stirred the imaginations of those around him on that remarkable day, and who sowed the seeds of a game of incredible value, would be worthy of immortality in the eyes of any nation. What his non-conformist move initiated ultimately caught the fancy of countless thousands; and the outcome of it all continues unabated today in a multitude of countries throughout the world.

That Ellis was a man of intellectual and spiritual resource is revealed by the fact that he was ordained a minister in the Church of England. Probably he would have subscribed to an interpretation of that passage from the Book of Proverbs in the Bible, 'A gift is as a precious stone in the eyes of him that hath it: whithersoever it turneth, it prospereth'. Had he been alive today and had he realised and appreciated what he had sparked-off, great would have been his wonderment and supreme pleasure at the thought of how his gift to sport had indeed prospered. Further, his versatility was confirmed when he felt moved to write a poem on the theme of ale! The beverage has been universally popular with rugby men from time immemorial. Their preferences are perhaps not far short of those of their benefactor in the handling game—a sustained love and enthusiasm for the amateur code, with a zest amounting to religious fanaticism, and an interest in the appropriate beverage in a game so robust and vigorous that the loss of body fluid needs replenishment!

That amateur code is derived from a clear-cut basic principle; 'one who cultivates a particular study or art for the love of it, and not professionally'. The concept is idealistic and entirely worthy, and it seems to me that throughout this history of the Scottish Rugby Union the motivation and deep involvement of successive committees have stemmed from the inspiration of William Webb Ellis and traditional values created by our early forebears in rugby in Scotland, as in other countries.

Undoubtedly there are aspects of society today which are under stress and attitudes leave much to be desired. Frequently worthy human values like fair play, restraint and tolerence are under attack, and any bulwark to safeguard such virtues is to be commended. Because the rugby ethic manages to retain its fundamental code of honour, it is a force for the positive rather than the negative; although complacency is not a word in the vocabulary of rugby and trends are carefully monitored so that the amateur spirit is safeguarded. Rugby has an astonishing knack of occupying a good deal of life without ever threatening to be all of life. Somehow it ensures its own continuity by retaining the interest and enthusiasm of so many men whose playing days have passed them by, but who are captivated by a way of life. Such men—and there are many of them—are strong strands in the fabric of this story, so meticulously and caringly researched by Sandy Thorburn and his contributors.

These committee-men of the Scottish Rugby Union have countenanced the challenges, the opportunities, the problems, the satisfactions, the valuable relationships of every facet of the game, for Scottish rugby and in the cause of Scottish rugby. They have come to realise and appreciate that its kinship does offer an astonishing variety and experience of dimensions of life.

Contrast the picture of an excited host of small boys indulging in mini-rugby prior to the 100th match between Scotland and England on 4th February 1984; for them an unforgettable and cherished experience in their young lives; and beyond the embankment of the south terracing of Murrayfield a War Memorial carrying the legend 'In proud memory of the Scottish Rugby Men who gave their lives in the Great War of 1914/18. Honour also those who followed them. 1939–45. . . '. Rugby cares. There is much which is objective; there is much which is subjective, and these generations of administrators have made a particular study of the subject and the art of rugby—for the love of it.

As the story unfolds, the human elements are inescapable: there are differences; there are disagreements. Yet these come about frequently through sincerely-felt principles, if on occasion perhaps misguided. But in the complex fabric of so many successive committees there is interwoven a golden thread of belief in all that is good in rugby football, and a determination, an ongoing resolution, to safeguard the best in the game and the quality of its traditions. There is the old adage that a man who knows the value of the past can be trusted with the present, although we must always be mindful of Samuel Johnson's remark which must have been prompted by his outlook on living, 'The business of life is to go forward'.

If there have been occasions throughout the decades when the Scots seemed slow to accept change, it has surely stemmed from a caution born of respect for a game which has offered so much to generations of players, where people are good company because they are doing what they enjoy, untainted and untarnished by deals and commercialism. Basically the values and safeguards in all their complexity have not altered, yet in the game itself there have been positive and impressive changes which radically influenced opportunity and scope on the field for a more adventurous style of play. For example, the International Board altered the Laws to discourage unnecessary kicking and looked again at creating more space for attackers by changing offside lines. That was not far short of twenty years ago. Such alterations for the good of the players and the game had the full support of the Scots.

On the other hand they have resisted, along with the International Board, the possibility of interference with the broad principle of Amateur Rugby Union Football that 'no-one is allowed to seek or to receive payment or other material reward for taking part in the game'.

It seems to me that these two examples epitomise the wide implications for those who love this game. There is the playing of rugby, a tough body-contact sport. What it continues to seek from individuals and teams are high standards of fair play and sportsmanship through self- and team-discipline; to know the value of give and take; to play hard and fast, but to be tolerant of opponents; to seek the ball and not the man; to be aware of the Laws and beyond them to that subtle element dubbed the Spirit of the Game—game by game. Then at the end of the day those simple niceties of the 'three cheers' and hand-shakes are not trite or mere formalities, but given genuinely and sincerely to opponents who may be about to become new friends or who are already friends for life. Then the game takes on that additional dimension of human relationships—where the satisfaction of participating is the just reward—which can do so much to encourage those who are in the playing of the game to stay with it in later life and thus ensure its continuity. Surely there are so many here involved in this history who have fallen under the spell of the pure amateurism of rugby and who, along with countless others in the club scene, have come to realise that it is a sport which is a right sport for generations to come on the Scottish scene.

Ultimately any game is about people, and our particular sport engenders a caring which transcends the game itself. Its internationalism in terms of fellowship, friendship and mutual respect is universally acknowledged. It is capable of eroding prejudices and overcoming barriers because it offers chance and scope to all, regardless of creed, class or political persuasion. Its traditions and folklore stimulate reminiscence and anecdote. It is a game of optimism in which hope springs eternal, a challenge to the young, a wellspring of associations and an ongoing vital source of interest to the middle-aged; also a splendid fount of contentment and containing the happiest of memories for the elderly. So be it. William Webb Ellis has a lot to answer for!

ADAM ROBSON
President, SRU, 1983—84

LIST OF ILLUSTRATIONS

AUTHOR'S ACKNOWLEDGEMENTS

I WISH to record my appreciation of the earlier work done by the late Bob Ironside, work which saw the production, in 1971, of the SRU booklet dealing with the first rugby International of 1871.

Since restarting on this present History I have been greatly indebted to two rugby-loving and knowledgeable friends. Firstly, to Bruce Stenhouse who, having read through the manuscript, offered much valued comment and put me on the track of some of the photographs which added to the text. Secondly, to John McI. Davidson whose expert guidance and assistance on the printing and publishing of the work cannot be over-emphasised. Throughout the latter difficulties that beset us, he gave freely of his time and knowledge to ensure that our timetable could be met. I would additionally acknowledge the help and assistance from Bill McMurtrie in factually checking the text and appendixes.

My thanks are also due to the ladies of the SRU office staff who so expertly found time to turn my manuscript into acceptable copy.

I would also thank the press (newspapers, magazines and photographers) and libraries for their willing help and assistance with photographs. Acknowledgement has been given to all sources which can be identified and I would ask all those whose names we could not trace to accept my thanks for use of their photographs and my apology for not being able to give acknowledgement.

Lastly, I offer sincere thanks to the following International players who, by answering our appeal for action photographs, sent in some splendid pictures which embellish the bare text: J. Aitken, W. D. Allardyce, J. L. Cotter, W. H. Crawford, J. T. Docherty, P. L. Duff, R. A. Gallie, R. J. C. Glasgow, R. A. Howie, J. M. Hunter, A. R. Irvine, T. G. H. Jackson, J. M. Kerr, D. G. Leslie, D. J. Macrae, I. G. McCrae, K. W. Marshall, J. A. Nichol, A. Robson, D. M. D. Rollo, B. M. Simmers, K. M. Spence, F. O. Turnbull, H. Waddell, T. G. Weatherstone, J. S. Wilson and R. L. Wilson; and Mrs Judith Smith.

A.M.C.T.

ACKNOWLEDGEMENT OF
ILLUSTRATIONS

THE Scottish Rugby Union wishes to acknowledge, with grateful thanks, the use of the following illustrations:

Jim M. Aird: plate 11.
Air View Ltd: plate 21.
Aerial Photographic Services (UK): plate 22.
The Arthur Family: plate 118.
Associated Newspapers Ltd: plate 97.
Associated Press: plate 80.
Alex. Ayton: plates 3, 4, 13(b), 17 and 18.
Balmain, Edinburgh: plate 8(b).
The Blair Family: plate 7(e).
Central Press: plate 107.
Mrs Cuthbertson: plate 8(c).
Edin. Acads. FC: plates 7(a), 7(d) and 14(b).
Edinburgh Evening Dispatch: plate 105.
Edinburgh University: plate 8(a).
The Football Association: plate 9(c).
The Glasgow Herald: plates 23, 72 and 88.
Hulton Press: plate 98.
A. L. Hunter: plate 115 and bookjacket.
Illustrated Sporting & Dramatic News: plate 20.
Illustrated London News: plate 110 and endpaper.
Irish Press: plate 90.
Mark Leech: plates 30, 75 and 76.
The Macdonald Family: plate 9(b).
Mayfair Studio, Port Elizabeth: plate 33.
Mitchell Library: plate 7(c).
National Library of Scotland: plates 13(a) and 14(a).
Photo Illustrated: plate 91.
Harley-Richmond Studio: plates 9(a), 114, 116, 117, 119, 120 and 121.
L. Robson & Son: plate 12(a).
Royal Bank of Scotland: plate 12(b).
Schola Regia: plates 7(b) and 7(f).
The Scotsman: plates 8(e), 24, 25, 26, 27, 28, 29, 31, 32, 66, 67, 73, 78, 79, 83, 84, 85, 86, 100 and 104.
Scottish *Daily Record*: plate 82.
Ian Smith: plates 111 and 112.
Sport & General Press: plate 106.
Bob Thomas Sports Photography: plates 69, 70 and 71.
Western Mail: plates 68 and 77.
Yerbury, Edinburgh: plates 1, 2, 5, 6, 8(d), 10, 36, 37, 39, 40, 41, 42, 43, 44, 45, 55, 56 and 65.

ABBREVIATIONS

AAA	Amateur Athletic Association
Aust.	Australia
BI	British Isles
Cos.	Counties
DL	Deputy Lieutenant
DRU	District Rugby Union
Edin. Inst.	Edinburgh Institution
Fet.-Lor.	Fettesian-Lorettonians
FFR	Fédération Française de Rugby
FP	Former Pupil(s)
GS	Grammar School
HS	High School
Hon. Sec. & Tr.	Honorary Secretary and Treasurer
IB	International Board
IRU	Irish Rugby Union
LI	London Irish
LS	London Scottish
LW	London Welsh
Mon.	Monmouth
NSW	New South Wales
NZ	New Zealand
R(D)VC	Royal (Dick) Veterinary College
RHS	Royal High School (Edinburgh)
RFU	Rugby Football Union (England)
SA	South Africa
SAAA	Scottish Amateur Athletic Association
SFU	Scottish Football Union (1873–1924)
SRU	Scottish Rugby Union (1924–)
Stew.-Mel. FP	Stewart's-Melville College FP
TC	Training College
USFSA	Union des Sociétés Françaises des Sports Athlétiques
Wrs.	Wanderers
WOS	West of Scotland RFC
WRU	Welsh Rugby Union
XV	Team of fifteen players
XX	Team of twenty players

1

THE BEGINNINGS

SINCE the development of the handling game of football in Scotland has been adequately covered elsewhere it is not necessary to look further back than the middle of the nineteenth century to lay a foundation for this history of the Scottish Rugby Union. The industrial upsurge of that age, demanding six long days of hard work each week, left the artisan population with little time or energy for vigorous recreation and it was almost only at various annual Fair Day festivities that the once popular pastime of football was seen. Indeed, if it had not been continued by the more leisured groups of school pupils and university students, the game might well have disappeared altogether.

In the Edinburgh area the pioneer work of a few schoolmasters, notably T. Harvey, J. J. Rogerson and H. H. Almond, who each held firm beliefs in the value of outdoor exercises for their pupils, saw the Rugby School rules of football successfully grafted on to the older Scottish game, and by 1863, the handling game was well established in schools in the Edinburgh area, particularly in The Academy, Merchiston, Loretto and The High School. These schools, each possessing their own playing-field, had earlier begun to play matches against one another. The earliest known inter-school match, Merchiston v High School, took place in February 1858; whilst the second, Edinburgh Academy v Merchiston in December 1858, can claim to be the oldest continuous fixture in the history of the game of rugby football.

The genesis of the future Union may be found in this closely linked group of Edinburgh schools. The Academy, Merchiston and Loretto (with Fettes College after 1870) attracted many pupils from other regions of Scotland; the Academy (1857) and Merchiston (1860) were the first to inaugurate Former Pupil clubs and many of the ex-pupils of these schools, after returning to their family homes and businesses, were to play prominent parts in originating new or sustaining existing senior clubs in their home areas. This was particularly true

1

for Glasgow, where the West of Scotland FC (1865) and the Glasgow Academical FC (1866) benefited greatly from such an influx of players from the Edinburgh schools. These early links between the first senior clubs of the two cities, helped by the existence of a good railway service, undoubtedly played an important part in the rapid establishment of fixtures between the two regions and the beginning of club rugby in Scotland.

At their inception these matches exposed undesirable variations in the rules followed by the different clubs, and eventually, in 1868, the Edinburgh Academical FC, after consulting with others, including the schools, drew up and printed a set of Rules which carried the title 'Laws of Football as played by the Principal Clubs of Scotland'. This, known as 'The Green Book', was to govern the main matches in Scotland until after the first International match with England in 1871. Neither the clubs nor the Green Book found it necessary to include the word 'Rugby' in their titles because the Association game only appeared in Scotland with the formation of the Queen's Park FC in Glasgow in 1867.

A similar diversity of rules existed in England, and when the Old Boys of the half-dozen or so well-known public schools met to play football at the universities the need for a unified code was discerned. It was, however, not until 1863 that a meeting of the club players in London formed the Football Association, whose Rules of play required only eleven players in each team and forbade the general handling or carrying of the ball. Blackheath and other city clubs who favoured a handling game refused to join this new body and apparently continued to use the Blackheath Rules printed in 1862 and based on the Rugby School Rules of 1846.

This new Association proved to be an active body, and after organising several successful games, staged in March and November of 1870 two matches in London labelled 'England v Scotland'. The Scotland teams consisted entirely of men resident in London and this engendered a newspaper correspondence (fully recorded in the SRU booklet on the 1871 Scotland v England game) which culminated in a letter dated 8 December 1870, placed in *The Scotsman* and *Bell's Life in London*, in which the captains of the West of Scotland, Edinburgh Academical, Merchistonian, Glasgow Academical, and St Salvator (St Andrews) clubs issued a challenge to the English rugby-playing clubs. This challenge was accepted by the Blackheath FC on behalf of the others and resulted in the first Rugby International match between Scotland and England being played at Raeburn Place, Edinburgh, on Monday, 27 March 1871.

It is quite possible this challenge accelerated another project, because the English Rugby Clubs, after a preliminary notice in late

2

December 1870, held a meeting in London in January 1871 at which they formed the Rugby Football Union. This body, though it did not take over the arrangements for the forthcoming International, quickly produced an official code of Rules of Play which was adopted at its first AGM in October 1871. Importantly, six Scottish Clubs (West of Scotland, Glasgow Academicals, and Edinburgh University in 1871 with Edinburgh Academicals, Royal High School FP and Edinburgh Wanderers in 1872), recognising that this code of Rules was more comprehensive and in keeping with recent developments, not only adopted it but also became members of the RFU.

By November 1871 the RFU invited the Scottish Clubs to play a return International match in London and also proposed that the fixture should continue on a home-and-away basis. This invitation was accepted and the committee of H.H.Almond (Loretto), the Hon. F.J.Moncreiff (Edinburgh Academicals), J.W.Arthur (Glasgow Academicals), B.Hall Blyth (Merchistonians), A.Buchanan (Royal High School FP) and Dr J.Chiene (Edinburgh Academicals and Edinburgh University), which had organised the 1871 match, again saw to the Scottish arrangements. On this occasion, the Rugby Football Union did a very thorough job of selection, and it was a fit and competent XX which brought them a victory at the Oval Cricket Ground on Monday, February 1872

THE INITIAL MOVES

In Scotland the success and the purposes of the RFU had not gone unnoted, and since the game was clearly spreading beyond the bounds of the two cities, the first steps to form a similar Scottish Union were taken sometime in the autumn of 1872 by a group of six people during an evening meal at the University Club in Edinburgh. The diners were Dr John Chiene, James Wallace, R.Craigie Bell and Harry Cheyne (all Edinburgh Academicals), B.Hall Blyth (Merchistonians) and Albert Harvey (Glasgow Academicals). All except Harvey were graduates of Edinburgh University. Chiene became a very distinguished Professor of Surgery; Wallace, then an Advocate, became a Sheriff; Bell and Cheyne were Writers to the Signet; Hall Blyth was a noted Civil Engineer, whilst Harvey was a very prominent and successful Merchant in Glasgow. In the following year the outcome of their discussion was the insertion of the following notice in the daily papers of the two cities:

'A meeting will be held on Monday, 3 March, in the GLASGOW ACADEMY, ELMBANK STREET, GLASGOW at Half-past Four o'clock (immediately after the conclusion of the International Match) to consider as to the propriety of forming a FOOTBALL UNION IN SCOTLAND on a similar basis to the Rugby Union in

3

England. All Members of Clubs playing the Rugby Union Rules are invited to attend.'

This meeting took place and, in spite of the very inclement weather which persisted throughout the afternoon of the match, was well attended. Dr J.Chiene, called to the Chair, briefly stated the objects of the proposed Union to be:

1. To provide funds for a cup.
2. To bring into closer connection the clubs playing.
3. To form a committee by whom the Scotch International team may in future be chosen.

These proposals having been accepted, James Wallace and Hugh Gibson proposed that the following clubs should form the Members of the Union: Edinburgh, Glasgow and St Andrews Universities, Edinburgh and Glasgow Academicals, West of Scotland, Royal High School FP and Merchistonians. It was agreed that other clubs would be admitted as soon as they demonstrated proper qualifications.

J.W.Arthur and Harry Cheyne then proposed the following committee to draw up a Constitution to be submitted to a General Meeting to be held before the opening of the next football season:

Edinburgh University: C.W.Cathcart, James Wallace.
Glasgow University: D.M.Brunton, Prof.Ramsey.
St Andrews University: P.Anton, A.N.Other.
Edinburgh Academicals: Hon.F.J.Moncreiff, H.Cheyne.
Glasgow Academicals: J.W.Arthur, Albert Harvey.
West of Scotland: A.Cochrane, R.McClure.
Royal High School FP: A.Buchanan, W.B.Neilson.
Merchistonians: B.Hall Blyth, Hugh Gibson.

These nominations were accepted and James Wallace was asked to act as secretary. For each Club, the first named player was the existing Club Captain.

THE FIRST ANNUAL GENERAL MEETING

The steering committee duly fulfilled its remit and the first AGM of the Union was held at 4.30 pm, on Thursday, 9 October 1873, within Keith & Co.'s Rooms, 65A George Street, Edinburgh.

The minutes record that the following six clubs were represented: Edinburgh Academicals, Royal High School FP, Edinburgh University, Glasgow Academicals, West of Scotland and Merchistonians, but *The Scotsman* states that Glasgow University were also represented.

Harry Cheyne, WS, took the Chair and the Acting Secretary, James Wallace, read out *seriatim* the proposed Bye-Laws of the Union, which with certain verbal alterations were adopted as follows:

1. The Union shall be called the Scottish Football Union.

4

2. All Clubs in Scotland playing the Rugby Union Rules shall be eligible for membership.

3. The objects of the Union are: (i) The encouragement of Football in Scotland; (ii) Co-operation with the Rugby Football Union; (iii) The selection of the International Team.

4. Each club shall be entitled to send four representatives to the AGM of the Union who shall form the General Council, two of whom shall be past players and two present, one of the latter being the playing Captain of the club. A third of the representatives to form a quorum.

5. The office-bearers of the Union, who shall be elected annually from among the members of the General Council at the General Meeting of the Union, shall consist of a President, a Vice-President, an Honorary Secretary and a Treasurer, all of whom shall be past players.

6. The Committee shall consist of the office-bearers, *ex officiis* and the Captains of each club. Five members of Committee to constitute a quorum.

7. The AGM of the Union shall be held alternately in Edinburgh and Glasgow on the second Thursday in October.

8. A Special General Meeting may be convened at any time on a requisition from any three clubs in the Union and such meeting shall be held in the place where the last General Meeting was held.

9. The Entrance Money from each club shall be one guinea and the Annual Subscription five shillings payable in advance on or before 1 January in each year. Should the subscription of any Club remain in arrears for more than one year the defaulting Club shall, if it remain unpaid after intimation from the Secretary, be removed from the list of the Union but shall be eligible for re-election.

10. Applications for membership must be sent to the Honorary Secretary not later than the last day of September in each year and the Secretary shall communicate to each Club in the Union the name and constitution of the club applying.

11. Admission shall be by vote of the members of the General Council at the General Meeting of the Union and a simple majority shall be sufficient to admit.

12. The byelaws shall not be altered except at a General Meeting and notice of any amendment or alteration together with the names of the proposer and seconder of every such amendment or alteration shall be given in writing to the Honorary Secretary on or before the last day of September in each year and the Secretary shall communicate to each club in the Union the proposed amendment or alteration.

The office-bearers for the ensuing year were then chosen:

President: John Chiene, Esq., MD.

Vice-President: Hugh Gibson, Esq.

Secretary and Treasurer: James Wallace, Esq., Advocate.

These three gentlemen along with the Captains of the clubs in the Union were nominated to act as a Committee for the year. The secretary then read applications for admission from the Wanderers FC, Edinburgh, and the Warriston FC, Edinburgh, both of which Clubs were unanimously admitted.

The meeting briefly discussed the qualifications for playing in the International match, but that matter along with several questions relating to the Rules of the game were remitted for the consideration of the Committee.

From the Minute of the first AGM several points are worthy of note:

1. Eight Clubs may be termed Founder Members of the Union: Edinburgh Academicals, Glasgow Academicals, West of Scotland, Royal High School FP, Merchistonians, St Andrews University, Edinburgh University, Glasgow University.

Two clubs may be termed Original Members of the Union: Edinburgh Wanderers; Warriston.

2. The idea of providing a cup had been dropped, a decision that was to be upheld for years.

3. Co-operation with the Rugby Football Union was to be maintained. Six of the ten clubs had been members of the RFU and accepted their Rules of 1871 only to withdraw on the formation of the SFU. However, the RFU at most of their early AGMs discussed and amended some of their Rules of Play with the result that the Scottish clubs, whose AGM was later in the year, were continually faced with new rulings some of which they did not favour but were more or less forced to accept. This situation gradually developed to a stage where the two Unions disagreed vigorously over a decision taken during the 1884 International at Blackheath and, in effect, this led to the formation of the International Board in 1886.

4. On the question of qualification for inclusion in the International team the meeting was inclined to favour birth rather than residence (which the RFU at first favoured).

5. One interesting difference between the composition of the Scottish Union with that in England is the exclusion of schools from membership. St Paul's School and Wellington College were founder members of the RFU and many other schools joined later. In Scotland, however, only clubs were regarded as eligible for admission, a matter of principle which comes out clearly in the Minutes of 1874–75 where it is recorded that an application from

Craigmount School was turned down as there was no Football Club separate from the School itself.

Doubtless the presence of FP Clubs among the early members of the SFU meant that the views of the rugby-playing schools could be represented if desired. It does, however, seem remarkable that H.H. Almond, Headmaster of Loretto, a member of the Committee responsible for the arrangements for the 1871 and 1872 International matches, and umpire at the first of these, should take no part in the SFU affairs. He might well have done if Loretto School had been a member of the Union, but Loretto in the 1870s was a small school with no FP Club.

In the 1880s, and again in the 1890s, small groups of schools including, as it happens, Loretto in each case, agreed to special rules for School Matches, 'to avoid danger and to improve forward play' it was stated on one occasion. For brief periods these schools were playing Rugby Football with a slight difference. Whether it was thought necessary to seek the approval of the SFU for all these variations to the Laws is not clear, but mention is made in the Minutes of 1898–99 of approval being given for different rules for School matches.

2

THE COMMITTEE

THE composition of the 1873 Steering Committee obviously followed that of the *ad hoc* body which organised the two first matches with England, because, in both seasons, a group of five arranged Trials and venues and, on consultation with the captains of the few clubs involved, selected the Scottish Twenties. It is no surprise, therefore, to find that the proposed and accepted structure for the new Union Committee was one of three office-bearers with the captains of all member clubs.

At the first AGM of 1873 this produced a Committee of thirteen. When three further clubs were admitted in the following year, a motion to reduce the Committee to nine was withdrawn, since it was considered that all the member clubs should be represented. This view was maintained until 1876, when another five clubs were admitted. The Constitution was then altered to give a Committee of three office-bearers with four representatives: two each from the Eastern and Western Districts. This District representation was increased to three each in 1880, because, by then, the game had spread well beyond the bounds of Edinburgh and Glasgow and many clubs had been admitted from the Borders, the Midlands and the North— even as far distant as Thurso.

At the AGM in 1887 a motion to have a team selection committee of President, Vice-President and two past players, one each from the East and the West, was defeated. A further motion that the Hon. Secretary and Treasurer should have no voting powers was also defeated. The attempt to establish a Selection Committee consisting only of past players probably reflected a growing concern over the number of Committee Members who were being capped. For example, between 1883 and 1888 either four or five of the six Members were being picked for the XV. It must, of course, be noted that from 1876 to 1880 it remained the custom to elect outstanding

8

club captains to the four places, and that after 1880 men of the calibre of T.Ainslie, J.B.Brown, J.Jamieson, W.A.Peterkin, C.Reid, J.P. Veitch and A.R.Don Wauchope, all really automatic choices for the xv, were elected to the Committee because of their ability and experience.

However, the introduction of other Inter-District matches in 1880, the serious dispute with England after the 1884 match, the formation of the International Board in 1886, and the increasing financial and other commitments of the Committee brought new factors into the choice of Committee men, and, by 1887, the selection was falling on older men who were highly qualified and well established in their professions. In 1887 two such newcomers were A.S.Blair, ws, who proved to be a most capable Hon. Secretary, and J.Aikman Smith, ca, who was destined to leave his mark on all levels of administration in Rugby circles.

The next change came in 1889 when it was passed that the District representatives should be eight past players, three each from Edinburgh and Glasgow with one each from the South and the North. These new representatives were: J.A.Smith (rhsfp), T.Ainslie (Ed. Inst. fp), H.F.T.Chambers (Edin. Univ.), D.J.Findlay (West of Scot.), R.Hutcheson (Glas. Univ.), J.S.Carrick (Glas. Acads.), J.K.Brown (Gala) and A.E.Pullar (Perthshire). The proposer urged that the game had made such strides in the South that the region was entitled to a seat on the Committee and that the North should have a similar privilege; further, that only past players should be elected '. . . as by that means there would be less likelihood of bias'. There is a suggestion here of a rising discontent amongst the Border clubs, and indeed such a feeling was clearly seen at the close of the 1890–91 season when the South clubs, meeting at St Boswells, seriously considered forming a separate South of Scotland Rugby Union. Perhaps the inclusion in the Scottish xv in 1890 of the Gala forward, A. Dalgleish, checked further action, but in 1894 the South succeeded in increasing their representation from one to two while reducing the numbers from Glasgow from three to two. The proposer of the motion made the point that '. . . this was not dictated by any hostility to Glasgow but from a sense of justice to the South who boasted as many clubs as the West and were not deficient in play'. The Glasgow clubs protested strongly and, almost annually, tried to restore their previous representation, especially when in 1896 a London District representative was added, and, for a while attempts were made to add a member from the South-West area. Further amendments to the Committee structure, raised by the West delegates in season 1899–1900, again failed although the status quo, when set against the favoured amendment, was retained only by the Chairman's casting vote.

Finally, the Committee was asked to study this vexed question of District representation and, for the 1905 AGM, produced a report which suggested that the bone of contention was really a question of the selection of teams and venues and not a matter of how many or how strong the clubs were in any one District. If any suggestion was to be made it would be to reduce the Edinburgh number to two, but in such a case it was felt that the South number should return to one, since the ratio in clubs was 15-5. It was further hoped that the office-bearers should not be regarded as representing Districts lest appointment to an office, which hitherto had been looked upon as an honour conferred, might become a bone of contention.

This report triggered off further annual motions until 1908, when one proposed by the Committee based on their 1905 report was passed. The Committee made it clear that 'it was set against an increase in its numbers as this would inevitably lead to the remitting of important business to sub-committees'. J. Aikman Smith (Hon. Secretary) pointed out that there appeared to be a prevailing opinion that a representative was there to represent the interests of his District, whereas it should be considered that the interests of the whole are identical and that a member merely represented the Committee in his District. The South, of course, strongly opposed the motion, maintaining that one man was not able to handle the supervision of their scattered District.

A most significant change came in 1910 when it was agreed to separate the offices of Secretary and Treasurer, leaving the Honorary Secretary as a Member of the Committee with a vote, whilst appointing a Treasurer who was not to be on the Committee nor to have a vote. J. Aikman Smith, who remained as Honorary Secretary, explained that the work had become too much for one man and that the Union was now well able to pay for proper assistance in its vastly increased financial affairs. Following this decision, the Union investments were put into the names of three Trustees and A. D. Flett, CA (Edinburgh Wanderers), was later appointed as the first salaried official of the Union.

In March 1914, with no knowledge of the disruption to come, the Committee intimated to their clubs that J. Aikman Smith felt compelled on medical advice to resign his office and that it had been decided to appoint a salaried Secretary. It was also proposed that five Special Representatives should be elected for a period of three years to sit on the Committee along with the seven District Representatives elected annually as hitherto. These Special Representatives would supercede the three immediate Past Presidents who, since 1913, had been *ex officio* Committee Members without a vote. It was also proposed that a Selection Committee of five should be appointed by the Committee after each AGM.

10

This new Constitution was duly passed at the AGM of 8 October 1914 and A.D.Flett was appointed as Secretary and Treasurer, but by this date practically no rugby was being played because of the beginning of the hostilities of the Great War.

A.S.BLAIR, CMG, CBE, TD, JP, DL, BA, WS (3.6.1865–10.9.1936)

A.S.Blair was one of the seven Old Lorettonians who played in the outstanding Oxford XV of 1884, but a knee injury finished his rugby-playing career when he was on the verge of a cap as a wing-threequarter. After graduating BA in 1886 he returned to Edinburgh to practise as a lawyer and was admitted as a Writer to the Signet in 1889.

In 1887, at very short notice, he took over the offices of Honorary Secretary and Treasurer of the SFU and very quickly put into order the perhaps rather neglected affairs of the Union. The pressures of his own business caused him to demit office in 1890, but he continued to act as Law Agent to the Union right up to his death in 1936.

In the early days of the International Board, particularly during the dispute with England when the SFU were represented by their President and Hon. Secretary, Blair was a valued member of its councils. In 1908, when the SFU changed its policy in representation on the Board, he returned as one of the Scottish members for a further two years. At the RFU AGM of 1886 one English delegate was reported as saying that he '. . . deprecated the few clubs of Scotland, Ireland and Wales making rules for the guidance of the Union, who were so vastly in the majority'. This drew from Blair the comment that 'numbers the English might have, but, to judge from results, Scotland could match them for quality in play'.

He served with distinction in France during the First World War, finishing as Lt. Colonel in the Royal Scots, and in later years, he worked unceasingly on behalf of ex-servicemen.

JAMES AIKMAN SMITH, CA (5.3.1859–6.2.1931)

ROYAL HIGH SCHOOL FPRFC
    Hon. Secretary, 1884–86
    President, 1886–89

SFU AND SRU
    East Representative, 1887–90
    Hon. Secretary and Treasurer, 1890–1910
    Hon. Secretary, 1910–14
    Acting Hon. Secretary and Treasurer, 1915–19
    Special Representative, 1914–25 and 1927–31
    Vice-President, 1925–26
    President, 1926–27

J. Aikman Smith attended the Royal High School and George Watson's College, but his contact with rugby lay solely with the former and older School and its FP Club. As a schoolboy he witnessed the first Scotland v England match at Raeburn Place in 1871, so he more or less grew up with the SFU and international rugby. After leaving school he entered the office of Messrs Murray & Romanes, CA, and was admitted a member of the Society of Accountants in 1881. At this time, the Royal High School FP Football Club (as with other early clubs the word 'Rugby' was not yet considered necessary) had begun a run of successful seasons under the captaincy of a renowned character, Nat. Watt, whose XVs, by their robust style of play, had earned themselves the sobriquet of 'Nat. Watt's Lambs'. Watt eventually 'collared' Aikman Smith as the Club's Hon. Secretary. This is almost literally true, for it is related that at the Club AGM of 1884, when such an office-bearer was being sought, Nat's burly brother more or less carried the relatively slight Smith into the meeting and dumped him down with the comment, 'Here's your . . . Secretary'. Small in physical size he may have been, but there is no question about the stature he reached in the world of rugby football during the next half century. As his Club's representative at the 1885 AGM of the SFU, he was most critical about the inadequacy of the annual financial statement and a year later had it passed that, in future, a proper financial summary would be issued with the notice calling the AGM.

After the sudden death in 1887 of J. A. Gardner, his successor, A. S. Blair, was joined on the Union Committee by Aikman Smith as one of the East representatives. It is clear that this combination of the lawyer and the accountant played important parts not only in tidying up the affairs and accounts of the Union but also in the councils of the recently formed International Board. When Blair stood down from the Union Committee in 1890 his administrative offices were taken over by Aikman Smith, but the combination probably remained *in esse* for Blair became the Union's Law Agent.

Aikman Smith was to continue in the Committee until his death in 1931; and his undoubted ability, intensity of beliefs and unbroken attendance in a constantly changing body, allowed him to play a major part in moulding and maintaining the thoughts and actions of the Union. By 1900 he had quite firmly established the authority and powers of his Committee and had placed the finances on such a sound basis that the Union had become the first National Union to own its own ground, along with stand and other facilities, at Inverleith. Twenty-five years later he was equally responsible for the move to the greater enclosure at Murrayfield. An uncompromising opponent of anything that suggested professionalism, he was a prime mover in the Union's actions against the Gould testimonial, the daily cash payments to the New Zealand tourists in 1905, the Macpherson affair in 1923 and the restrictions on the travelling expenses and prizes associated with the very popular Border Sevens.

He was completely unwavering in his determination to maintain the highest standards in the game in Scotland, not only on the field but in its administration. Like Blair, he would have preferred that the four Unions had equal representation on the IB but was quite firm that this latter body should not admit other Unions – and so retain control of the game as played by the four Home Unions. He was openly critical of changes in the Laws suggested by the Dominions whose proposed alterations he felt were mainly intended to make the game faster or more entertaining to the spectators. He maintained that the game should remain one to be played comfortably by amateurs and schoolboys.

He died in office, having to be taken off the train carrying the Committee and players to the Welsh match at Cardiff in 1931.

THE COMMITTEE: 1914-1939

At the AGM in October 1914, two months after the outbreak of War, the President, Dr J. R. C. Greenlees, was unable to be present because he was by then on military duty in France. It was also reported that two International caps, R. F. Simson and Dr J. L. Huggan, had already died in action. The meeting passed the proposed new Constitution and elected a Committee which, for the first time, included five Special Representatives. The War, however, brought club rugby to a halt and only two Committee Minutes were recorded during the period 1915–1918.

In March 1915, seven of the Committee met and decided to inform the Clubs that no Annual Subscriptions would be asked for the coming season. Repayment was made of the last Debenture, left standing in the name of J. Aikman Smith, and a sub-committee of J. M. Dykes, J. D. Dallas, J. Aikman Smith and A. D. Flett was appointed to deal with any business that might arise.

In August 1916, five of the Committee met and approved the Treasurer's Accounts for 1915-1916 and decided that, during A. D. Flett's absence on military duties, J. Aikman Smith would act in his place, thus confirming the situation that had existed since the previous year. Sadly, the names of eighteen International players killed in action were intimated. Two Committee members, J. M. Usher and J. H. Lindsay, had also fallen and A. D. Flett was killed in 1917.

By January 1919 several clubs had restarted and the Union held its first post-war meeting at which the two Committee vacancies were filled and steps taken to appoint a successor to the late A. D. Flett. At the AGM in 1919, now held in May, it was agreed that the existing

13

Committee should continue in office for another season and, shortly afterwards, H.M.Simson, ws (Watsonians), was appointed as the new Secretary-Treasurer. A Selection Committee of five which included four non-Committee men was nominated, and this arrangement lasted for three seasons before the team selection was taken back into the hands of the full Committee. After failures in 1928, 1930 and 1931 to re-establish a Selection Sub-committee, such a body of five, drawn from the elected Committee Members, was established in 1932.

The South repeatedly tried, without success, to double its committee representation, yet in 1937 the Midlands were granted separate representation. The Constitution had been revised in 1924 when five District Unions were set up and given some authority to deal with local affairs. At this time the title of 'The Scottish Rugby Union' was adopted, replacing the original 'The Scottish Football Union'.

THE COMMITTEE: POST-1939

The Committee elected at the AGM in 1939 issued a directive designed to cope with the problems created by the outbreak of War and then, at the next AGM in 1940, the Bye-Laws were altered where necessary to permit the Committee to continue the adminstration of the affairs of the Union, without calling a General Meeting, so long as the National Emergency existed. This situation continued until March 1946, but by then the Committee had lost, through death, its President, four Special Representatives and two District Representatives. Three of these vacancies were filled during 1945, but it was not until the first peace-time AGM in 1946 that the Committee was restored to its full complement. One important change was passed without dissent at the AGM in 1949: the South representation was increased to two.

During the full season of 1946-47 the great increase in Union business forced H.M.Simson to ask for some assistance, and in August 1947 F.A.Wright, CA (Edin. Academicals), was appointed as Treasurer and Assistant Secretary. Oddly enough, this dual arrangement brought its own troubles, because within a couple of seasons the two men reported difficulties arising from having two part-time officials each operating from his own business premises. A sub-committee proposed that the Union should, as soon as possible, appoint a single full-time Secretary-Treasurer who, with an adequate staff, would work from an office owned by the Union. It was recommended that this office should be located at Murrayfield, but in the meantime, accommodation was purchased at Coates Crescent, where H.M.Simson had his own business offices. When he retired in 1951, after thirty years in office, F.A.Wright, working from Coates Crescent, took over as a full-time Secretary-Treasurer. However, within a year, F.A.Wright announced his impending return to private practice,

14

whereupon J. Law (Kelvinside Academicals) was appointed as Joint Secretary-Treasurer and the entire property at Coates Crescent was purchased by the Union. In 1954, J. Law took over solely as Secretary-Treasurer, remaining at Coates Crescent until the planned move to Murrayfield took place in 1964.

During the 1950s, clubs in the Edinburgh area were clearly dissatisfied with some aspects of the Committee structure. In 1952, perhaps influenced by the very disappointing International results of the past season, they sought to change the composition of the Selection Sub-committee, proposing that it should be composed of members elected by the Districts with a Union Committee member as Chairman. It was also stipulated that no member of this body should serve for more than four years. However, this motion was firmly rejected at the AGM. The Edinburgh District clubs returned to the attack at the AGM in 1956 and the Meeting was faced with thirteen motions proposing various changes in the Bye-Laws. However, the clubs from the other Districts, while expressing some sympathy with the underlying intentions, felt that any proposed alterations to the Bye-Laws deserved much fuller consideration and succeeded in passing an amendment which decided that the entire position should be considered by a separate sub-committee containing representatives from both Union Committee and each District.

This sub-committee duly produced some rewritten Bye-Laws which were presented and accepted at the next AGM in 1957 and two changes were particularly significant:

1. The District Representatives would henceforth be elected by their District clubs at an annual meeting. (Previously the Representatives, though nominated by clubs in the District concerned, were selected by the votes of all clubs at the AGM of the Union.)

2. The Union Committee could now co-opt annually not more than two Past Presidents (with vote) for any special purposes for which their services might be of use to the Committee.

A second Vice-President was added to the Office-Bearers in 1981 (a proposal to effect this had been rejected in 1964). The change was made to ensure that the junior Vice-President, if he had not already been a member of the Committee, should gain experience in Committee affairs and methods.

The widening of Union commitments brought about increases in the office staff. During 1974-75 an Assistant Secretary (J.D. Cockburn) and a Technical Administrator (J.H. Roxburgh) were appointed. An Assistant Technical Administrator (D.W. Arneil) was added during 1981-82.

Lastly, I.A.L.Hogg, CA (Watsonians), was appointed Treasurer in 1978 and, anticipating the retiral of J.Law in 1983, was appointed Secretary-Designate in April 1982, to take full office after the AGM in 1983. His position as Treasurer was then filled by I.A.Forbes, BA.

3

GENERAL UNION AFFAIRS

THE FIRST DECADE: 1873–1883

DURING this period every Annual General Meeting was recorded in the Minutes, but it is clear that many Committee meetings were not entered. This is certainly true of those at which Trial and International teams were chosen. Several such meetings, missing from the Minutes, were well reported in the leading newspapers.

At each October AGM important matters were discussed and frequently these involved changes in the Laws of the Game agreed to by the RFU at its own AGM, held in early October. Such proposals then came second-hand to the Scottish clubs, who did not always find them without fault but had no choice but to accept them while passing on their objections to the RFU. One discussion, which dragged on for three seasons until 1876, centred on the legality of picking up a rolling ball. Those who wished to encourage the traditional Scottish forward dribbling game fought hard to allow only a bounding ball to be taken up, but eventually they had to accept the other Law. On the other hand, the important introduction in 1875 of the scoring value of a try was accepted at once, because the Scottish Green Book of 1868 had suggested this as a Rule to be decided on by the two Captains prior to a game.

In another two cases the SFU did have its views prevail. First, when England proposed that residence should be the qualification for selection for an International team, Scotland, who were continually losing players going south to the Universities, to business in the cities or into the armed forces, insisted that parentage or place of birth should be the deciding factor. In the first International of 1871, England played B.H.Burns, a Scot and an Edinburgh Academical resident in London, and offered a place to A.G.Colville, a Merchistonian playing with Blackheath. The latter declined, choosing to play for the Scottish Twenty, which also included A.Clunies-Ross, a Malaysian-Scot from the Cocos Island and J.L.H.Macfarlane from Jamaica, both of whom were educated in Scottish schools.

Secondly, when in December 1875 the SFU suggested that the number of players in an International Team should be reduced from twenty to fifteen, the RFU declined, believing that the season was too far advanced for such a change to be introduced. When the request was repeated in October 1876 it was accepted by the RFU, and thereafter, fifteens were played. Scotland first played a XV when in 1877 they accepted an invitation from the Northern Football Union of Ireland to play an Irish XV in Belfast. At this time there was also an Irish Football Union in Dublin and disagreement between the two Unions forced the cancellation of a return match in Glasgow in 1878. However, the two Unions combined to form an Irish Football Union and the fixture was resumed with a second match in Belfast in 1879.

The Calcutta Cup was first played for in 1879. Members of the Calcutta Football Club had decided to disband, on account of dwindling numbers of both players and opponents. They offered to use their remaining funds to present a Challenge Cup to the RFU for use in whatever way the Committee of that body thought best for the encouragement of the game. After correspondence it was agreed that this should be a challenge cup to be played for annually by England and Scotland.

The Club's funds, amounting to about £60 stg., were withdrawn from the bank in rupees, and these were melted down and fashioned into a splendid cup with three snake handles and an elephant surmounting the lid. The trophy stands about eighteen inches high. The year of every match from 1879 onwards, with the name of the winning country and the names of the two captains, are engraved around the base.

The first match for the Cup, at Raeburn Place in 1879, was drawn. England won the next, at Manchester in 1880; and after another draw at Raeburn Place in 1881, Scotland were winners at Manchester in 1882. When the First World War caused a break in fixtures, Scotland had won the Cup 15 times to England's 12: in 1939, the number of wins was equal at 23 each: but, since the 1950s, the tide has run in England's favour and they are now 10 ahead, up to 1984.

In 1881 the match with England at Raeburn Place ended in a draw, Scotland equalising with a late converted try. The validity of this try had been disputed and the English President was later reported as saying that '. . . the Scotch team was strong, their strength being in umpiring'. He hoped '. . . in future to have unbiased referees who understood their duties'. This comment considerably upset the SFU Committee and some acrimonious correspondence followed. There was one important sequel to this difference of opinion. For the 1882 match in Manchester, England invited an Irish referee to officiate and neutral referees have been used ever since then.

In 1881 R.W.Irvine, who had captained Scotland during the previous five seasons, retired. When it was discovered that the honour had passed to J.H.S.Graham, another Edinburgh Academical, rather than to the senior cap, A.G.Petrie (Royal High School FP), considerable indignation was generated among some of the Edinburgh clubs. A Special General Meeting was convened to demand the resignation of the Committee. In the face of some concessions the motion was withdrawn and the affair died down, but there were repercussions. Several excellent Edinburgh forwards, including A.G. Petrie, withdrew from the Irish match, which was lost for the first time. Later, at the AGM, there were wholesale changes in the Committee, with A.G.Petrie being elected President.

Wales came on the scene, playing England for the first time in 1881 and Ireland in 1882. A match with Scotland followed in 1883, at Raeburn Place, Scotland winning by 3 goals to 1. Regular fixtures then started, with a match at Newport in 1884.

THE FORMATION OF THE INTERNATIONAL BOARD

The start of the 1883-84 season saw a further set of amendments to the Laws issued by the RFU. In December 1883 these were accepted by the SFU, but several objections and suggested alterations put forward by the Scottish clubs were communicated to the RFU. The season began with satisfying wins over Wales and Ireland, but, in the English match at Blackheath in March 1884, a hotly disputed score by England, which won them the game, sparked off a controversy which was to have far-reaching consequences in the history of rugby football.

At that time a game was controlled by two umpires, each carrying a stick, and a referee not yet provided with a whistle. The players (and the umpires) could voice an appeal against some irregularity. An umpire who agreed with the appeal would immediately hold up his stick. If both umpires held up their sticks, play was halted, but if only one stick went up, the referee had at once to indicate whether or not he accepted the appeal.

The dispute at Blackheath arose over the interpretation of a 'knock-on'. In 1874, the RFU had defined 'knocking-on' as 'deliberately hitting the ball with the hand' (without any indication of the direction in which the ball was propelled), whereas 'throwing forward' was stated to be 'throwing the ball in the direction of the opponents' goal line'. Both were 'not lawful'. The Laws continued: 'If the ball be either "knocked-on" or "thrown forward" the captain of the opposing side may (unless a fair catch has been made) require to have it brought back to the spot where it was so knocked or thrown on and there put down'. In 1883 the RFU deleted the word 'deliberately', leaving the definition of 'knocking-on' as 'hitting the ball with the hand'. In Scotland, a knock-on in any direction was regarded as being illegal and was greeted by the cry of 'Fist!'.

In the second half of the match at Blackheath in 1884, Scotland was leading by an unconverted try to nil when, at a line out, C.W. Berry of Scotland knocked the ball back and a Scot made the usual appeal of 'Fist'. The Scottish umpire, J.H.S.Graham (the SFU President), raised his stick. All the players, except two Scottish and four English, halted, but R.S.Kindersley of England, who had seized the ball, ran on to touch down near the posts, virtually unimpeded. For half an hour play was at a standstill while the point of Law and the relatively unopposed score were discussed by the umpires, the referee, the players, and even by G.Rowland Hill, the Hon. Secretary of the RFU, who came on to the field armed with a copy of the Laws. The dispute was left unsettled. The referee (G.Scriven of Ireland), while agreeing that a fist had knocked the ball back, decided that the game should be restarted with the kick at goal. This was successful and was instrumental in winning the match for England.

Almost at once the SFU, claiming that the try was invalid, asked that the matter should be put before and judged by some neutral body, but the RFU, though admitting that a disagreement over interpretation existed, steadfastly refused this request, holding that the referee must stand as the sole judge of fact and whose decision must be adhered to. The facts, of course, were not in dispute: the referee agreed that the ball had been 'fisted' back—but had this been illegal or not? A.R.Don Wauchope, who played in the match, said 'The fact that no Englishman had appealed was never raised at the time, and to judge by the fact that eleven of the English team ceased play, it would appear that their interpretation was that the game should stop.' A later English comment that Scotland could not expect to benefit from their own infringement certainly seems reasonable in 1984, but a hundred years earlier there was no Advantage Law: this did not come into being until 1896.

To the Scottish clubs, the RFU's refusal to submit the dispute to a neutral party strengthened a growing feeling that the English Union was determined to maintain its position as the sole authority on the Laws of the game. At the AGM of the SFU in 1884 the clubs' views were voiced in the following terms: 'That the recent match in March between Scotland and England may be held null or a draw, or be satisfactorily settled by reference; that the independence of the Scottish Union be fully recognised and arrangements made for the settlement of future disputes by reference; and that when these points are settled the Secretary shall either issue or accept a challenge for the ensuing season'.

20

At this time, a gap occurs in the Minutes of the SFU, caused by the deterioration of the health of its Hon. Secretary, J.A.Gardner, who died in 1887, but the dispute with England is reasonably well discussed in the newspapers of the time. It is obvious that no settlement had been reached for there was no English match in 1885, and at the AGM in October of that year, it was noted that 'Scotland was willing to have the dispute terminated, but not by an unconditional surrender to England'.

The Committee was instructed by the Meeting to approach the other Unions on the subject and there was an immediate response. In December 1885 the Irish RU proposed that the four Unions should meet not only to discuss the affair but also to give consideration to the formation of an International Board which could handle the settlement of international disputes. Such a meeting did take place in Dublin on the day of the Irish-English match on 6 February 1886, and there Scotland conceded the 1884 match to England on the understanding that the latter would join with the other Unions on equal terms in the proposed International Board. Later, on 13 March 1886, the English match was played in Edinburgh. This Dublin Conference brought about the formation of the IB whose further development may be very fully followed in its own History published in 1961. The RFU, however, reluctant to yield control over the framing of the Laws of the game, declined to join the IB and stayed aloof until 1889. As a result, neither Scotland, Ireland nor Wales played England during seasons 1887-88 and 1888-89. Then, at the request of both the SFU and the RFU in December 1889, the entire dispute was put into the hands of two arbitrators, who by April 1890 produced the regulations of the International Rugby Football Board which all four Unions accepted. The two arbitrators were Lord Kingsburgh (The Lord Justice Clerk, nominated by the IB) and Major F.A.Marindin (President of the Football Association, nominated by the RFU). Their services were later recognised by the presentation to each of a silver rose bowl bearing emblems of the home countries. That given to Lord Kingsburgh is now in the care of The Edinburgh Academy, his old school.

As already described, this period of development in the international control of the game was also one when some significant changes took place in the personnel of the SFU Committee. The sudden death of J.A.Gardner in September 1887, a mere fortnight before the AGM, led to the appointment of A.S.Blair, and then, at the AGM itself, there came the election of J.Aikman Smith as one of the East representatives. These two last-named, one a lawyer and the other an accountant, were almost certainly responsible not only for the tidying up of the affairs of the SFU but also for a firm establishment of its authority in Scottish rugby circles. Furthermore, they, along with another lawyer, A.R.Don Wauchope, were valuable members in the councils of the young International Board.

In home affairs the Union accounts were brought up to date. The first investment of £150 at 4½%, with the National Bank of India, was made in 1888 and a proper financial statement was now produced for each AGM.

THE 1888 TOUR TO AUSTRALIA AND NEW ZEALAND

The first rumblings of professionalism appeared in the SFU Minutes of 1888-89 following on a tour of Australia and New Zealand by a team organised by two English professional cricketers, A.Shaw and A.Shrewsbury, who had previously managed a cricket tour to Australia. The tour was not under the auspices of any of the Home Unions, and before the party set out, one English player selected had to be withdrawn on being declared a professional by the RFU. On their return home, three Hawick players were closely examined by the SFU Committee regarding the expenses of the trip, which had occupied eight months from start to finish. The Minutes of the SFU dryly report:

> Their assurances being satisfactory, the matter was dropped until such time as direct evidence might be adduced in support of any alleged professionalism.

THE NINETIES

After the conclusion of the dispute with England in April 1890, A.S.Blair did not stand for re-election, and, at the 1890 AGM, J.Aikman Smith was elected as Hon. Secretary and Treasurer, a joint office he was to hold until 1910. He then continued as Hon. Secretary until 1914 and had actually demitted office when the events of the First World War forced him to carry on until the 1919 AGM.

The Committee found itself much occupied in settling many questions of law and play, brought before it by the member clubs. It was decided to take control of all District and Trial matches, retaining a voice in team selection and the governing of the finances. On one occasion some trouble arose over the selection of a North XV. A very stern letter to the District was prepared before the Committee broke for lunch, but later, apparently in a more benign mood, the letter was rewritten in less severe terms.

In 1892 the qualifications for selection to the International team were outlined and it was also decided that in future the International trophy caps would be presented by the Union instead of being purchased by the players themselves.

The growing control and authority of the Committee already established by A.S.Blair was now further strengthened by his successor, and following what now seems a minor and really rather amusing controversy over the wearing of shin guards, the deeper powers of the Committee were clearly set out at a Special General Meeting in 1893, when the following motion was passed: 'That this meeting, in order to put an end to all doubts on the subject, hereby recognises the power of the Committee of the SFU to pass any Resolution which in its opinion tends to the encouragement of Rugby Football in Scotland, so long as the written Bye-Laws of the Union or Laws of the Game are not altered, and to enforce the same until said Resolution is disproved by a Special General Meeting . . .'.

The strength of the Committee was soon sternly tested. For some time Border club spectators, who had rather less regard than some for the Union and for the background of the members of the Committee, had been causing concern with their outspoken behaviour during and at the end of matches. Things came to a head with an adverse report from the referee at the Gala-Watsonians game at Mossilee in 1894. The Committee carefully investigated the affair and finished by dealing severely with the Gala club and its Captain. The latter, supported financially by several club members, raised a law suit against the Union. That body immediately defended itself and the referee. When the Gala case collapsed, with the pursuers unable to sustain the cost let alone the legal point, the Union took severe retribution by suspending *sine die* not only the Captain but also all the club members known to have financially supported the law suit. It was further unanimously resolved that no Union club be allowed to play at Galashiels until March 1895. When the Gala case was concluded, the Union issued a very comprehensive summary of the affair to the member clubs, explaining the final decision taken to suspend several members of the Gala club.

At this stage it is worth while looking briefly at the changing background of the game. During the 1870s the Committees of the Scottish and English Unions and most club players were men with prosperous backgrounds, well educated, usually pupils at the principal rugby-playing schools or the universities and well able to afford both the time and expense involved in playing the game. It should be recalled it was not until 1880 that the English game was played on a Saturday instead of a Monday, and even then, it was only a minority who could take a half-day off on Saturdays.

By 1880 the game in Scotland had spread beyond the bounds of the two cities, particularly into the Borders whose town clubs rapidly became formidable opponents but whose robust style of play, standards of umpiring, fierce local pride and quite outspoken supporters began to disturb the Committee. The Border clubs, although gaining one Committee place in 1889 were, by 1891, still unhappy with the administration. Perhaps it was the selection of Adam

Dalgleish in 1890, the first Border cap, and a second Committee seat gained in 1894, that quietened things down, as mentioned earlier.

The Northern Union. In 1893 there occurred the 'broken time' crisis in England. The point at issue was the difficulties faced by players, especially in the industrial areas of Yorkshire and Lancashire, who endured loss of wages in order to take part in games—especially those played at some distance from home. At the AGM of the RFU in that year, two Yorkshire representatives moved 'That players be allowed compensation for *bona fide* loss of time'. The motion was rejected by 282 votes to 136, and shortly afterwards, twenty-two Yorkshire and Lancashire clubs withdrew from the RFU. The establishment of the Northern Union, permitting 'broken time' payments, followed and the RFU suspended all clubs which joined this new body. The SFU, in 1895–96, decided that '. . . the Union shall recognise suspensions by the National Unions of England, Ireland and Wales', and later warned Scottish clubs to check the standing of any 'foreign clubs' before accepting a fixture with them. Any Scottish player signing forms for a Northern Union club was regarded as a professional and, as such, was barred from being either a playing or non-playing member of a club in membership of the SFU—a policy which has continued to this day.

The A.J.Gould Case. In 1896 the SFU received a request for contributions to a testimonial fund for A.J.Gould, an outstanding Welsh player. The matter was passed on to the IB, who strongly disapproved of the Testimonial Fund which proposed to purchase a dwelling-house for the player. The Welsh RU were not prepared to concur, and in spite of a clear warning from the IB to the Union and the player, the Fund was passed over to Gould. In 1896–97, the Welsh RU passed certain resolutions in which the power of the IB to interfere in such an internal Welsh affair was challenged. The Welsh RU thereafter resigned from the IB, and as a result, their matches with Scotland and Ireland in 1897 were cancelled (their English game had already been played). In 1897–98, with Gould having retired from the game, the case was virtually allowed to die away. The Welsh RU requested to be re-admitted to the IB and this request was granted with a firm insistence on certain conditions. The Welsh RU then asked for a resumption of fixtures. As far as Scotland was concerned a mutually acceptable date in 1898 could not be found, but matches began again the following year.

Prior to 1888, Scotland had no contacts with countries outwith those that were members of the Home Unions. In that year, a team comprising UK players was selected to tour Australia and New Zealand, and some Scots players were included in the party. Several years later, in 1896, an Edinburgh XV played a Paris XV. In the years

24

that followed, reciprocal visits to the UK were made by a French XV and also by a team made up of New Zealand 'native' groups.

Having been making enquiries about a suitable ground of its own, the Scottish Rugby Union purchased land at Inverleith. This, the first rugby field owned by the Union, was opened in 1899, the first International match being against an Ireland XV on 18 February in that year.

THE PRE-WAR PERIOD 1900–1914

At this time the Union, now possessing its own ground and with a firmly established authority, might have hoped for a period of quiet development. On the domestic scene it was still faced by the annual dispute over the representation of the Districts on the Committee, a controversy which, as we have seen, finally produced a New Constitution at the AGM in 1914.

In 1901 a request that a Union XV should play a German XV at the Glasgow Exhibition was not entertained, but a proposed Canadian tour was viewed sympathetically and, during the Christmas and New Year period of 1902–03, a team under the auspices of a Canadian Rugby Union played some six closely contested matches in the cities and Borders.

This was followed by visits from New Zealand, South Africa and French teams, a sequence which will be taken up in a later chapter.

The G. Boots Case. In 1903–04 there was again a 'Welsh problem'. The Welsh RU were allowing G. Boots, of Newport, to play in Rugby Union matches even though he had signed Northern Union forms. The SFU advised their clubs not to play against any team which included Boots and the Welsh RU questioned this action. The matter was referred to the IB, who, while deciding this did not come under its jurisdiction, upheld the Scottish attitude that 'each Union has full jurisdiction over its own clubs and it is in its power to prevent them playing against any individual player'.

Writing of Articles to the Press. In 1904–05 the SFU passed a resolution of considerable significance: 'No player shall be permitted to take payment for an article on Rugby Football'.

Seven-a-Side Tournaments. At this time the SFU had become increasingly concerned over payments to players taking part in seven-a-side tournaments and it was decided that in future all Sevens should be under the jurisdiction of the Union. In 1905–06 it was laid down that no prizes other than medals or badges were to be allowed in these tournaments, but this rule was relaxed for the 1905–06 season because clubs had already purchased prizes.

The D. G. MacGregor Case. A year later, it was back to Wales again. D. G. MacGregor, a member of the Pontypridd Club, had been capped

25

for Scotland for the first time in 1907, playing in all three matches. Pontypridd asked permission to mark this achievement by presenting a gift to the player, but the SFU refused to grant this. Later the SFU reminded MacGregor that he must not play for or against any team that included G. Boots of Newport and this resulted in a letter being received from the Newport Club, regarding this restriction. The SFU declined even to discuss the matter with the club, pointing out that their ruling in the matter had already been intimated to the player.

BETWEEN THE WARS 1919–1939

Club rugby was fully re-established during the 1919–1920 season and the Union Committee dealt very sympathetically with numerous requests for grants to allow clubs to lease or purchase their playing-fields or to erect pavilions or other accommodation. From the outset there was an obvious upsurge of public interest in the game. The long-established clubs in the cities and Borders found themselves strongly challenged by younger clubs such as George Heriot's School FP in Edinburgh and Glasgow High School FP in the West, whilst a decade later, Hillhead High School FP and Dunfermline were noticeably successful. Club matches were well supported, frequently requiring special trains to be run between the cities and the attendances at the International matches began to tax the capacity of Inverleith.

On the International scene relations with France, proposed for 1915, were resumed, whilst the New Zealand and New South Wales Unions continued their pressure for a voice in the framing of the Laws and for a place on a wider International Board; but the older and more conservative minds amongst the Home Unions were not yet ready for such moves. It should be noted that a New South Wales Union dated from 1874; a Queensland Union from 1878; a South African Union from 1889 and a New Zealand Union from 1892.

The SFU's stern opposition to anything hinting of professionalism continued after the First World War. Believing that some Northern Union players had been involved, the SFU queried the Welsh RU over the composition of a Welsh XV that played against a New Zealand team in 1919.

A. Wemyss. Andrew Wemyss (Gala and Edinburgh Wanderers), first capped in 1914 and again after the War (although he had lost an eye), was queried about his writing articles about matches, and a Bye-Law forbidding any club member to write such material, was produced. 'Jock', having pointed out that he had finished playing, raised some blood pressures by turning out for Leicester six months later in a mid-week holiday match against Heriot's FP—which was

26

played at Inverleith! A decade later, another cap, F.H.Waters (Cambridge University), asked for a reinstatement stating that he had stopped his journalistic work, but this request was not granted. Two Aberdeen players were also suspended for supplying reports on their club matches and six Border players were suspended for taking part in trial games with Northern Union clubs.

The N.C.Macpherson Affair. In 1923 the Newport (Mon.) club went through the season undefeated and the enthusiastic supporters organised a fund which resulted in each player receiving a splendid gold watch valued at £21. When the sfu learned of this, they wrote to Neil Macpherson, Newport's Scottish cap, inviting him to hand back this quite expensive gift. Macpherson, however, politely declined to dissociate himself from his clubmates, whereupon the sfu suspended him *sine die* and placed a ban on Scottish clubs playing against Newport. The matter was promptly brought before the ib, which body ruled that all mementos to a player (other than a wedding present) should not be of a value greater than £2, whereupon the sfu, having made their point, removed the suspension—but Macpherson was not capped again. The watch still exists in the possession of Macpherson's son, now resident in Hong Kong.

The Numbering of Players. In December 1911, and again a year later, it was decided that numbered jerseys should be supplied for the players in all Trial matches, but no such step was taken for the International matches where the match programmes were apparently considered adequate enough to provide any identification required. In 1914, at a meeting of the ib, a suggestion that International players should be numbered was met with strong disapproval from certain members of the Board and so the matter was dropped.

It was not until the Wales v England match in Cardiff in 1922 that numbers were first used in an International game, and both countries continued the practice whenever their opponents approved. In January 1926, the Irish ru, stating that they were favourably inclined to the course, asked the views of the sru with regard to the numbering of players, but the latter Committee replied that they preferred, in the meantime, to adhere to their then present practice of not numbering the players.

After the New South Wales match in December 1927, in which each visiting player carried his individual tour number, the question was discussed and the Committee, by a narrow majority, decided to number its xv for the French match at Colombes in January 1928. However, J.M.Bannerman was asked to check on the views of the players, and later, a letter objecting to the innovation, signed by a majority of the team, was handed to the Secretary, H.M.Simson. This letter was duly placed before the Committee, which, respecting the wishes of their players, reversed their previous decision by an equally narrow margin, and so the Welsh and Irish matches of 1928 were played without numbers. Some apocryphal stories have been told about this action. It was said that the Border players were advised how they should vote; that John Bannerman, the 'senior cap' and a critic of numbering, rather 'leaned' on his team mates to support his views!

Noticing the change in policy, the RFU wrote asking the SRU to give favourable consideration to numbering their XV for the English game at Twickenham, but the SRU declined to alter their decision. This refusal found its way rather too rapidly into the English Press, whose adverse and caustic comments definitely irritated the members of the Scottish Committee. HM King George V attended this match, and it is said that he asked J. Aikman Smith why his team was not numbered and received the terse reply that 'This is a Rugby match, not a cattle sale'. That evening, at the after-match dinner, the Committee members were again upset to hear further critical references of their decision made, in their presence, by the President of the RFU. However, after writing a strongly phrased letter, in which they bluntly voiced their feelings and firmly asserted their right to conduct their affairs as they saw fit, the matter was allowed to pass—but the SRU held to its decision until the opening of the 1932-33 season, when it finally decided to number its players in all International and Trial games.

After long and devoted service to rugby football, J. Aikman Smith died in 1931 and John Bannerman, after an unbroken run of 37 caps, retired from the International scene in 1929. One may speculate how far the absence of these two deeply intense characters affected the decision to change the policy.

The Dominions. Apart from the topic of numbering the players, the SRU had, for some time, been disturbed by the continued attacks in the English Press which alleged that Scotland alone was responsible for the refusal to increase the grant asked by the NZ tourists in 1927. In answer to these criticisms the Committee issued in May 1928 a very comprehensive circular to its member clubs which revealed that each decision reached in that particular issue had been unanimously approved by all the four Home Unions and later endorsed by the IB. They also took the opportunity to clarify their position with reference to other matters concerning rugby in the Dominions.

1. The reasons (mentioned elsewhere) for their refusal to accept fixtures with the NZ tourists in 1925 were fully set out.

2. They appreciated why a Dominion might find it necessary to adopt variations in the Laws, but they could not accept that any

Dominion by admission to the IB should have a say in the control of the game in the Home countries. In particular, they firmly opposed some proposed alterations designed to make the game faster, more interesting to spectators and, so, beneficial to the gates.

SCOTLAND, THE DOMINIONS AND FRANCE

THE MAORIS 1888–89

THE first overseas Touring Team to visit Scotland was 'The New Zealand Native Football Representatives', usually referred to as 'The Maoris'—though several members of the team were of other racial origin. The tour was organised by the RFU to which the New Zealand Rugby Union, like other similar bodies, was affiliated. In twenty-five weeks the team played no fewer than seventy-four matches, including three on successive days. This massive programme was undertaken to help to finance the tour. Only one of these fixtures was in Scotland, the Maoris defeating Hawick by a goal to a try.

CANADIANS 1902–03

The first reference in the SFU Minutes to a team from the Dominions or Colonies appears in 1900–01. A Canadian team proposed to visit Scotland and this tour duly took place in 1902–03, with matches against Club sides. The success of the tour was recorded and a contribution out of Union funds was made to those Clubs who had played and entertained the visitors.

NEW ZEALAND 1905–06 AND SOUTH AFRICA 1906–07

In 1902–03 the RFU raised the possibility of a tour by a New Zealand side, with the Home Unions offering fixtures and giving guarantees for each match. This proposal put the SFU in a difficult position. While very willing to help to meet the costs of the tour, the SFU were, at that time, not well placed financially to provide the guarantees suggested for two matches. By December 1903, when it was decided to offer the New Zealand tourists two fixtures in Scotland, the SFU had used its new field at Inverleith for five seasons and were still committed to debts totalling £6,600. The Annual Accounts reveal that the average surplus from the International matches played on Inverleith from 1899 to 1903 were:

5. SRU COMMITTEE, 1972-73

Standing: J. Law (Secretary), A. W. Harper, J. T. McNeil, W. L. Connon, G. Burrell, C. W. Wilton, J. R. B. Wilson, G. W. Thomson, T. Pearson, J. D. Cockburn (Asst. Secretary). *Seated:* J. W. Y. Kemp, H. Lind, H. S. P. Monro, Dr J. R. S. Innes (Vice-President), A. W. Wilson (President), C. W. Drummond, A. D. Govan, A. Bowie, F. MacAllister.

6. SRU COMMITTEE, 1983-84

Standing: J. D. Cockburn (Admin. Sec.), J. Thain (Head Groundsman), C. Ritchie, G. D. M. Brown, Dr I. M. Todd, A. C. W. Boyle, R. D. S. Munro, F. C. H. McLeod, F. M. McDougall, I. A. L. Hogg (Secretary), I. A. Forbes (Treasurer). Seated: J. B. Steven, I. A. A. MacGregor, J. T. McNeil, W. L. Connon, J. W. Y. Kemp (Vice-President), A. Robson (President), G. Burrell (Vice-President), T. Pearson, G. B. Masson, R. G. Charters, G. K. Smith. Insets: l. J. H. Roxburgh (Technical Admin.); r. D. W. Arneil (Asst. Technical Admin.).

7. HONORARY SECRETARIES

(a) J. Wallace (Edin. Acads.), 1873-75; [A. R. Stewart (Edin. Wrs.),
1875-79 (no photograph available)]; (b) J. Brewis (RHSFP), 1879-81; (c)
A. S. Paterson (Edin. Univ.), 1881-83; (d) J. A. Gardner (Edin. Acads.),
1883-87; (e) A. S. Blair (Fet.-Lor.), 1887-90; (f) J. A. Smith (RHSFP),
1890-1914 and 1915-19.

8. SECRETARIES

(a) A. D. Flett (Edin. Wrs.), 1914-15; (b) H. M. Simson (Watsonians), 1919-51; (c) F. A. Wright (Edin. Acads.), 1951-54; (d) J. Law, OBE (Kelvinside Acads.), 1954-83; (e) I. A. L. Hogg (Watsonians), 1983-

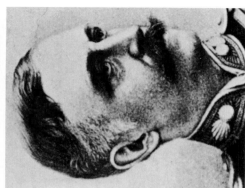

b

c

Marindin. Lord Kingsburgh (The Lord Justice Clerk) and Major F. A. Marindin (President of the Football Association) were the nominees of the International Board and the Rugby Football Union who acted as arbitrators in the dispute between the two parties (see pp.21-22). They produced the Award which defined and established the Regulations of the International Rugby Football Board in April 1890. Their services were recognised by the presentation to them of silver rose-bowls suitably inscribed. That presented to Lord Kingsburgh is now in the keeping of The Edinburgh Academy, his former School. It was he, then simply J. W. A. Macdonald, who sat at the entry gate collecting the money for the first international at Raeburn Place in 1871.

a

10. THE CALCUTTA CUP

On Christmas Day 1872 a rugby match was played in Calcutta by a Twenty representing Scotland, Ireland and Wales. By January 1873 the Calcutta Rugby Club had been formed and joined the R F U in the following year. For four years the club struggled on against the difficulties created by the climate, the lack of opposing clubs and the emergence of other sports such as lawn tennis and polo but, by 1877, it became clear that the club would fold up. A problem arose over the disposal of the ample club funds and eventually it was suggested that a trophy of Indian workmanship should be presented to the R F U. This offer was made and accepted in 1878, the R F U replying, 'The Committee accept with very great pleasure your generous offer of the Cup as an International Challenge Cup to be played for annually by England and Scotland—the cup remaining the property of the Rugby Football Union'.

The Cup was made from the actual silver rupees withdrawn from the club's account at its bank. Later, a wood base was added and round this are the dates of every Calcutta Cup match with the name of the winning country and those of the two captains.

It was first played for at Raeburn Place in 1879 and the record stands at: England, 44 wins; Scotland, 34 wins; 13 draws. Fifteen games were cancelled because of the dispute in the 1880s and because of the two World Wars.

11. WAR MEMORIAL ARCH

Erected at Inverleith, 1921. Transferred to Murrayfield, 1937.

12. (a) The handsome First Division Trophy awarded annually to the winners of Division I of the Scottish Rugby Union Championship for the Schweppes Trophies. (b) This striking bronze sculpture is awarded annually to the winners of the final in the Scottish Rugby Union Youth Leagues for the Royal Bank Trophy.

Public Notices.

A MEETING will be held, on Monday the Third March, in the Glasgow Academy, Elmbank Street, at ½-past Four o'clock (immediately after the Conclusion of the International Match), to consider as to the propriety of Forming a Football Union in Scotland, upon a similar basis to the Rugby Union in England.

All Members of Clubs Playing the Rugby Union Rules are invited to Attend.

R OYAL CLYDE YACHT CLUB.

The FIRST GENERAL MEETING of the SEASON will be held in Maclean's Hotel, No. 198 St. Vincent Street, on Tuesday Evening, 4th inst., at Eight o'clock. There will be a Ballot, on same Day, in the Secretary's Office, from One till Four P.M.; and in the Evening, at the Place of Meeting, from Eight till Ten.

WILLIAM YORK, Hon. Secy.

a

b

13. (a) 1873, *Glasgow Herald*: The newspaper notice of the inaugural meeting of formation of the Scottish Football Union. (b) Dr John Chiene, President 1873-74 and 1877-78.

Dr John Chiene, CB, MD, FRCSE, DSC, FRS, LLD, 1843-1923. John Chiene was educated at The Edinburgh Academy (1854-60) and studied at Edinburgh and Sheffield Universities. He had a long and distinguished career in medicine being the Professor of Surgery in Edinburgh University from 1882 until his retiral in 1909. As a surgeon and medical author he was frequently honoured, being President of the Royal Medical Society (Edin.) and President of the Royal College of Surgeons (Edin.) and having the degree of LLD conferred upon him by both Edinburgh and Glasgow Universities. In 1900 he received a CB for his services as Consulting Surgeon to HM forces in South Africa. He was one of the six people who, at an evening dinner, took the first steps to found the Scottish Football Union and was the first President of the Union.

The ANNUAL MEETING of the SUBSCRIBERS is to be held at the INSTITUTION, HENDERSON ROW, TO-MORROW (TUESDAY), at Two o'clock.

WELLINGTON REFORMATORY FARM SCHOOL.

The ANNUAL MEETING of the SUBSCRIBERS to and FRIENDS of this INSTITUTION will be held in 5 ST ANDREW SQUARE, on WEDNESDAY the 29th of MARCH, at Two o'clock.
JAMES WATT, Esq., Provost of Leith, in the Chair.

INTERNATIONAL FOOTBALL MATCH.—

This MATCH will take place TO-DAY on the ACADEMY CRICKET GROUND, RAEBURN PLACE, at Three o'clock.
Admission—ONE SHILLING.
Academicals are requested to leave their Cards at the Gate.

LODGE ST CLAIR, 349—

MONTHLY MEETING in FREEMASONS' HALL, THIS (MONDAY) EVENING, 27th inst., at 8.30 P.M.   A. B., Secy.

FREE CHURCH PRINCIPLES AND UNION.

(Extract from Appendix to Speech by Dr Charles J. Brown, 1868.)
"I embrace the present opportunity of noticing a charge—often brought against some of us—of *inconsistency* between our present thoughts and utterances on the subject of State endowments and our thoughts and utterances respecting them in other days. You

a

b

14. (a) *Scotsman*, 1871: The newspaper notice of the first International Rugby match, which took place at Raeburn Place. (b) Commemorative Stone, donated by Mr William Mackay of Aberdeen and placed in the Raeburn Place grounds as a Centenary memorial.

15. Raeburn Place, Scotland *v* England, 1886

This work by W. H. Overend and L. P. Smythe, was obviously intended to be
accurate because the Scottish forward in the right foreground is clearly Charles
Reid. It is believed that D. A. MacLeod is further to the right and A. T. Clay always
asserted that he was the Scot lying on the ground. It can be guessed that the backs
shown are (left-to-right) A. R. Don Wauchope, G. R. Wilson, A. G. G. Asher and R. H.
Morrison. The English forward with the ball is surely E. T. Gurdon. The umpire
must be either G. Rowland Hill or J. S. Carrick and appears to be signalling an appeal
for some infringement since his flag is raised. Note the mounted police who
appeared for the first time at an International match. The artists have depicted the
pitch as being placed too near to the pavilion. One copy of the work (uncoloured)
hangs at Murrayfield but coloured versions may be seen in the pavilion at Raeburn
Place and in the Clarkston Committee Room.

16. Raeburn Place, Scotland v England, 1894

This shows the temporary stand erected for this match. Note that there is still no stone wall along the lane to the park. The Wanderers pitch in the Grange ground has been moved to the north end of the cricket field and some form of stand has been erected along the line under which the covered ditch ran. The Scottish left half-back is looking for the ball and the right half is clearly 'standing off'. The referee's apparel is worthy of note.

17. Powderhall, Scotland *v* Ireland, 1897.

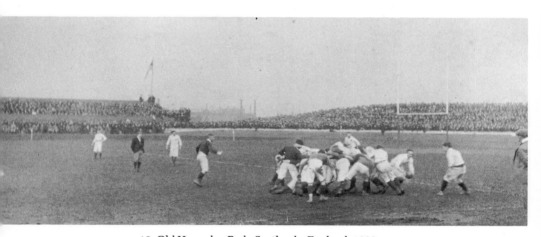

18. Old Hampden Park, Scotland *v* England, 1896.

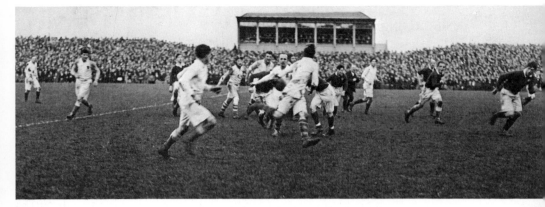

19. Inverleith, Scotland *v* England, 1914.

20. Murrayfield, aerial view, 1925.

21. Murrayfield, aerial view. The wing extensions to the stand were added in 1936.

22. Murrayfield, 1984. An aerial view including the East Stand and the surrounding grounds. This panorama shows clearly the extent of the property owned by the Scottish Rugby Union.

23. Murrayfield, 21 February 1976, Scotland v England. HM The Queen accompanied by HRH The Duke of Edinburgh about to meet the teams. In attendance were J. H. Orr and G. T. Bainbridge, the Presidents of the two Unions.

24. Murrayfield, 26 March 1983. HRH The Princess Anne formally opens the new East Stand. She is accompanied by the President of the SRU, G. W. Thomson.

England, £1,049; Ireland, £698; Wales, £770.
During the same period the surplus from the Inter-City games played in Glasgow averaged about £100.

With all these figures available, the Committee, with a declared intention of helping the finances of the tourists, stated that, since it believed that it had no right to impose a guarantee on its Debenture and Bond holders, it would hand over the net gates from both matches because it was clear that the total would certainly exceed the two guarantees asked.

Faced with this decision the New Zealand Tour Manager, apparently worried about the Scots and their climate, wrote asking what expenses would be deducted from the gates and what would be the situation if a match was cancelled. After receiving the Union's reply, he informed them that his party did not wish to be entertained after the matches. One gets the impression that relations were then less than cordial! In the end the SFU were proved correct, for the tourists received £1,700, a sum which greatly exceeded the two guarantees asked for.

At that period (1903–05) the Union Committee contained many well-educated and intelligent members. Men such as J.D.Dallas (Sheriff), A.S.Pringle (Advocate), W.Neilson (Barrister), J.C.Findlay (Solicitor), R.Welsh (Farmer), A.B.Flett and J.W.Simpson (Doctors), R.C.Greig and J.Aikman Smith (CAs) lacked neither legal, financial nor business background. These men knew what they were doing; they publicly made it clear that they wished to do their best for the tourists and, far from being upset at the amount given to the New Zealanders, they offered precisely the same terms to the South Africans for their visit in the following season, 1906–07. In addition they announced that the tourists would be entertained after the matches at the Union's expense. (The net gates provided the South Africans with £1,100.)

From the outset the SFU had been concerned at the dearth of information regarding the financial arrangements of the New Zealand tour. They were even more disturbed after they had handed over such a large sum without knowing how it was being used, but it was not until October 1907, after they had received the financial statement for the South African tour, that they requested the RFU to provide a similar statement for the New Zealand tour. This became available in late 1908 and at once the SFU queried an entry of £1,041. The Hon. Secretary of the RFU replied that this represented a daily allowance of three shillings (15p) to each player and the manager to cover incidental expenses and that this had been made with the approval of his Committee. The SFU at once decided that cash payments of this kind were contrary to the principles of amateur rugby and, in view of the

RFU's approval of such payments, the SFU then wrote cancelling the next English match. As recently as 1895, the RFU had taken a firm stand against 'broken time' payments and, as a result, had been badly disrupted by the breakaway of the Northern Rugby Union clubs. Matters were laid before the IB, who agreed by six votes to two with an English motion that Scotland were not entitled, without reference to the IB, to cancel their fixture with England. The Scottish motion to determine the status of players receiving cash payments was not passed, the voting being 4–4 with the Chairman having no casting vote. Though the SFU failed to get retrospective action over the payments they did get tacit approval when the meeting unanimously agreed 'That the making of any allowances to players in cash in the opinion of this Committee is contrary to the principles of amateur Rugby Football and in future no such allowances be made to any player'. The meeting finally recommended that the IB should now consider the amendment of its Bye-Laws generally. While, inevitably, these decisions were not entirely to their liking, the SFU 'in the best interests of the Game, decided not to press their views' and so resumed the fixture with England. The SFU then convened a Special General Meeting in March 1909 at which their member clubs gave their unqualified support to the Committee for its stand on cash payments and then moved that steps be taken to alter the Constitution of the IB to allow equal representation to each of the Home Unions. The discussion also showed that there was no support for the formation of an Imperial Board which included the Colonial Unions. J. Aikman Smith spoke out against changes in the Laws recently introduced by the New Zealand Union which tended to make the play faster and so more spectacular while demanding more from the players. On the financial side, he hoped that 'the condition would always remain that the player had to pay something out of his own pocket to play'. An ex-President, R.D. Rainie, echoed this by declaring that such changes would cause the game 'to deteriorate into an amphitheatre display by hired players'. It was also agreed that Scotland should take part only in Colonial tours that were managed by a Committee equally representative of the four countries.

AUSTRALIA 1908–09 AND SOUTH AFRICA 1912–13

During 1906–07 the SFU declined to support a tour in the UK proposed by the New South Wales RU, and a year later, deeming it inadvisable to have a visiting team in the following season, the SFU decided not to ask for any fixtures. Accordingly, when the Australians (New South Wales and Queensland) came in 1908–09, they played no matches in either Scotland or Ireland.

In 1910–11 the IB tentatively agreed on allowable expenses for visiting teams, who had to come as guests. The expenses included third-class fares, all medical attention, first-class hotel accommodation, laundry and a drink at meals only. A Tour Manager had to be appointed.

A year later the Home Unions agreed to a South African tour in the UK in 1912–13 and the financial arrangements proposed by the RFU were approved. The Minutes specified only one problem—a decision by the Oxford University authority to ban any of their players from accepting a place in the Scottish XV against South Africa on 23 November, as the University match was less than a month later. Following letters to the RFU and Oxford University, the edict was cancelled and two Oxford players turned out for Scotland.

BRITISH TOURS OVERSEAS

Reference has elsewhere been made to the Tour to Australia and New Zealand in 1888, organised by Messrs Shaw and Shrewsbury, and to the subsequent inquiry carried out by the SFU into the expenses of the trip.

The Minute Books are silent about the first four overseas tours organised by the RFU—to South Africa in 1891, 1896 and 1902, and to Australia in 1899. The SFU were presumably not 'supporting' any of these, but there is no indication that players with Scottish Clubs were actively discouraged from taking part in them. In the 1891 tour there were five Scottish players, including the captain, W.E.Maclagan (London Scottish). The team won all 19 matches, scoring 220 points to 1 (the 1 being the value of a try at that time). The 1896 party did not contain any Scots; that in 1899 had two, while in 1903 there were seven, with M.C.Morrison (RHSFP) as captain.

During 1903–04 the SFU declined to recognise officially, in any way, a proposed tour to Australia in 1904. Only one Scottish player went, D.R.Bedell-Sivright (Cambridge Univ.), who was appointed captain. (He had been in the tour to South Africa the previous summer.)

In 1906–07 the SFU declined to support a proposed tour to New Zealand in 1908. They also objected, apparently (for the Minutes do not mention this), to any Scottish players taking part and suspended a Clydesdale player who had accepted an invitation to go. The matter was closed by his withdrawal from the touring party. The team (as usual, under the auspices of the RFU) which went to New Zealand and also Australia in 1908 contained only English and Welsh players.

However, the SFU agreed to support a tour to South Africa in 1910. The team was to be chosen by a committee of four, one from each of the Home Unions, and was to be the guests of the South African Union. Five players from Scottish Clubs were included in the party.

33

This tour, the first in which the SFU seem to have been 'officially' involved, was the last before the outbreak of war in August 1914.

In 1912–13 a New South Wales RU request for a visit by a touring team was regarded favourably by the Home Unions. Early in August 1914 the RFU had written with regard to a proposed tour to Australia and New Zealand in 1915. The SFU decided that it was 'injudicious to proceed with such a scheme in the existing state of National affairs'. The Committee went on to state that in any case they would not permit any of their players to visit New Zealand. No reasons were given, but it seems to indicate that the SFU were not happy about the state of the game in that country.

AN IMPERIAL BOARD

From time to time, prior to 1914, proposals for the establishment of an Imperial Board as the ruling body of the game were put forward. In 1905–06 the New South Wales RU circularised the following suggestions:

1. It was now time to constitute an Imperial Board for the control of the game.

2. This Board would contain representatives from each of the four Home Unions, with New Zealand, New South Wales, Queensland, Griqualand West, Nova Scotia, Transvaal, Western Province, British Columbia and any others to be admitted.

The IB, and indeed the four Home Unions, refused to consider these proposals, maintaining that the IB must be the controlling body of the game in the UK.

In 1906–07 New South Wales again suggested the formation of an Imperial Board and the SFU reiterated its refusal to accept such a body. A year later, New South Wales, New Zealand and Queensland were continuing to press for the establishment of such a Board, but the IB and the four Home Unions did not change their views.

RELATIONS WITH FRANCE

Both styles of British football were carried across the Channel by young businessmen. Such helped to form the Le Havre Club in 1872 and started the playing of rugby in Paris by 1877. In 1887 the Union des Sociétés Françaises des Sports Athlétiques (USFSA) was formed as the controlling body in France for a grouping of several sports of which Rugby Football was one.

In 1896 an Edinburgh XV travelled to play a match against a Paris XV, and two years later, a French team played two matches, one at Myreside, Edinburgh, and the other at Hamilton Crescent, Partick. The SFU challenged the financial arrangements of this latter visit and finished up by suspending two of the Scottish organisers whose expense remunerations were considered to be excessive.

In January 1907 the Committee were stirred to deal with a report that a club in membership of the SFU had played a match in France on a Sunday. This produced a sternly worded circular forbidding Sunday play anywhere and finishing with the rebuke 'The Committee regret that there should be any necessity for giving this intimation'.

The first contact with the French ruling body came in March 1907 when the USFSA suggested that a mutual agreement should be signed recognising the other's jurisdiction over rugby football in their respective countries. This the SFU declined, since they could see no object in becoming parties to such an agreement. Later that year the SFU received another request written by C.F.Rutherford (a man of Scottish parentage who was to play a prominent part in the development of rugby in France). This letter asked for an International fixture with Scotland or at least a visit from a strong Scottish club. A decision on this was held over to observe the outcome of the forthcoming French matches against England and Wales, and when Rutherford at the end of the 1908–09 season repeated his request, the SFU offered France an International fixture to be played at Inverleith on 22 January 1910. A fortnight before the game the SFU intimated that the Scottish team would play in white jerseys so that their visitors might play in their usual uniform, which included a light blue jersey. However, they adhered to their policy of only awarding caps for matches against the other three Home Unions.

The fixture was continued until 1913, but the match that year in Paris was marred by the alarming behaviour of the spectators, who throughout the game took great exception to the very firm rulings of the English referee, who at the close was physically threatened and had to be escorted from the field by the players, police and mounted soldiers. The reaction of the RFU was a refusal to provide a referee for any further match in Paris. The SFU took a serious view of the verbal and physical attacks on the referee and cancelled the fixture for 1914, even though it would have been at Inverleith. The Committee took pains to emphasise that their action was directed solely against the spectators and not in any way against the French players and officials. French rugby circles, while deeply regretting the severity of the Scottish decision, were openly critical of the behaviour of their own spectators. Further discussions were halted by the 1914–18 war, but the fixture was resumed in 1920.

In November 1912 the *Scottish Referee* carried the following advertisement: 'The Stade Bordelais, Rugby Champions of France, wish a good Stand-off Half [left-half] for their team. A good business situation will be found in Bordeaux for a capable player.' This was regarded as smacking of professionalism and the French Rugby authorities were contacted. They at once investigated the matter, suspended the committee of the club concerned, dismissed the club coach and banned the club President and one other member for life.

5

SCOTLAND'S INTERNATIONAL
RUGBY GROUNDS

INVERLEITH

FROM Cassels' *Old and New Edinburgh* we learn that Inverleith was
the only baronial estate of any extent that lay to the north-east of
Stockbridge. At the time of Robert I the charter lay with a William
Fairley. By the time of David II it lay with William Ramsay and, by
1381, with David Ramsay.

The lands then passed into the possession of the Touris (or Towers)
family and, by 1678, to the Rocheids (pronounced Rougheid). In 1704
Sir James Rocheid received a baronetcy, but on his death, being
unmarried, the title and grounds passed to his cousin. On the death of
this second baronet the title lapsed and the estate passed to his
daughter, who married Sir John Kinloch, Bart. Their third son
eventually succeeded to the estate of his maternal grandfather and
thereupon assumed the name of Rocheid of Inverleith. His son,
apparently an eminent agriculturalist, was recorded as being 'of in-
ordinate vanity and family pride' and dwelt in the family mansion of
Inverleith House, but after his death, the estate was gradually sold off.
The houses of Inverleith Row were built along the eastern boundary
and, in 1822, the Royal Botanic Garden moved into the same area from
its previous site off Leith Walk.

When the Garden was extended in 1881, Inverleith House and its
grounds were acquired to become the official residence of the Regius
Keeper, but the Trustees of Sir William Fettes and Mr Rocheid were
required to provide proper access to the Garden and to Inverleith
House. It was about this time that Inverleith Place was formed to run
westwards to the entrance of the then relatively new Fettes College.
That the Rocheid family had removed from Inverleith House is
evident from a disposition of 1894 made by Rocheid in favour of the
Governors of the Fettes Trust. This shows that some 53 acres were
conveyed to the Fettes Trust and it was part of this ground that the
SFU purchased in 1897 for their own field of Inverleith. This field lay

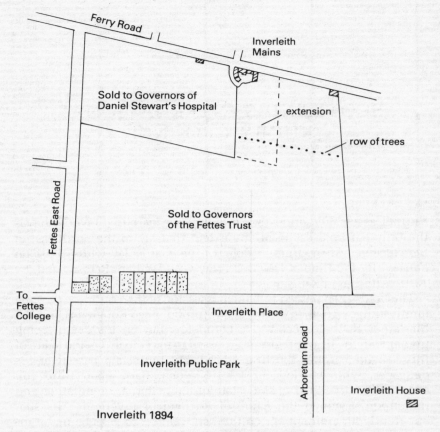

Inverleith 1894

immediately to the south of the steading of Inverleith Mains and to the east of an area bought from the Rocheids by the Governors of Daniel Stewart's Hospital. This disposition was signed by Charles Henry Alexander Frederick Camillo James John Rocheid of Inverleith and Darnchester residing at Pieverstorf Kratzeburgh, Mehlenburg Schuir, Germany – and from another source he is named as Baron Rocheid.

INVERLEITH: THE FIRST UNION FIELD

In the early days of the game no special fields existed for football and play took place on some convenient open area or on a cricket ground, and so it is not surprising to find the *ad hoc* Committee of 1871 asking for the use of The Edinburgh Academy cricket field at Raeburn Place for the first English match. The first nine International matches at least were all played on well-established cricket fields. The second home International match in 1873 was played on the West of Scotland CC ground at Hamilton Crescent, Partick, and these two venues were to be used for International and Trial matches up to 1895 with the SFU making a payment which gradually increased. In 1875, £25 was paid for the English match. This had risen to £30 by 1881 but, by this time, the gate had more than doubled and a temporary stand was erected at a cost of £45.

The Academy, however, remained unhappy about the use of Raeburn Place because their pupils were constantly using the field, especially on Saturdays, and on the day of an International or Trial the SFU had trouble getting the field and ground ready for the match. From 1889 there were frequent discussions between the two bodies over rental and conditions of use, and by 1890 J. Aikman Smith, the newly appointed Hon. Secretary and Treasurer, began a search for an area to be the exclusive property of the Union. The Fettes Trust was approached to secure the use of an area lying south of the College and behind Comely Bank, almost certainly the site of the present Broughton High School. The matter fell through when the Trust decided that the presence of a ground housing International crowds near to the College was not acceptable and declined to feu the area, The Union was thus forced to continue uneasy alliances with both cricket clubs. The clubs complained about the stresses put on their grounds by the crowds, the erection of temporary stands and an insistence that their members should pay for entry to a match. The Union were concerned over the ground being used during the morning of a match and the loss of revenue and control created by members and others gaining entrance without payment. Finally, in October 1895, the Academical Club wrote to say that it was with the greatest reluctance that they had resolved not to lease Raeburn Place in the future. The Union recorded its genuine regret at this interruption of the association of the Union with Raeburn Place which had continued for so many years.

Faced with this, the Committee secured the use of the Queen's Park Football Club ground at Old Hampden Park for the English match in 1896. The District and Trial games were played on the School field at Merchiston Castle and on the Royal High School FP ground at Newington.

By March 1891, J. Aikman Smith reported that he was negotiating terms for a field which he considered would be in every way suitable for the purposes of the Union and accordingly Messrs R. D. Rainie and R. M. M. Roddick were appointed to join him in a sub-committee to handle and report on the matter. Various planning difficulties held the affair back and it was not until after a Special GM in August 1897 that it was agreed to purchase Inverleith for £3,800, a sum to be met mainly by the issue of Debentures. Then, in December 1897, the SFU became the first of the Home Unions to own and run its own rugby field and stand. While the ground was being prepared, the sports ground at Powderhall in Edinburgh was used for the home matches against Ireland in 1897 and England in 1898 (the Welsh match in 1897 was cancelled because of the Gould dispute). The ground at Inverleith was ready for the Welsh match in January 1899, but the game was postponed because of inclement weather and the field was opened by the Irish match on 18 February 1899.

Later, two further strips of land were purchased, one in 1901 to allow the erection of a splendid reporters' box and telephone office opposite the Stand and another in 1905 to allow the straightening of the fencing at the south-east corner. Up to 1914 there was little change: some further enclosure seats were added and there were the usual repairs and painting done to the stand seats and metalwork.

A groundsman, A.E.Sellars, was settled in the cottage attached to the ground and almost certainly it was he, a keen cricketer, who encouraged the Leith Caledonian CC to apply for and be granted a lease and the summer use of the field for their practice and matches. As well as this, by 1901, Edinburgh Wanderers FC, who had been using the Grange CC field at Raeburn Place, were granted a controlled winter lease of the ground. In 1913, when the Newington RFC dissolved because of their failure to get a ground of their own, their co-tenants, Bruntsfield RFC, asked the Union if it would pay the rental of their field, which was part of the Edinburgh Polo Club field at Murrayfield. The Union discussed the point and resolved to approach the Polo Club in an attempt to obtain the whole area for the following season and throw it open for the use of several Junior Clubs, but this move came to nothing.

THE SECOND UNION GROUND: MURRAYFIELD

During the 1914–18 War, Inverleith had been made available for military matches, but little, if any, maintenance work was carried out and, by 1919, the condition of the wood and metalwork was causing concern. Some badly needed painting was done and the wooden enclosure seats were replaced by a double row of metal ones. It was not long before other relevant matters were troubling the Committee.

It was quickly evident that Inverleith would barely cope with the greater numbers now attending the International matches and the demand for stand seats could not be met. The Western clubs were pressing for one International match to be played in Glasgow, where only an existing Association field such as Hampden Park could be used. The former Royal High School PP and FP grounds at Corstorphine, leased in 1920 for the use of Junior clubs in Edinburgh, were lost when the City took over the ground in 1921. An approach was made to the Fettes Trust for the leasing of ground to the east of

Inverleith and two estimates were obtained for a second Stand to be built on that side of the field. This project would have proved to be costly, but then J. Aikman Smith reported the possibility of acquiring the ground belonging to the Edinburgh Polo Club, some 19 acres at Murrayfield, and, inside 3 months in late 1922, the area was purchased and the initial steps taken to raise embankments and erect a stand. Straightaway another successful issue of Debentures made this venture secure and, eventually, the last International game was played at Inverleith against France in January 1925. The second Union field was opened with the English match in March 1925. This proved to be a memorable game watched by a record crowd of some 70,000 spectators, an attendance which from the outset, justified the move to the more spacious ground. In 1927 more ground to the west was purchased; two access bridges across the Water of Leith were built, extra pitches for the use of Junior clubs were laid out and eventually, a car park was brought into use. The demand for stand tickets did not lessen and so, in 1936, two wing extensions to the stand were added, raising the seating capacity to 15,228. About this time, several improvements were made to the dressing-rooms and the Committee acquired a box in the stand and a bigger Committee room. Inverleith was sold to the Merchant Company in 1926 and the War Memorial Arch, erected there in 1921, was transferred to Murrayfield in 1936. There were some notable gifts to the Union. In 1929 Sir David McCowan presented the clock tower, in 1930 J. Aikman Smith presented the first score box and in 1931 Sheriff Watt, KC, presented the flag staff and flag.

MURRAYFIELD: THE SECOND WAR BREAK 1939–1945

As early as May 1939 the Union, perturbed by the political situation, advised The Edinburgh University RFC not to take part in a proposed tour in New Zealand by the Home Universities, yet three months later, following a decision by the Home Unions Board, it was agreed to resume relations with the FFR and France was offered a fixture in Paris in January 1940.

The outbreak of war in September brought everything to a halt; the newly arrived Australian touring team returned home without playing a single game. The Union cancelled all its Trials and Matches but did encourage the clubs to carry on as far as possible. Some clubs were forced to close. Others, like Edinburgh Academicals with Edinburgh Wanderers, and West of Scotland with Kelvinside Academicals, amalgamated, and the surviving clubs, short of petrol, oil, coal, food and clothing coupons, carried on playing neighbouring clubs and filling in blank Saturdays by entertaining teams from the Forces stationed in their areas.

The Union at once remitted all annual subscriptions, postponed Debenture payments and at the 1940 AGM altered its Bye-Laws to permit the existing Committee to continue and administer the affairs of the Union for the duration of the National Emergency. The ground and accommodation at Murrayfield were offered for National purposes and were immediately taken over as a Supply Depot by the RASC.

Thus club rugby remained alive and, in addition, the Services' sports authorities from 1942–1945 arranged two Scotland v England Services Internationals each season, the 'home' matches being played at Inverleith for two seasons with a return to Murrayfield made after the ground was derequisitioned in 1944.

With the virtual end of hostilities in 1945, the Union urged the District Unions and the clubs to restart the game in their regions and during 1946 selected Scottish XVs to play a number of Victory International matches (no caps being awarded) against the Home Countries and also a strong New Zealand Army team.

At the first post-war AGM in 1946 the state of emergency was regarded as ended and the original Bye-Laws were restored; the full International card was resumed and this included a fixture in Paris against France.

MURRAYFIELD: POST WAR

The five war years of comparative neglect meant that much costly remedial work had to be done to the ground and stand. The weathered terracing steps and barriers were gradually brought back to standard whilst the enclosure seating was repaired and additional rows added. In the stand, the roofing, metalwork, seating and woodwork were all thoroughly overhauled and, in certain sectors, the seating was repositioned to produce a more satisfactory grouping. Following on a decision, taken in 1949, that the Union Office should eventually be transferred to Murrayfield a survey was begun into the possible further use of the areas within the stand. This resulted in many improvements and extensions being made to all the players' and referees' dressing-rooms and showers. Additional tea-rooms were provided for lady guests and International players, and by 1972, the present Committee Box, with its direct access to improved Committee Rooms, was built. The projected move of the Union Office from Coates Crescent took place in late 1964, since which time the accommodating of the increase in administrative personnel has been met by opening or adapting other areas within the stand.

The most outstanding innovation was the introduction of undersoil heating on the field of play. As early as 1952 the constant threat of cancellation of matches because of wintry conditions moved the

Committee to investigate the possibility of installing such a system, but the cost, at that time, was considered prohibitive. However, when in 1959 Dr C. A. Hepburn (Hillhead High School FP) offered to meet the entire cost of the installation, his generous proposal was most gratefully accepted. The system was laid and ready for use by the start of the following season. Today, its success is an established fact and the gift is acknowledged on a plaque placed on the wall at the rear of the stand.

During this same period, the provision of floodlighting was examined, but it was decided that it was not expedient to erect such a system, which at Murrayfield would have a fairly limited use. Instead, noting that in the Borders, the Kelso club had erected their own set of lights, it was decided, with the intention of aiding the playing of Inter-District matches, to support the financing of such installations at suitable fields in Glasgow, Edinburgh and the North. Eventually this led to floodlighting being installed at the Hillhead HSFP ground at Hughenden. Elsewhere, nothing developed immediately although, once again, Dr Hepburn expressed a desire to help install flood-lighting at Murrayfield. This further proposal was examined, but the discussions and the design and placing of the lights became so pro-longed that the project came to a halt when Dr Hepburn found it necessary to withdraw his offer.

Serious consideration was also given to the provision of either covered enclosures for the embankments or the erection of a second stand along the east side of the field. Estimates were studied but again the high cost caused the scheme to be laid aside. In 1975 the Welsh match was played before a world record of some 104,000 spectators whilst many other hundreds failed to get sight of the game. There followed a decision that future International games at Murrayfield would be all-ticket affairs with an upper limit of 70,000 spectators. This restriction, the keen annual demands for stand tickets and various aspects of spectator control on the terracing, gave cause for rethinking and, by July 1981, a decision was taken to erect the new East Stand at Murrayfield. It was agreed to finance part of the cost by the issue of 5,000 Interest-free Loans of £400, the cash to be repayable in 20 years and giving the lender the right to purchase one ticket for each home International. These financial arrangements were formally agreed at a Special GM in December 1981. The complete cost was expected to be £3.15 million, towards which the Scottish Sports Council offered a grant of £250,000. In March 1982, the President, Mr Fraser MacAllister (Clarkston), symbolically cut a turf on the Inter-national pitch to mark the start of the construction work on the new Stand. This was actually completed in December 1982 and in use for the Irish and Welsh games early in 1983 but was officially opened by

HRH The Princess Anne before the match against the Barbarians on 26 March 1983.

During this season Marketing Agents for the Union were appointed and subsequently the Royal Bank of Scotland agreed to sponsor International matches on the ground for three seasons from 1982–83.

The old score-box having been demolished during the building of the East Stand, two electric scoreboards were installed, one on each Stand. An offer from Mrs G. P. S. Macpherson to contribute the cost of a clock at the rear of the East Stand in memory of her late husband was accepted, and a plaque affixed to the back of the stand acknowledges this gift.

The pitch and other facilities have continually been made available to various bodies: The Edinburgh and District Charity Sevens; the Edinburgh Highland Games; the Scottish Women's Hockey Association; the Scottish Ladies' Lacrosse Association; the Clan Gathering and World Pipe Band Competition; Jehovah's Witnesses; a pop concert by David Bowie; and for a Youth Rally to welcome to Edinburgh His Holiness The Pope.

The Harlem Globetrotters succeeded in staging their own style of entertainment on a floor laid in front of the stand. In 1947 the Heart of Midlothian FC, faced with the possibility of meeting the Hibernian FC in a cup tie, asked if Murrayfield could be made available for such a meeting. This was actually agreed to, but the tie did not materialise. Serious consideration was given to housing part of the Commonwealth Games of 1970, but, since this would have entailed the widening of the field by moving back the east embankment, the idea fell through.

The secondary pitches behind the stand were soon fully used by Edinburgh Wanderers, several Junior clubs (Bruntsfield, Kenmore and Royal (Dick) Veterinary College), Scotus Academy and Edinburgh Ladies' Lacrosse Club. Wanderers were later given permission to set up training lights and to erect a small stand (the inscription on the front of which gives a subtle reminder of the very early foundation of the club), but when they sought permission to build a pavilion for their own use within Murrayfield, the club received an explicit and very firm refusal.

44

6

THE DEVELOPMENT OF COACHING
IN SCOTLAND

THERE is no doubt the teaching, instructing, training and 'coaching' of rugby in some form or another has been carried out in schools and clubs since the inception of our game. This chapter on coaching indicates in the first instance how the Scottish Rugby Union, as a body, showed interest in giving a lead in this field, and, in the second, the way the coaching structure has evolved into the sophisticated, well-organised form of today.

The disastrous results of the National XV in the very early 1950s seem to have been the stimulus which motivated the Scottish Rugby Union, in turn, to attempt to do something about improving the game in Scotland. It was agreed that the starting-point must be to emphasise to players and schoolboys the importance of performing the basic skills. The problem was—how to get this over.

The first mention in the SRU minutes of this is a 'Training Course in Glasgow in the Summer of 1952 organised by J.M.Anderson and R.W.Shaw, where loop films on the basic skills were shown to the performers'. The loop films were taken from an RFU film and were reported to be quite satisfactory, but the equipment necessary to show the films was cumbersome and difficult to operate efficiently. Following this Course the SRU, in September 1952, formed a sub-committee of three, which was composed of the Glasgow Members—J.M. Anderson, H. Waddell and R.W.Shaw. Its remit was to advise on material for loop films, and liaise with the Scottish Instructional Film Unit. Permission was granted by the RFU to use their film, and the Committee also authorised that copies of the RFU Manual be made available to clubs and schools.

At a General Committee Meeting on 22 May 1953 great concern was shown as to where all the promising rugby players at school were going after they left, because many did not seem to be joining clubs. On 2 October 1953 J.M.Bannerman was most adamant that the SRU should be giving a lead to clubs and schools as to the type of game that should be played in Scotland. H.Waddell undertook to get the loop films and instructions on the basic skills out to schools and clubs, along with diagrams of 3-2-3 scrum formation, and the 'wheel'.

In the Autumn of 1954 the President, J.M.Bannerman, to endorse his philosophy, arranged meetings in each District to meet the head-masters of schools, and the presidents and captains of clubs, to preach his gospel. The outcome of this was that a sub-committee of the Union was formed to liaise with schools. The Committee, J.M.Bannerman, H.Waddell, D.S.Kerr, R.W.Shaw, C.W.Drummond and A.W.Wilson, was instructed to look into the matter of organising a Coaching Conference for schoolmasters. Its main belief was expressed emphatic-ally: that coaching was for schoolboys and every effort be made to help schoolmasters who taught rugby.

At the Committee meeting prior to the SRU AGM on 19 May 1955, the President reported on the proceedings of the first finding of the Sub-committee to liaise with schools, and asked approval for the objectives laid down:

1. That in any district where such did not exist already, school-masters should be urged to form local Associations on the lines of the Edinburgh and District Schools' Rugby Association.

2. That there should be close liaison between these District Associations of schoolmasters, and the SRU Representative for the area on matters of purely local interest.

3. That each District Association of schoolmasters should be invited to nominate two representatives to meet the SRU Schools' Liaison Committee from time to time to discuss matters of national interest.

4. That the SRU should sponsor a rugby coaching conference for schoolmasters at the beginning of season 1955–56. Enquiries to be made to ascertain which one of the public schools would grant facilities for the conference.

5. An early meeting between the Schools' Liaison Sub-Com-mittee and schoolmasters' representatives should be held to discuss the proposed coaching conference.

6. That a letter should be sent to the headmasters of all rugby-playing schools, outlining the above proposals.

The above was approved and acted on.

This first National Coaching Conference organised by the SRU took place on 8 and 9 September 1955 at Fettes College, Edinburgh, where 148 schoolmasters attended. The course was staffed by prominent past international players, along with F.McDonald, rugby master at Fettes College. The cost to the SRU was £530.

The Convener of the Conference was R.W.Shaw (SRU). His 'summing-up' of the Conference is interesting:

Aims of Conference
1. The SRU interest in schools.
2. Co-operation with masters in charge of rugby.
3. Bringing them together.
4. Helping boys to obtain more enjoyment out of the game.
5. Improvement in Scottish club rugby standards.
6. Improvement of International Team.

Design of Conference and Choice of Subjects, Speakers and Demonstrators
1. Physical fitness.
2. Individual requirements.
3. Combined efforts: (a) forwards; (b) half backs; (c) three-quarters; (d) full back; (e) the team; (f) the captain.
4. Coaching methods.
5. Hints to referees.
6. Demonstrations.
7. Use of aids: (a) loop films; (b) diagrams; (c) blackboard.
8. Discussion groups and questions.

Conclusions
1. Have we achieved our aims?: (a) short term; (b) long term.
2. Work to be done by masters: (a) sacrifice of time; (b) production of better citizens; (c) rewards.

Responsibilities of SRU
1. To clubs.
2. To Scotland.

As a follow-up to the National Course, the District Representatives were requested to spread the 'word' and 'deeds' still further, as they thought fit, in their own District.

The Midlands District Schools' Rugby Association was quick to react and held a Course for Schoolmasters in the Midlands at Dollar on 27 November 1955. This was well attended and derived praise from A. W. Wilson, SRU Representative.

The SRU Sub-committee and Schools' Representatives from each District, and Representatives from Headmasters Conference Schools and Preparatory Schools, met in the North British Hotel, Edinburgh, on Friday, 9 December 1955. Thus the first Schools' Liaison Committee, as we know it today, was formed. Two main conclusions from the meeting were as follows:
1. Districts should organise Courses for Masters who had little knowledge of the game of rugby, and who were taking junior school teams.
2. There should be a National Course for Masters taking 1st XVs.

The Border clubs held a Training Course for players on 26 August

1956, and on 9 September 1956, a course was held for schoolmasters in the Borders. C.W.Drummond indicated that a further two courses would be held in September 1957, one for forwards and one for backs, because he felt the best way to 'spread the policy' of the Union was via the senior players. G.G.Crerar reported that the West had similar courses organised for September 1957.

The SRU Committee decided, at their meeting on 26 September 1956, to further emphasise their policy, and to improve communication with clubs and schools, that the notes prepared by H.Waddell, for the Borders courses at Melrose, be revised and printed in booklet form for sale at a nominal price to individual players, clubs and schools. Consequently, *Raise the Standard* was available for sale at one shilling on Saturday, 1 December 1956. Over 4,000 copies were sold in the following months. The Committee was complimented for their efforts by the President, W.M.Simmers.

Two factors put a temporary brake on course development: (a) opposition from the clergy concerning Sunday participation in rugby authorised by the Scottish Rugby Union, and (b) financing of courses. The Committee decided they could not give their 'blessing' to official organised training courses, which took place on a Sunday, '... but had no objection to individuals being associated with the running of such courses as be deemed necessary, either as speakers or demonstrators'.

On 2 November 1957 R.W.Shaw, Convener Schools' Liaison Committee, felt that the Committee should consider at the very earliest opportunity:
1. Financial policy in regard to coaching: (a) towards clubs; (b) towards referees; (c) towards schools.
2. SRU District Representatives must report on all courses held or to be held.

On 30 November 1957 the Committee accepted the financial responsibility for approved courses. A sum of £150 was allocated to each District for this purpose, but was not to be used for financing the operation of District Schools' Associations.

The convener of selectors, A.W.Wilson, was asked to state the policy which the National XV would be following in the 1958–59 season, and all Districts, clubs and schools should be made aware of this. Close contact should also be kept with the Schools' Liaison Committee to ensure all courses were on a similar 'tack'—so essential for the development of the game in Scotland.

Extracts from the Minutes illustrate interesting developments:
30 August 1958. Glasgow District Schools held a coaching conference at Jordanhill College. Cost to the SRU, £18.
6 December 1958. The topic of international rugby for schoolboys was raised at a Schools' Liaison Meeting, but the SRU very

definitely turned it down. The principle of 'say no, and think again' was applied once more.

6 February 1959. C.W.McGeorge of Larchfield School volunteered to coach Glasgow University 1st XV. This was given full support by the SRU Committee.

8 January 1960. The subject of international rugby for schoolboys was again brought up. The SRU now agreed that it should be left to the schools to work out their own policy on this matter, but keep the Union informed of every step. (NB. It was on 27 March 1966 that the schoolmasters resolved to form the Scottish Schools' Rugby Union, and the constitution was placed before the SRU for approval on 16 June 1968.)

The first schoolboys' international was played v England at Murrayfield on 14 April 1967 and resulted in a 3-points each draw. A great deal of assistance in these matters was given willingly by the SRU, and M.S.Stewart, R.W.Shaw, A.W.Wilson and C.W.Drummond have to be commended for their tactful guidance.

At a meeting on 24 June 1960, the Convener of Selectors again reaffirmed his policy for the season 1960–61. C.W.Drummond informed the SRU of the advantages gained, and lessons learned on Scotland's short tour to South Africa in May 1960. This first short tour proved invaluable. He recommended that Districts, clubs and schools be asked to concentrate on (a) fitness; (b) the practice of basic skills; and (c) emphasis on attack. The players on the South African tour were to be invited to visit schools and clubs, and attend the courses organised throughout the coming season.

At the same meeting it was stated that attention must be given to Referees' Courses, but once again kept under the strict jurisdiction of the SRU Representatives. Clubs were to be encouraged to run Colts XVs to cater for boys leaving school at 15.

A sum of £150 was again given to each District, and part of this could be used to assist clubs with Colts XVs.

In September 1960, in a further effort to put the message across to as many schoolmasters as possible, it was agreed to invite Representatives of the Scottish School of Physical Education, Jordanhill, to attend the Schools' Liaison Meetings, and invitations were sent to Messrs Orr and Dickinson. W.Dickinson was later to become the first Adviser to the Captain of the National XV.

The game in Scotland in the early 1960s was certainly developing and branching out in many ways. More schools, including junior secondary schools, were giving more boys the opportunity to play rugby. District Schools' Rugby Associations were established in all Districts apart from the North, who were still finding one or two

49

difficulties—although support for the game was growing in the Inverness area. Many inter-district school games were now played. The talk of international rugby for schoolboys was developing into a possibility. The number of new rugby clubs was increasing, with clubhouses becoming a necessary requirement of the rugby scene. Floodlights were appearing at some grounds in each District. Referee Societies and Allocation Committees were also formed, and television was attempting to show its value in portraying the game with resultant financial proceeds enabling the Union to assist clubs in general. The SRU was living with this expansion, but was still determined that the improvement in the quality of the game was of prime importance. They continued with this policy of encouraging courses in Districts (a) for schoolmasters coaching boys; (b) for club referees and schoolmaster referees; (c) for players; (d) for boys at under-15½ age level.

There was a great deal of talk about courses, but putting courses into operation, and their ultimate success, depended on the enthusiasm and expertise of the District members. An indication of the varied type of course available to participants included:

1. Edinburgh District, in addition to their annual course for schoolmasters in September 1961, organised a Camp Course at West Linton for boys of under 15 from non-rugby playing schools.

2. Glasgow District held a one-day Conference on 9 September 1961 at Jordanhill for masters and representatives of clubs.

3. Glasgow District had a Coaching Conference for players in June 1962 likely to help with coaching.

4. Midlands District had a Course in October 1962 for schoolmaster referees.

5. There is no doubt that South District organised numerous courses that were never recorded in the SRU minutes.

Pressure was increasing for the SRU to become more involved in the coaching sphere. There was a greater demand for National Courses to set the standard and dictate the policy, with a resultant follow-up at District level.

The SRU accepted the challenge, conscious of the cost, and decided to organise a National Course for boys of under 15, to develop and improve their basic skills. The Union hoped that greater interest would be created, to encourage those boys who left school at an early age, to continue to play the game.

Two courses, with 120 boys in each, took place at Fettes College on 11 and 12 September and 14 and 15 September 1963. (The course was held on a Sunday and a church service was incorporated in the programme.) Boys from every type of school were invited and, ultimately, there was a satisfying response. The courses were claimed to be invigorating and, at their conclusion, two factors were very much in evidence: (a) the boys from junior secondary schools benefited most and, (b) the staff coach with the 'professional' technique of delivery, expertise in handling groups, plus rugby-playing knowledge was a great asset.

The following year, in September, the SRU organised a further course at Fettes College, for schoolmasters. This time both coaching and refereeing were on the programme. The coaches, many with a teaching background, staffed the above courses, and were to play an important part in laying a sound foundation to the SRU coaching structure in the future. Many are still contributing today.

In 1965, £200 was the allocation given to Districts. On 20 November 1965 a sub-committee was set up '... to investigate and report on what can be done by the SRU for the furtherance of the interests of rugby football in Scotland'. The terms of reference included all school rugby matters; provision of playing-fields for rugby; courses of all descriptions; and the financial commitment to the SRU. This *ad hoc* Committee, convened by A. W. Wilson, took the task in hand. The attitude of this Committee was 'proceed positively but hasten slowly'.

On 4 November 1966 at the SRU Meeting, under the Presidency of M. S. Stewart, the *ad hoc* Committee made some of its findings known—one of the most significant concerning coaching. The President asked the full Committee to give complete support to the *ad hoc* Committee's proposal, i.e. 'to set up a panel of volunteer coaches comprising experienced players, to go around clubs, if and when requested by clubs'.

The Committee also supported the motion to organise a National Course for club referees to take place at Murrayfield on 1 October 1967, in addition to a National Course for schoolmaster referees, at Fettes College, on 7 September 1967.

Some thought was given to a course for the 'panel of volunteer coaches', but action was delayed at the time.

The season 1967–68 was vital as regards decisions on coaching by the SRU. The Minutes indicate that a great deal of time, thought and discussion was given to coaching matters, including (a) the escalation of coaching in other Home Countries; (b) the formation and assembly of squads; (c) the 'threat' of National XVs being coached and (d) types of course for intending coaches.

At this juncture, an invitation from the RFU was sent to all Home Countries to attend a Meeting of their Sub-committee responsible for coaching, on 23 April 1968, at the East India Sports Club in London. The *ad hoc* Committee recommended acceptance, and also that the President, G. G. Crerar, should attend accompanied by a member of the Selection Committee, appointed by the Convener of Selectors. G.W.Thomson was appointed to attend. A great deal of valuable information was gained from the meeting, including the current position of coaching in the UK.

The SRU, at their meeting on 27 June 1968, after a lengthy discussion on 'what is good for Scottish rugby?', agreed to form a sub-committee for coaching, and appoint a convener with powers to choose his Sub-Committee—but '. . . to keep in close liaison with the National Selection Convener and Schools' Liaison Convener, and report expediently and regularly to the full Committee, particularly on finance'. G.W.Thomson was appointed Convener. The simple remit was to develop a coaching structure in Scotland, in order that a standard of play would be maintained, at a level which would allow Scotland to continue to compete as a major force in world rugby.

The Coaching Sub-committee, established under the Convenership of G.W.Thomson, was A.Bowie, G.Burrell and J.W.Y.Kemp. G.W. Thomson held the Convenership until his election as President in 1982–83, when T.Pearson took over. This Committee was to oversee many changes in both coaching and the structure of the game in Scotland.

As a first step towards achieving the aim of having a coach for every club in Scotland, a Coaching Advisory Panel was established in 1968 to act as a 'think tank' in coaching development, putting forward ideas to the Sub-committee for consideration. Advisory Coaches were appointed in each of the five Districts as a means of spreading the word around the clubs.

Coaching Advisory Panel

L. Tatham (Chairman), W.Dickinson (Jordanhill College), T. Pearson (Howe of Fife), A.Robson (Dollar Academy, President SSRU), A.T.Ross (RHSFP), J.W.Shearer (Galashiels Academy).

Lin Tatham proved an able and progressive chairman in the formative years.

District Advisory Coaches

Edinburgh: G.Sharp, R.M.Tollervey, J.Young.

Glasgow: J.Coletta, I.N.Cosgrove, J.H.Roxburgh, A.W.A.Sproul.

Midlands: W.D.Allardice, D.M.D.Rollo, J.B.Steven.

South: J.L.Allan, R.P.Burrell, R.G.Charters, D.Grant.

North: C.A.D.Baillie, A.Hamilton, N.A.McEwan, A.J.K.Munro, J.B.Morrison.

In 1969 the SRU staged its first National Course for Club Coaches, with all clubs being invited to send a representative. This course still continues as an annual event, thus enabling clubs to develop their own coaching structure.

The National Course itself continues to develop and now comprises

52

Parts I and II of the National Coaching Course for Club Coaches, the SRU Club Coach Award Course, the National Under-21 Player Improvement Course and the National Course for Referees. It is a course well-respected throughout the rugby world, and many visitors from other Home Nations and from overseas have attended and enjoyed the experience.

Over the years many other types of Coaching Courses have become part and parcel of SRU coaching policy; in any season the following activities are likely to be available to clubs and schools:

National

Annual National Course for club coaches, referees and invited under-21 players.

Youth Camp held at Struan, Perthshire, run in conjunction with the Scottish Schoolboys' Club.

Residential courses for 13–16 year olds.

District

Coaches and teachers involved with under-18 teams.

Coaches and teachers involved with mini/midi-rugby.

Player improvement at under-18 and under-21 levels.

Skill clinics for 13–16 year olds.

Referee courses for referees, schoolmasters and club members.

Special

Teacher certificate courses.

Individual school-based in-service.

Individual club visits by the technical staff and advisory coaches.

This wide workload is administered by two full-time Technical Staff—the Technical Administrator, J.H.Roxburgh (appointed in 1974) and the Assistant Technical Administrator, D.W.Arneil (appointed in 1981). The practical aspects are handled by the Technical Staff, the Coaching Advisory Panel and the Advisory Coaches.

As well as developing coaching at senior club level, the Coaching Sub-committee took on the role of developing a Youth Rugby structure to provide rugby for boys between the ages of 8–18 outwith the normal school structure. This development became necessary with the broadening Physical Education Curriculum and with the lessening commitment of teaching staff to extra-curricular activity. This in no way signified the Union's withdrawal of support for school rugby, which is still regarded as extremely important in terms of Scottish rugby. It was, however, an acceptance of reality and a genuine attempt to ensure a fruitful future for the game in Scotland.

In 1974 Mini-Rugby was introduced as an activity suitable for Primary Schools. For whatever reason, the game did not develop in this sphere, but it did catch on and grow quickly within the Club structure. The SRU, whilst encouraging this development, was most careful to issue strict rules governing the number of matches and tournaments to be undertaken by boys in this age group to avoid unnecessary pressure on the youngsters. Mini-Rugby needs to be about participation and enjoyment; it is an introduction to the game of rugby, and should never be seen as an end in itself.

A consequence of Mini-Rugby was the growing number of boys in the 12–16 year age group who wished to continue their connection with a rugby club. The SRU realised that the majority of these boys would be able to play their rugby at school and wished to encourage them to do so. However, Midi-Rugby (as rugby in this age group has become known) has been allowed to develop naturally within the club structure, and is proving to be a productive source of playing talent in areas where school rugby is not as strong as might be desirable. Boys who play club rugby in this age group can be nominated by their clubs to attend the annual Youth Rugby Camp which the SRU run in conjunction with the Scottish Schoolboys' Club. The first Camp was held in 1978 at Bruar, and although life is somewhat spartan, some 140 boys are encouraged to develop the full range of rugby skills in an atmosphere of competitive companionship, which is the very soul of Rugby Union Football.

It has been on the next stage of the ladder, i.e. 16–18 age group, that perhaps the biggest development has taken place in recent years with the emergence of a Club-based Youth Rugby structure. The SRU in conjunction with sponsorship from the Royal Bank of Scotland introduced in 1980 a District League competition, with the District League winners meeting in the semi-finals to determine which two clubs would meet on the international pitch at Murrayfield, and compete for the magnificent Royal Bank Trophy. Further developments in this age group have been a full Inter-District Championship with teams chosen exclusively from Youth League Clubs, and the progression to National and International matches.

The development of club rugby in this age group has not been without its problems, particularly the potential clash of interests between school and club. However, the SRU has continued to support and encourage school rugby, and, gradually, the level of co-operation between schools and clubs has improved.

Season 1985–86 sees the introduction of International rugby at Under-19 level. The vast majority of the players will come from the SSRU, and Scotland Under-18 squads of the previous season. This development is seen as a means of retaining highly talented players within the game at a vital stage in their careers—which is the time to transfer from under age to senior rugby.

It is the aim of all those involved in the Coaching structure of Scottish rugby to ensure that all players at all levels of the game have

54

the opportunity to fulfil their potential, and to maximise their enjoyment in playing the game.

Coaches and referees, who contribute so much to assist the players to achieve this aim, are given positive guidelines in the Scottish Rugby Union publications.

Following the early days when there was the very commendable initiative in the production of the booklets, *Raise the Standard* which extolled truths so applicable today, and *Laws of the Game* simplified by the international referee A.I.Dickie, numerous publications have appeared in recent years.

Mini-Rugby, Touch Judging, Positioning of Referees, Coaching Handbook, Fundamentals of Coaching, Scrummage and Back Play from Scrummage have all been covered. Others dealing with Ruck/Maul, Lineout, and Defence are in preparation. These illustrate the confidence the SRU has in portraying the game as they wish it to be played.

In conclusion it is fair to say that, since the Course at Fettes in 1955, the development of coaching in Scotland has been spectacular in comparison with any previous 'changes' in our game. Financially, this progressive development has seen the expenditure in coaching rise from £1,000 in 1965 to £52,000 in the 1983–84 'Grand Slam' Season. This outlay is an expression of the Union's pursuit of its prime objective 'to promote, encourage and extend the game of Rugby Football in Scotland'.

G.W.THOMSON, Coaching Convener 1968–82
T.PEARSON, Coaching Convener 1982–
J.H.ROXBURGH, Technical Administrator
D.W.ARNEIL, Asst. Technical Administrator

7

THE SCOTTISH RUGBY UNION
CHAMPIONSHIP

BEFORE the formation of the Scottish Football Union in 1873 rugby clubs in Scotland arranged their own fixtures. Consequently, over the years the longer-established clubs gradually built up fixture lists, which were perpetuated with an apparently inherent disinclination on the part of these clubs to depart from what had become traditional and, to that extent, permanent fixtures. This meant that as the game spread more widely the emerging clubs found it virtually impossible to break into the pattern of these arrangements except on an occasional or temporary basis.

Through the medium of the newspapers there was introduced an unofficial championship—so called because the SRU very properly refused, officially at least, to condone what was essentially an arbitrary situation—comprising eventually some 33 of the older clubs. This unofficial championship did little to facilitate the introduction of new clubs to the established order: certainly it took clubs many years of hard work and good results to be admitted. The anomaly of this situation was never better illustrated than when Boroughmuir FP, having been admitted to the unofficial championship in season 1954–55, promptly won it at the first attempt!

It was largely the acknowledgement of the difficulties posed to the more recently-established clubs to improve their fixture lists that encouraged Heriot's FP, supported by Glasgow High School FP, at the 1969 AGM of the SRU to propose:

That the Committee of the Scottish Rugby Union should investigate the introduction of a system of competitive club rugby in Scotland, such system to be introduced at the earliest possible date.

As no one reasonably could cavil at an 'investigation' the motion was carried unanimously.

The SRU Committee of the day did not waste time and drafted provisional proposals—suggesting a series of district leagues followed by a knock-out competition among the leading clubs in each league—which were sent to clubs for consideration. Thereafter the then Vice-President, R. W. Shaw, visited clubs in each of the districts to confirm that it was agreed that some form of organised competitive rugby was desirable and to discuss the provisional proposals as to how it should be structured.

No clear generally agreed view emerged, so there was put to the 1970 AGM a Motion on behalf of the SRU Committee proposing a system of regional leagues culminating in a knock-out tournament embracing the leading clubs in each of these leagues. After much discussion a view emerged that preference was for a national competition and it was agreed to introduce as soon as possible a system of competitive rugby composed of a national league or leagues and that a consultative committee be appointed to make the necessary arrangements.

The Consultative Committee—comprising five representatives of the SRU Committee (W.L.Connon, A.W.Harper, F.MacAllister, T.Pearson, J.R.B.Wilson) and one club representative from each of the four districts (I.Cameron, T.Henderson, J.K.Hutchison, J.S. Methven)—was set up under the chairmanship of the new Vice-President A.W.Wilson. The Committee worked hard and quickly brought forward a proposal that there should be three divisions of 16 clubs each and a fourth division embracing the remaining full-member clubs which wished to participate. It also put forward provisional rules to regulate the competition.

These proposals were discussed with club representatives at a special meeting held a month before the 1971 AGM. At the AGM some optional ideas proposed by clubs were discussed but no conclusion was reached. It was agreed to appoint an organising committee to pursue matters.

The Organising Committee was formed on the same basis as the Consultative Committee but under the chairmanship of Special Representative W.L.Connon. Taking into consideration the many and varied views which previously had been expressed the Committee eventually recommended that the Championship should comprise four divisions of 12 clubs each plus a fifth division split into an east section (9 clubs) and a west section (14 clubs).

The main problem faced by both the Consultative and Organising Committees had been the composition of the various divisions. Clubs were consulted about their perception of which clubs should be in which division: attempts were also made to compare records over the preceding three years although the then-existing structure of widely-varying fixture lists inevitably meant that it was often impossible to compare like with like. Nonetheless the composition of the new leagues was achieved and, generally, it was accepted that any marginal errors or anomalies in allocation would be corrected within the first year or two of the Championship.

The proposals were accepted at the 1972 AGM when it was agreed that the Championship would commence with effect from season 1973–74—this to facilitate the re-arranging of existing fixtures. Thereafter the name of the Organising Committee was changed to the Championship Committee.

Initially, attempts were made, when compiling the Championship fixture lists, to embody existing fixtures between clubs in the same division. However, it was revealed that this would create an imbalance of home and away games and the Championship Committee undertook the arrangement of all fixtures in all divisions so as to provide an equitable distribution of home and away matches. The Committee also finalised the Championship Rules.

During the inaugural year of the Championship only two minor points for consideration arose. The first was that, because some clubs had difficulty in agreeing dates for the playing of postponed games, the Rules were changed to empower the Championship Committee to direct when and where such matches be played in the event of clubs failing to agree. It is praiseworthy that, in subsequent years, these powers seldom have been invoked—a tribute to all clubs for operating within the spirit of the game. The other point to emerge was the desirability of arranging representative matches on dates other than those allocated to the Championship. Since then, with the exception of occasional early-season visits of touring sides, clashes of dates have generally been avoided. A more major decision was to adopt the suggestion made by several clubs that, with effect from season 1975–76, the dates of fixtures would be rotated by one week each season to avoid clubs having the same opponents on the same Championship Saturday every year.

One situation which had not been foreseen was the desire expressed by many junior clubs to participate in the Championship. During 1973–74 no fewer than nine District Union clubs (five in the east and four in the west) applied for Full Member status in order to be included in Division V in season 1974–75.

All applicant clubs were admitted at the 1974 AGM. However, to avoid a flood of similar applications, it was agreed that, henceforth, the Championship would be based on merit only and that all clubs would have the opportunity to advance through the District Leagues to the bottom division of the Championship and, thereafter, as far as their ability would take them.

This decision posed further problems for the Committee. For example, there was no guarantee that the clubs relegated from Division IV would belong to the same District as those promoted from

58

Division v. Furthermore, to create Division v, to say nothing of possible sixth and seventh divisions on a national basis, might involve some clubs, both Full Member and District Union, with limited financial resources, having to travel considerable distances at great cost. However, having consulted the clubs, it was agreed to recommend to the 1975 AGM that the Championship should be extended on a national basis by creating Divisions v, vi and vii each containing twelve clubs. This was adopted and the new divisions came into effect in season 1976–77 with non-participating clubs subsequently having the opportunity to gain entry from the District Leagues on a promotion and relegation basis.

The next season saw another innovation. Following discussions between the SRU Committee and a well-known soft drinks firm, the Championship attracted sponsorship and became known officially as 'The Scottish Rugby Union Championship for the Schweppes Trophies'. A laudable feature of this commercial support was that every competing club benefited directly by receiving a cash distribution each year.

Unhappily, season 1979–80 saw for the first time a situation in which not only could two clubs not agree on a date for playing a postponed fixture, but one of them eventually ignored the Committee's directive and forfeited the Championship points. Consequently, as no match points were earned, this might have prevented the other club from winning the Division in question, although, fortunately, it did not prevent it from gaining promotion. In an attempt to avoid future similar situations the Championship Rules were changed to make any club guilty of failing to obey a Championship Committee directive regarding a postponed fixture liable to relegation or even suspension from the Championship.

The first major change in the structure of the Championship took place with effect from season 1982–83. After much discussion and some dissension on a number of options as to how the Championship might be improved, it had been agreed at the 1981 AGM to extend the number of teams in each Division to 14 and to retain Division vii thereby admitting a further fourteen clubs to the Championship.

One of the perceived benefits of thus extending the number of clubs in each Division was that it would reduce pressure on players in clubs which lost the first few matches of the season. It is conjectural whether this has happened or whether the pressure has simply been delayed or transferred to other clubs.

Be that as it may, there has since then been continuing discussions on whether or not the optimum structure has been achieved. There are many who believe that at least the top two or three Divisions should each comprise eight clubs playing on a home-and-away basis. This, it is thought, would improve the quality of play of these teams by their being exposed to a hard match every week. As well as this, taking the Welsh analogy, it is considered that such a system would ultimately lead to a richer supply of talented players to the National xv. Another view is that the present situation is fine and that any more obvious hierarchical structure would tend to denude clubs lower down the order of their better players, who would be encouraged to gravitate to the higher clubs. The argument as to which option better serves the interests of Scottish rugby is a fascinating one!

Over the first eleven years of the Championship there have been other matters which have exercised the minds of the Committee from time-to-time. The October start to the Championship has posed particular difficulties for nearly all the university clubs participating and the incidence of vacations has compounded the situation. However, by-and-large, the universities have coped well, albeit with difficulty. Nonetheless, it may be that, if the number of Saturdays allocated to Championship matches is increased, the position of the universities may have to be reconsidered.

Although there has been a certain amount of player-movement to different clubs this has not been significant. To prevent undue movement during the season, players can only transfer to another club for Championship purposes if their domicile has changed.

Inevitably, the weather has played an important if varied part during the first eleven years of the Championship: the worst was season 1983–84 when no fewer than 112 games were postponed due to unfavourable ground conditions. The seven divisions were affected as follows: Division I, 16 games postponed; Division II, 13; Division III, 13; Division IV, 15; Division V, 16; Division VI, 19; Division VII, 20. It is a tribute to all clubs that the overwhelming majority of postponed games over the years has been re-arranged timeously and by the clubs themselves concerned—occasionally for a second time when the weather has again intervened.

Among the most important contributions to the success of the Championship to date has been that of the referees. Originally appointed by the SRU Referees Committee and allocated by the Championship Committee to the first four Divisions only, referees are now appointed and allocated to these four Divisions by the SRU Referees Committee. Generally the standard has been high and all players and clubs owe a debt of gratitude to these gentlemen who give voluntarily of their time each week so that rugby enthusiasts may enjoy the game. It is a further tribute to them that they have responded well at all levels to the initiative being taken by the SRU to arrange training courses for referee education.

What then of the Championship itself? Has it achieved or begun to achieve what it was designed to do?

When Heriot's FP put forward the original proposal they argued that organised competitive rugby would do two things: enable all clubs to gravitate to the level at which they were capable of sustaining fixtures and encourage the better players to move to the better teams. Contrary to popular belief it was not argued that such a system necessarily would improve the quality of the National xv—although it was hoped that this might be a by-product. Certainly the first objective has been achieved—and in spectacular fashion by some clubs. Clubs like Clarkston, Gordonians, Haddington and Highland were among those to take full advantage, in the early years, of the opportunities provided. Later, such as Corstorphine, Preston Lodge and Stirling County moved up several Divisions as did Glenrothes who having won access to Division vii in 1977–78, promptly won that division and proceeded to win Divisions vi and v in the ensuing two seasons. But pride of place in this context must surely go to Portobello FP who, having won Division vii in season 1978–79 at only the second time of asking, thereafter, in successive seasons, moved right up to Division ii having won Divisions vi and v and been runners-up in Division iv and iii in the process.

The second objective has been achieved to a limited extent and a number of players have come to prominence who might otherwise have remained 'unknown Miltons'. There are those who argue that more could be done by clubs in the lower Divisions actively to persuade players with obvious potential to transfer to clubs higher up. That many clubs are reluctant to do this is entirely understandable.

Where the Championship has been an unqualified success is in identifying Hawick as the outstanding and most consistent club in Scotland. Their record speaks for itself. In the first eleven years of the Championship (up to 1983–84) Hawick have won Division i no fewer than seven times, with the only other clubs to win being Heriot's FP (1978–79) and Gala (1979–80, 80–81 and 82–83). On these four occasions, Hawick were, respectively, fourth, third, third and second.

It is interesting to speculate how significant is the fact that there are four junior clubs in Hawick which prefer to act as feeder clubs to the 'Greens' rather than to seek promotion through their own participation in the Championship.

What then of the future? There is no doubt that the introduction of organised competitive rugby has created a better and fairer system so far as fixture lists are concerned. Matches generally are closely contested affairs and in most divisions the struggles for promotion or to avoid relegation tend to continue until virtually the last game of the season.

61

Increasingly, however, it is believed that the Championship must somehow be fashioned so as to have a more direct effect on the quality of the National xv. If this is to be achieved, more thought will have to be given as to how fixtures in the first division generally can be made more competitive. At present there is too wide a gulf between the top and the bottom of the division. Further consideration will also have to be given as to how the better players at all levels can be encouraged to develop their full potential. To that end the Championship must not be viewed in isolation but in relation to representative games at a variety of levels and age-groups. It is a complex but far from insuperable problem and, when resolved, will augur well for the future success of Scottish rugby.

J. K. HUTCHISON
Member of Consultative, Organising and
Championship Committees, 1970–

25. Murrayfield, May 1982. His Holiness The Pope attends a Youth Rally during his visit to Scotland.

26. Murrayfield, July 1983. The Watch Tower Convention hold their Annual Gathering.

27. Murrayfield, 1956. Highland Games: a competitor in action.

28. Murrayfield, March 1977. Lacrosse International: Scotland v Wales.

29. Murrayfield, June 1983. The popular singing star, David Bowie, stages a concert.

30. Murrayfield, 26 March 1983. View of the East Stand from the s w corner of the ground. Taken during one of a series of games played prior to the Scotland v Barbarians match. The ceremonial opening tapes can be seen.

31. Murrayfield, February 1959. Anti-freeze plan in action prior to the Scotland *v* Wales game on 7 February 1959.

32. Murrayfield, Summer 1959. Laying the electric blanket during the summer of 1959. Second from the right is D. S. Kerr, Convener of the Field Committee and, on his right, T. S. Sellars, Head Groundsman.

Scotland Tour to South Africa, 1960. Scotland Party and South Africa Team and Officials. South Africa v ...tland, Boet Erasmus Stadium, Port Elizabeth, 30 April 1960. *Back row*: P. J. Burnet* (LS), I. Kirkpatrick, ... Hastie (Melrose), G. P. Lochner, T. O. Grant* (Hawick), D. Hopwood, R. H. Thomson* (LS), R. Twigge, ... Neill (Edin. Acads.). *4th row*: J. W. Y. Kemp* (Glas. HSFP), T. Allen (Manager, SA Team), G. D. Stevenson* ...wick), H. van Zyl, T. McClung (Edin. Acads.), M. Gerber, R. C. Cowan (Selkirk), D. Holton, R. M. Tollervey ...riot's FP), J. Gainsford, R. W. T. Chisholm* (Melrose), J. F. Louw (Executive, SARB). *3rd row*: Dr E. A. Strasheim ...) Referee, F. W. Mellish (Chairman, SA Selection Committee), C. E. B. Stewart (Kelso), P. Allen, A. R. Smith* ...ow Vale), D. van Jaarsveldt (SA) Captain, G. H. Waddell* (Cambridge University) Captain, A. van der Merwe, ...B. Edwards* (Heriot's FP), M. Bekker, D. M. D. Rollo* (Howe of Fife), B. Erwee (SA Representative with Scotland ...r Party), S. Swart (Baggage Master with Scotland Tour Party). *2nd row*: K. G. McLeod (Scotland 1906), ...arolin (SA 1906), A. Stegmann (SA 1906), Dr G. L. Potgeiter (Vice-President, SARB), R. W. Shaw (SRU, Hon. ...nager), Dr D. H. Craven (President, SARB), C. W. Drummond (SRU, Hon. Assistant Manager), J. J. de Kock ...cretary, SARB), A. Morkel (SA 1906), Dr A. Rabie (President, EPRU). *Front row*: F. H. ten Bos* (Oxford ...versity), J. Claassen, W. Hart* (Melrose), J. Engelbrecht, H. F. McLeod* (Hawick), D. Stewart, ...B. Shillinglaw* (Gala), F. Gericke, N. S. Bruce* (LS). *(Photograph provided by Mr D. B. Edwards)*
* Played for Scotland in International

...cotland Tour to Canada, 1964. *Back row*: J. Buchanan (Jordanhill Coll), D. Grant (Hawick), G. W. E. Mitchell ...n. Univ.), B. C. Henderson (Edin. Wrs.), W. J. Hunter (Hawick), J. W. Telfer (Melrose), J. A. P. Shackleton (LS), ...uddon (Hawick). *Middle*: A. J. Hastie (Melrose), A. J. W. Hinshelwood (Stewart's Coll. FP), K. R. F. Bearne ...erpool), J. P. Fisher (RHSFP), D. H. Chisholm (Melrose), R. G. Young (Watsonians), F. A. L. Laidlaw (Melrose), ...I. Simmers (Glas. Acads.). *Front*: C. Elliot (Langholm), K. J. F. Scotland (Aberdeenshire), N. S. Bruce (LS), ...V. Drummond (Hon. Manager), J. B. Neill (Edin. Acads., *Captain*), H. S. P. Monro (Hon. Manager), D. M. D. Rollo ...we of Fife), G. D. Stevenson (Hawick), I. H. P. Laughland (LS).

35. Scotland Tour to Argentina, 1969. *Back row*: A. D. Gill (Gala), J. R. Murchie (wos), B. Laidlaw (rhsfp), G. K. Oliver (Gala), N. Suddon (Hawick), D. T. Deans (Hawick), W. C. C. Steele (Langholm & raf), J. McLaucl (Jordanhill). *Middle*: J. Ellis (Heriot's fp), A. B. Carmichael (wos), A. F. McHarg (ls), P. K. Stagg (Sale), G. L. Br (wos), W. Lauder (Neath), M. A. Smith (ls), A. V. Orr (ls). *Seated*: D. S. Paterson (Gala), C. F. Blaikie (Heriot's I. Robertson (Watsonians), J. W. Telfer (Melrose, *Captain*), G. G. Crerar (Hon. Manager), A. D. Govan (Hon. Assistant Manager), R. J. Arneil (Edin. Acads.), F. A. L. Laidlaw (Melrose), C. W. W. Rea (wos).

36. Scotland Tour to Australia, 1970. *Back row*: C. M. Telfer (Hawick), J. N. M. Frame (Gala), G. L. Brown (w P. C. Brown (Gala), G. K. Oliver (Gala), W. Lauder (Neath), D. S. Paterson (Gala). *Middle*: C. W. W. Rea (wos A. D. Gill (Gala), A. B. Carmichael (wos), P. K. Stagg (Sale), A. G. Biggar (ls), M. A. Smith (ls), D. T. Deans (Hawick), I. S. G. Smith (ls and Army). *Front*: G. C. Connell (ls), N. Suddon (Hawick), I. Robertson (Watsonia H. S. P. Monro (Hon. Manager), F. A. L. Laidlaw (Melrose, *Captain*), G. Burrell (Hon. Assistant Manager), R. J. Arneil (Leicester), J. W. C. Turner (Gala), T. G. Elliot (Langholm). *Absent*: J. McLauchlan (Jordanhill).

, Scotland Tour to New Zealand, 1975. *Back row:* C. M. Telfer (Hawick), A. R. Irvine (Heriot's FP), J. M. Renwick
awick), D. W. Morgan (Stew.-Mel. FP), A. J. M. Lawson (Edin. Wrs.), C. D. Fisher (Waterloo), L. G. Dick
rdanhill Coll.), B. H. Hay (Boroughmuir), N. E. K. Pender (Hawick). *Middle:* M. A. Biggar (LS), J. N. M. Frame
ala), G. Y. Mackie (Highland), A. J. Tomes (Hawick), I. A. Barnes (Hawick), D. G. Leslie (Dundee HSFP),
Lauder (Neath), G. A. Birkett (Harlequins), W. S. Watson (Boroughmuir). *Front:* D. L. Bell (Watsonians),
C. C. Steele (LS), I. R. McGeechan (Headingley, *Vice-Captain*), G. Burrell (Hon. Manager), J. McLauchlan
rdanhill, *Captain*), W. Dickinson (Hon. Assistant Manager), A. B. Carmichael (WOS), A. F. McHarg (LS),
F. Madsen (Gosforth).

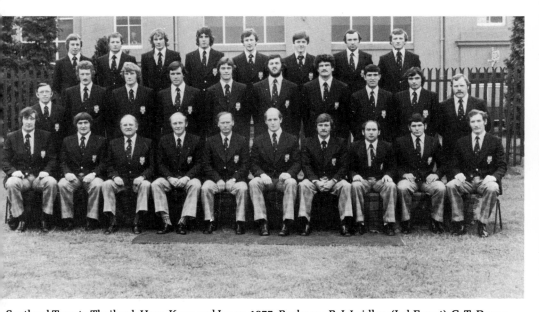

Scotland Tour to Thailand, Hong Kong and Japan, 1977. *Back row:* R. J. Laidlaw (Jed-Forest), C. T. Deans
awick), J. Y. Rutherford (Selkirk), R. A. Moffat (Melrose), K. W. Robertson (Melrose), M. J. T. Hurst (Jordanhill),
M. Berthinussen (Gala), L. G. Dick (Swansea). *Middle:* R. C. McNaught (Hon. Physio.), G. Dickson (Gala),
B. B. Gammell (Edin. Wrs.), R. F. Cunningham (Gala), A. E. Kennedy (Watsonians), A. J. Tomes (Hawick),
S. M. Macdonald (LS), C. D. R. Mair (WOS), R. Wilson (LS), G. M. McGuinness (WOS), *Front:* I. A. Barnes
awick), J. McLauchlan (Jordanhill), G. W. Thomson (Hon. Assistant Manager), N. A. MacEwan (Player/Hon.
ach), T. Pearson (Hon. Manager), M. A. Biggar (LS, *Captain*), C. D. Fisher (Waterloo), J. M. Renwick (Hawick),
G. Cranston (Hawick), W. S. Watson (Boroughmuir).

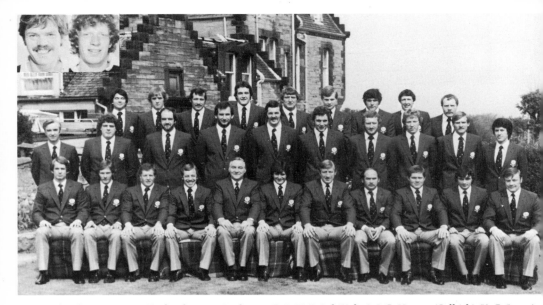

39. Scotland Tour to New Zealand, 1981. *Back row*: G. R. T. Baird (Kelso), I. G. Hunter (Selkirk), K. G. Lawrie (Gala), J. H. Calder (Stew.-Mel. FP), N. A. Rowan (Boroughmuir), S. Munro (Ayr), A. G. Cranston (Hawick), P. W. Dods (Gala), G. M. McGuinness (WOS). *Middle*: D. A. D. Macleod (Hon. Medical Officer), I. G. Milne (Herio FP), W. Cuthbertson (Kilmarnock), T. J. Smith (Gala), A. J. Tomes (Hawick), I. A. M. Paxton (Selkirk), G. Dicks (Gala), D. B. White (Gala), R. W. Breakey (Gosforth), D. A. McLean (Hon. Physio.). *Front*: D. G. Leslie (Gala), J. Y. Rutherford (Selkirk), C. T. Deans (Hawick), R. J. Laidlaw (Jed-Forest), G. K. Smith (Hon. Manager), A. R. Irv (Heriot's FP, *Captain*), J. W. Telfer (Hon. Assistant Manager), J. M. Renwick (Hawick), B. H. Hay (Boroughmui R. Wilson (LS), J. Aitken (Gala). *Insets*: l. A. J. M. Lawson (Heriot's FP); r. P. M. Lillington (Durham Univ.). (B these players joined the party as replacements for injured players.)

40. Scotland Tour to Australia, 1982. *Back row*: G. R. T. Baird (Kelso), K. W. Robertson (Melrose), I. G. Milne (Heriot's FP), R. E. Paxton (Kelso), J. H. Calder (Stew.-Mel. FP), F. Calder (Stew.-Mel. FP), J. A. Pollock (Gosfor C. J. Williamson (WOS), D. I. Johnston (Watsonians). *Middle row*: B. M. Gossman (West of Scotland), N. A. Rowa (Boroughmuir), I. G. Hunter (Selkirk), D. B. White (Gala), I. A. M. Paxton (Selkirk), I. D. McKie (Sale), W. Cuthbertson (Kilmarnock), R. J. Gordon (LS), R. Cunningham (Bath), G. M. McGuinness (WOS), P. W. Dods (Gala). *Front row*: A. J. Tomes (Hawick), C. T. Deans (Hawick), R. J. Laidlaw (Jed-Forest), I. A. A. MacGregor (Ho Manager), A. R. Irvine (Heriot's FP, *Captain*), J. W. Telfer (Hon. Assistant Manager), J. Y. Rutherford (Selkirk), J. Aitken (Gala), D. A. McLean (Hon. Physio.). *Replacement*: J. Calder (Stew.-Mel. FP), not present.

41. Scotland Tour to Romania, 1984. *Back row*: I. Tukalo (Selkirk), F. Calder (Stew.-Mel. FP), G. J. Callander (Kelso), A. E. Kennedy (Watsonians), T. J. Smith (Gala), A. J. Tomes (Hawick), A. D. G. Mackenzie (Highland), D. I. Johnston (Watsonians), N. A. Rowan (Boroughmuir). *Middle*: P. D. Steven (Heriot's FP), D. S. Wyllie (Stew.-Mel. FP), S. K. McGaughey (Hawick), D. G. Leslie (Gala), J. Jeffrey (Kelso), A. J. Campbell (Hawick), J. R. Beattie (Glas. Acads.), J. Y. Rutherford (Selkirk), J. A. Pollock (Gosforth), R. Cunningham (Bath), J. M. Renwick (Hawick). *Front*: Dr J. C. M. Sharp (Hon. Medical Officer), R. J. Laidlaw (Jed-Forest), K. W. Robertson (Melrose), J. Aitken (Gala, Captain), R. G. Charters (Hon. Manager), C. M. Telfer (Hon. Assistant Manager), I. G. Hunter (Selkirk), P. W. Dods (Gala), D. A. McLean (Hon. Physio.).

42. 1971. 27 March, Murrayfield. Centenary Celebration Match with England. *Back row*: D. J. Duckham (Coventry), A. L. Bucknall (Richmond), F. E. Cotton (Loughborough Coll.), P. J. Larter (Northampton), C. W. Ralston (Richmond), A. F. McHarg (Ls), R. J. Arneil (Leicester), G. L. Brown (wos), J. N. M. Frame (Gala), Q. Dunlop (wos), A. R. Brown (Gala). *Middle*: R. Hiller (Harlequins), R. B. Taylor (Northampton), J. V. Pullin (Bristol), A. Neary (Broughton Park), J. P. Janion (Bedford), T. F. E. Grierson (Hawick) Touch Judge, M. Joseph (Wales) Referee, R. P. Burrell (Gala) Touch Judge, A. B. Carmichael (wos), W. C. C. Steele (Bedford), N. A. MacEwan (Gala), C. W. W. Rea (Headingley). *Front*: D. L. Powell (Northampton), N. C. Starmer-Smith (Harlequins), A. R. Cowman (Loughborough Coll.), C. S. Wardlow (Northampton), J. S. Spencer (Headingley) *Captain*, Sir William Ramsay, CBE, President RFU, R. W. Shaw, President SRU, P. C. Brown (Gala) *Captain*, A. G. Biggar (Ls), J. W. C. Turner (Gala), J. McLauchlan (Jordanhill), D. S. Paterson (Gala).

This was a second match against England, played a week after the Calcutta Cup match at Twickenham.

3. 1972. 14 October, Murrayfield. Scotland & Ireland v England & Wales. Centenary Year Match. *Back row:* . M. Knight (Bristol), J. P. R. Williams (Lw), J. V. Pullin (Bristol), A. Neary (Broughton Park), M. G. Roberts (Lw), . M. Davies (Swansea), W. J. McBride (Ballymena), G. L. Brown (wos), J. F. Slattery (Blackrock Coll.), T. O. Grace it Mary's Coll.), J. N. M. Frame (Gala), N. Suddon (Hawick). *Middle:* C. B. Stevens (Harlequins), J. Taylor (Lw), . T. E. Bergiers (Llanelli), P. J. Larter (Northampton), T. G. R. Davies (Lw), D. C. J. McMahon (Heriot's FP) Touch idge, M. G. Domercq (France) Referee, H. B. Laidlaw (Hawick) Touch Judge, A. R. Brown (Gala), W. C. C. Steele Langholm), N. A. MacEwan (Gala), J. M. Renwick (Hawick), J. J. Moloney (St Mary's Coll.). *Front:* R. M. Hopkins Llanelli), P. Bennett (Llanelli), A. J. L. Lewis (Ebbw Vale), D. J. Lloyd (Bridgend) *Captain,* V. J. Parfitt (President, 'RU), R. M. A. Kingswell (President, RFU), A. W. Wilson (President, SRU), Judge J. C. Conroy (President IRU), . C. Brown (Gala) *Captain,* C. M. H. Gibson (NIFC), A. B. Carmichael (wos), K. W. Kennedy (LI).

4. 1973. 31 March, Murrayfield. Scotland v President's XV. Centenary Year Match. *Back row:* D. R. Burnet (Aust.), . H. Ellis (SA), P. J. F. Greyling (SA), A. R. Sutherland (NZ), B. Dauga (France), D. A. Dunworth (Aust.), G. L. Brown Wos), P. C. Brown (Gala), A. F. McHarg (LS), I. W. Forsyth (Stewart's Coll. FP), D. Shedden (wos), N. A. McEwan Gala). *Middle:* I. N. Stevens (NZ), R. Benesis (France), J. Iracabal (France), R. A. Carlson (SA), T. F. E. Grierson Hawick) Touch Judge, M. Joseph (Wales) Referee, A. M. Hosie (Hillhead HSFP) Touch Judge, I. R. McGeechan Headingley), A. R. Irvine (Heriot's FP), G. M. Strachan (Jordanhill), A. D. Gill (Gala), D. W. Morgan (Melville Coll. P). *Front:* G. B. Batty (NZ), G. L. Colling (NZ), D. A. Hales (NZ), J. J. McLean (Aust.), A. J. Wyllie (NZ) *Captain,* r I. R. Vanderfield (Vice-President, Australian RFU), Dr D. H. Craven (President, SA Rugby Board), A. W. Wilson President, SRU), P. Dwyer (President, NZRFU), J. McLauchlan (Jordanhill) *Captain,* C. M. Telfer (Hawick), . B. Carmichael (wos), R. L. Clark (Edin. Wrs.). *Inset:* J. N. M. Frame (Gala).

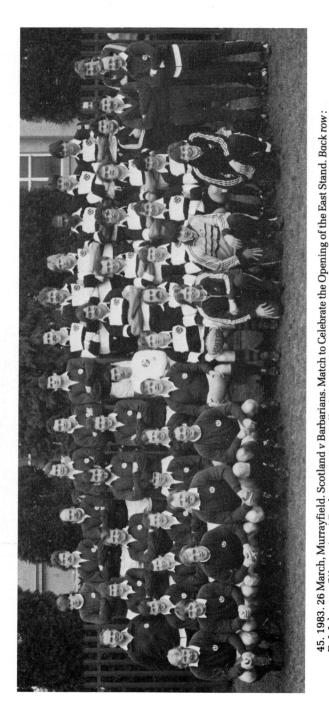

45. 1983. 26 March, Murrayfield. Scotland *v* Barbarians. Match to Celebrate the Opening of the East Stand. *Back row:*
D. I. Johnston (Watsonians) Replacement, J. A. Pollock (Gosforth), J. M. Renwick (Hawick), D. G. Leslie (Gala), J. H. Calder
(Stew.-Mel. FP), J. R. Beattie (Glas. Acads.), R. L. Norster (Cardiff), J. P. Scott (Cardiff), P. J. Winterbottom (Headingley),
E. G. Tobias (Boland), J. B. Lafond (Racing Club), D. M. Gerber (Eastern Province). *Second row:* J. A. Short (Hawick) Touch Judge,
J. Y. Rutherford (Selkirk), N. A. Rowan (Boroughmuir), T. J. Smith (Gala), I. A. M. Paxton (Selkirk), R. Hourquet (France) Referee,
H. J. Bekker (Western Province), P. A. G. Rendall (Wasps), R. Paparemborde (Pau), P. Dintrans (Tarbes), W. J. James (Aberavon)
Replacement, A. Simpson (Sale) Replacement, S. Bainbridge (Gosforth) Replacement, J. B. Anderson (Corstorphine) Touch
Judge. *Third row:* K. W. Robertson (Melrose), P. W. Dods (Gala), C. T. Deans (Hawick), G. R. T. Baird (Kelso), R. J. Laidlaw
(Jed-Forest), J. Aitken (Gala) *Captain*, J. F. Slattery (Blackrock Coll.) *Captain*, C. F. W. Rees (Lw), J. Carleton (Orrell), T. D. Holmes
(Cardiff), W. G. Davies (Cardiff). *Front:* A. J. Campbell (Hawick), R. Cunningham (Bath), I. G. Hunter (Selkirk),
G. M. McGuinness (wos), B. M. Gossman (wos), H. P. MacNeill (Oxford Univ.), M. Douglas (Llanelli), R. A. Ackerman (Lw)—all
replacements.

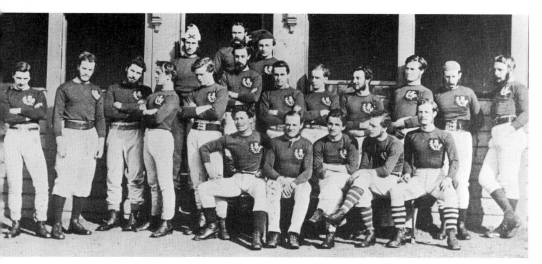

1871. Scotland v England. The First Rugby International. The Scotland xx. *Back row*: R. Munro (St Andrews Univ.), J. S. Thomson (Glas. Acads.), T. Chalmers (Glas. Acads.). *Middle*: A. Buchanan (RHSFP), A. G. Colville (Merchistonians), J. Forsyth (Edin. Univ.), J. Mein (Edin. Acads.), R. W. Irvine (Edin. Acads.), J. W. Arthur (Glas. Acads.), W. D. Brown (Glas. Acads.), A. Drew (Glas. Acads.), W. Cross (Merchistonians), J. F. Finlay (Edin. Acads.), J. Moncreiff (Edin. Acads.) *Captain*, G. Ritchie (Merchistonians). *Front*: A. Clunies-Ross (St Andrews Univ.), J. C. Lyall (Edin. Acads.), T. R. Marshall (Edin. Acads.), J. L. H. Macfarlane (Edin. Univ.), A. H. Robertson (WOS).

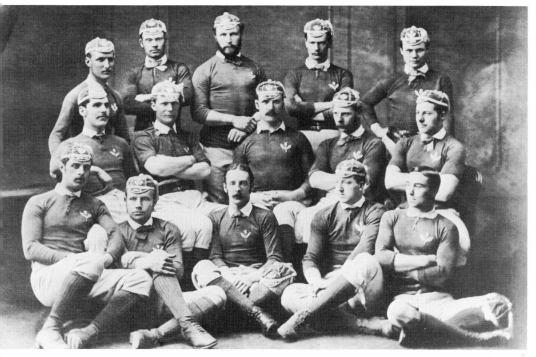

1879. Scotland v England. First Calcutta Cup Match. The Scotland xv. *Back row*: R. Ainslie (Edin. Inst. FP), N. Ewart (Glas. Acads.), H. M. Napier (WOS), D. R. Irvine (Edin. Acads.), J. B. Brown (Glas. Acads.). *Middle*: J. Finlay (Edin. Acads.), R. W. Irvine (Edin. Acads.) *Captain*, A. G. Petrie (RHSFP), J. H. S. Graham (Edin. Acads.), A. Neilson (Glas. Acads.). *Front*: N. T. Brewis (Edin. Inst. FP), J. E. Junor (Glas. Acads.), M. Cross (Glas. Acads.), E. MacLagan (Edin. Acads.), J. A. Campbell (Merchistonians). (The cap and jersey belonging to H. M. Napier may be seen in the Museum at Murrayfield.)

48. 1899. Scotland v Ireland. First International at Inverleith. The Scotland xv. *Back row*: H. O. Smith (Watsonians), R. C. Stevenson (ls), A. Mackinnon (ls), W. M. C. McEwan (Edin. Acads.), M. C. Morrison (rhsf R. T. Neilson (wos), J. M. Reid (Edin. Acads.). *Second row*: T. L. Scott (Langholm), J. T. Mabon (Jed-Forest), J. H. Couper (wos), W. P. Donaldson (wos) *Captain*, G. C. Kerr (Edin. Wrs. & Durham), G. T. Campbell (ls), L. Harvey (Greenock Wrs.). *In front*: D. B. Monypenny (ls).

49. 1906. Scotland v South Africa. *Back row*: A. Burger, K. G. Macleod (Camb. Univ.), D. Brooks, L. M. Spiers (Watsonians), H. H. Corley (Ireland) Referee, D. Brink, J. C. MacCallum (Watsonians), J. G. Scoular (Camb. Uni H. A. de Villiers. *Second row*: W. H. H. Thomson (wos), A. F. Burdett, I. C. Geddes (ls), J. A. Loubser, M. W. Wal (ls), A. B. H. L. Purves (ls), J. C. Stegmann, T. Sloan (Glas. Acads.), A. F. W. Marsberg, G. M. Frew (Glas. hsfx Seated: D. S. Mare, D. R. Bedell-Sivright (Edin. Univ.), H. J. Daneel, L. L. Greig (Utd. Services) *Captain*, H. W. Carolin (*Captain*), W. P. Scott (wos), J. W. E. Raaff, H. G. Monteith (U. Hospitals), W. S. Morkel. *Front*: Dobbin, P. Munro (ls), J. D. Krige.

(This was the second match against a touring Dominion team. K. G. Macleod scored a memorable try. No tea photograph is available from the first match v nz in 1905.)

1914. Scotland v England. *Back row*: W. M. Wallace* (Camb. Univ.), E. T. Young* (Glas. Acads.), I. M. Pender
), A. W. Symington (Camb. Univ.), R. M. Scobie (LS), J. L. Huggan* (LS). *Seated*: J. G. Will* (Camb. Univ.),
M. Usher (LS), F. H. Turner* (Liverpool and LS), E. Milroy* (Watsonians) *Captain*, A. W. Angus (Watsonians),
R. Ross (Edin. Univ.), G. H. H. P. Maxwell (Edin. Acads.). *Front*: A. D. Laing (RHSFP), T. C. Bowie (Watsonians).
The last match before the War. The six players marked * died on active service.)

. 1920. France v Scotland. G. B. Crole (Oxford Univ.), G. L. Patullo (Panmure), G. Thom (Kirkcaldy), A. D. Laing
HSFP), A. Wemyss* (Edin. Wrs.), C. M. Usher* (LS), F. Kennedy (Stewart's Coll. FP), A. W. Angus* (Watsonians)
ptain, D. D. Duncan (Oxford Univ.), A. T. Sloan* (Edin. Acads.), E. C. Fahmy (Abertillery), J. Hume* (RHSFP),
S. Hamilton* (Headingley), R. A. Gallie (Glas. Acads.), W. A. K. Murray (LS).
(This was the first post-war International. The six players marked * were pre-war caps.)

52. 1939. Scotland *v* England. *Back row :* G. Roberts* (Watsonians), J. R. S. Innes (Aber. Univ.), I. N. Graham (Ed Acads.), D. K. A. MacKenzie* (Edin. Wrs.), W. C. W. Murdoch (Hillhead HSFP), I. C. Henderson (Edin. Acads.) W. Purdie (Jed-Forest), R. B. Bruce-Lockhart (LS), Ivor David (Wales) Referee. *Front :* W. H. Crawford (Utd. Services), A. Roy (Waterloo), G. B. Horsburgh (LS), R. W. Shaw (Glas. HSFP) *Captain*, D. J. Macrae (St Andrew Univ.), W. B. Young (King's Coll. Hosp.), T. F. Dorward* (Gala).

(The last match before the War. The players marked * died on active service.)

53. 1946. Scotland *v* New Zealand Army XV. *Back row :* C. H. Gadney (England) Referee, D. W. C. Smith (Aberde Univ.), R. Aitken (LS), A. G. M. Watt (Edin. Acad.-Wrs.), W. I. D. Elliot (Edin. Acad.-Wrs.), J. Kirk (Edin. Acad.-Wrs.), J. H. Orr (Heriot's FP), D. W. Deas (Heriot's FP), I. J. M. Lumsden (Watsonians). *Second row :* W. H. Munro (Glas. HSFP & Army), J. Anderson (LS), I. C. Henderson (Edin. Acad.-Wrs.), K. I. Geddes (LS) *Captai* C. R. Bruce (Glas. Acads. & Army), G. Lyall (Gala), A. W. Black (Edin. Univ.).

(This was the first of six 'unofficial' international matches played in the first post-war season. No Internatio caps were awarded.)

8

SUCCESSES IN TRIPLE CROWN
AND GRAND SLAM PRIOR TO 1984

THE mythical Triple Crown could not be a reality in the minds of rugby men for some years after the first Internationals were played. Scotland had, of course, met England in 1871 for the first time, while Ireland became involved in 1877. However, it was not until 1883 that Wales met Scotland at Raeburn Place and they suffered the same fate of England 12 years before—a defeat.

Scotland played well in the decade of the 1880s and for several years, notably in 1883, 1884, 1886 and 1887, were narrowly deprived of Triple Crown successes—by England on each occasion. Indeed in the latter two years drawn games with the wearers of the Rose were all that stood between heady success and the anonymity of failure. Even the International campaign of 1890 was close, oh so close, and yet again England pipped Scotland by a goal and a try to nil. Probably Scotland's first success in 1891 came as no surprise to the initiated, but all the tremendous satisfaction of achievement would no doubt be a great joy to players, officials and spectators just as it was in the most recent 1984 high point.

Scotland met Wales at Raeburn Place on 7 February 1891 and won comfortably by 1 goal, 2 drop goals and 6 tries (15) to nil. Scotland completely dominated the game, for Wales had no answer to a pack which scored six of the seven tries, while giving their backs plenty of the ball. Scotland were still playing the three-back formation and G. MacGregor, who specialised in feeding his wide-set wingers with long, accurate passes, struck up a good partnership with P. R. Clauss, a small man—but fast and aggressive. H. J. Stevenson, who had been an automatic and outstanding choice as centre back for four seasons, refused to play this passive type of game, but being too good to omit, was placed at full-back. Even here his ability to turn defence into attack was not lost and on several occasions he dashed up-field and set the backs off on a passing run. Indeed he could well be classed as the first attacking full-back.

The success continued against Ireland at Belfast on 21 February

1891 to the tune of 3 goals, 1 drop goal and 2 tries (14) to nil. This match was played on the Ulster ground at Ballynafeigh in fine weather. It was a good open game with plenty of action from the Irish forwards and some hard running from their backs, but overall Scotland were in complete control. W. Wotherspoon and Clauss were outstanding in attack. For Ireland S. Lee played well and H. G. Wells had one run the length of the field to touch down but a score was not allowed. It was in this season that touch judges replaced the umpires on the field.

It came to pass then that Scotland, without a point against them faced the always-powerful England at Richmond on 7 March 1891. A severe storm and rain did not keep away a crowd of 20,000 who came hoping to see England win the Triple Crown (they had beaten Wales 7–3 and Ireland 9–0) but they had to go away bitterly disappointed. The critics blamed the forwards and the halves who were completely outplayed by their opponents. Scotland began well and within ten minutes C. E. Orr, getting the ball from a scrum, let G. MacGregor away and when he in turn passed to Clauss the winger dropped a very good left-footed goal. After the restart MacGregor got the ball after a line-out and sent J. E. Orr off on a fast run round the English forwards and backs to score between the posts. Then D. G. Anderson, who had been playing very well, let MacGregor away, and a good pass let W. Neilson (who was still a schoolboy at Merchiston) away for another try. The English defence had crumbled badly but Lockwood, who had tackled well, showed his paces and scored just on time. At full-back H. J. Stevenson again showed himself to be a player of infinite resource and skill in defence and attack. Scotland had at last laid the England bogey and became winners of their first-ever Triple Crown by the overall handsome margin of 38 points to 3. England had been defeated by 2 goals and 1 drop goal (9) to 1 goal (3).

Games over the next few years were closely contested and indeed in 1892 only defeat by England denied another Scottish triumph. In 1895 the wearers of the Thistle again tasted sweet success.

It began with a win over Wales at Raeburn Place on 26 January 1895 by 1 goal (5) to 1 drop goal (4), a single point margin under the scoring system of the period. After protective straw had been removed from the field, the north end proved to be too hard and at the request of the Welsh—who refused to play otherwise— the pitch was shortened by some eighteen yards to eliminate this area. Even so, the ground remained unpleasantly hard, and one dangerous run by A. J. Gould (Wales) finished when he swerved and slipped. There was a lot of fine play nevertheless, with the Scottish pack showing up well in the loose. Behind them, M. Elliot, in his first game, did well in attack and defence. In the second half Wales did a fair amount of attacking but the defence and kicking of G.T.Campbell saved several situations. J.J.Gowans went over for a try which was converted by H.O.Smith. Wales fought back but the defence, notably A.R.Smith, was sound. Then W.M.C.McEwan, on his own goal-line, marked a dangerous kick-ahead and kicked for touch only to see W.J.Bancroft (Wales) catch the ball in the field of play, move infield and drop a fine goal from near half-way. This finished the scoring although Gowans had one fine run only to be collared on the line in front of the posts.

A victory over Ireland, also at Raeburn Place, followed with a 2 tries (6) to nil win on 2 March 1895. The match was postponed twice from February and both team selections were much influenced by influenza. Play was fairly even in the first half, both sides showing good defence but Scotland's R.Welsh ran dangerously. Ireland started the second half confidently with a fine run by J.T.Magee but Scotland gradually got on top. W.B.Cownie had a run, passed to J.W.Simpson and the ball went via W.Neilson to Welsh who scored. Shortly afterwards, Simpson and the familiar Clauss had a good passing bout before giving the ball to W.Neilson who sent G.T.Campbell off on a grand dodging run through a mass of opponents to score.

The final match of the season against England at Richmond on 9 March 1895 was a closely-fought affair, Scotland winning by 1 penalty goal and 1 try (6) to 1 penalty goal (3). The Scottish pack controlled the game throughout and tended to keep the ball tight, so there was relatively little back play, especially as W.P.Donaldson, as was his custom, did a lot of kicking to touch. Scotland began well but were startled to find themselves trailing when J.F.Byrne kicked England's first-ever penalty goal from mid-field. However, G.T. Neilson with an equally fine kick from the touchline, equalised with Scotland's first penalty goal and it is interesting to observe that it took another 30 years before another penalty goal was kicked in a Calcutta Cup match. Before half-time, G.T.Neilson caught Byrne with the ball and, securing it, was able to run in for a try. England had lost the Calcutta Cup and Scotland had gained another Triple Crown.

After the successes of 1891 and 1895, followed by another in 1901, Scotland had the satisfaction of knowing that the triumph was coming with most acceptable regularity. The 1901 campaign began with a flourish against Wales who were defeated by 3 goals and 1 try (18) to 1 goal and 1 try (8) at Inverleith on 9 February 1901. A feature of the crowd was the wearing of black as a mark of respect for the death of Queen Victoria. The Scottish team had eight new caps and contained seven of the outstanding Edinburgh University xv. A heavy Welsh pack of forwards (who were criticised for rough play) did well in the scrums but could not match the Scots in the loose and the Welsh backs were greatly troubled by the speedy and clever Scottish backs.

A.N.Fell all but scored for Scotland early on, then Wales were prevented from scoring only by the efforts of A.W.Duncan. Then came the turning point of the match. From a maul, the ball came out on J.I.Gillespie's side. The Scot pounced on it, tricked two opponents with a dummy, and with a sprint drove over the line with two Welshmen hanging on to him. Next, P.Turnbull, with his characteristic ability to slip past defenders, wandered through the backs up to Bancroft, the Welsh full-back, and gave a scoring pass to A.B.Flett. The Scottish backs continued their brilliant running in the second half, Turnbull making several deceptive weaving runs and two more tries were added. A late rally brought two consolation tries for Wales.

At their next hurdle against Ireland at Inverleith on 23 February 1901, the Scots contained early forward rushes. C.A.Boyd, the Irish full-back, was caught in possession; the Scottish forwards worked the ball loose and a passing run by Fell and J.M.Dykes let Gillespie score. The Scottish backs continued to attack and well-timed passing by Turnbull and A.B.Timms let W.H.Welsh away on a run where his great pace took him round the defenders for a score. From the kick-off an almost similar move by the same three gave Welsh a second high-speed try—three inside ten minutes. The Irish forwards replied and there was a good try at the posts. Again the Scottish backs made several fine runs but did not break through, Boyd putting in some fine tackles on Welsh. In the second half there was no scoring but plenty of action. D.R.Bedell-Sivright broke away and A.E.Freear (Ireland) was hurt stopping him. Fell had a hard run halted, then A.W.Duncan was instrumental in stopping the Irish pack. The two Ryans, J. and M. of Ireland, threatened trouble with a strong rush, but Scotland held on to what had been the half-time lead of 3 tries (9) to 1 goal (5). Interestingly, with J.B.Allison playing for Ireland, all the Edinburgh University threes and the full-back were present at this match.

In the final game of the season, Scotland faced England at Blackheath on 9 March 1901 and they had a comprehensive victory by 3 goals and 1 try (18) to 1 try (3). Early on, A.Frew went over for Scotland but the referee gave England the benefit of the doubt. England pressed for fifteen minutes but from then onwards the Scots were clearly on top and scored thrice in ten minutes. The pack was in good form with dribbling rushes, whilst the backs combined beautifully at full pace. Fell and Turnbull combined to put Gillespie in (which meant he had scored in every International of the season). J.A.Bell, from the middle of a crowd of forwards, flung the ball wide to Welsh whose pace carried him clear to score behind the posts, and then Fell and Turnbull made another opening for Timms to score. The second half was less spectacular. Turnbull missed a chance when, with Fell outside him, he kicked past the English full-back Gamlin, but lost the touch. Some slack Scottish defence let England in for a solitary score to which Scotland responded through a last try by Fell. The Scottish backs had shown great attacking ability and pace in a well-deserved third Scottish Triple Crown success.

All three International matches in 1902 had been lost and for the first game of the 1903 season Scotland faced Wales at Inverleith on 7 February 1903 in a fierce gale of wind and blinding rain coming from the south-west. The water-logged pitch was swept clear of pools by workmen just before the start. Scotland began with the gale behind them but could only score a penalty goal (given for feet-up in the scrum) and drop-kicked by A.B.Timms from just inside halfway. The Welsh pack played to their backs who made one or two sallies only to be halted by stern tackling and the conditions, which were really against all handling. On restarting, the Scottish forwards took a most determined grip on the game and gradually took control. Wales did get into the Scottish 25 for a while only to be thwarted by firm defence. Eventually grand play by H.J.Orr and J.E.Crabbie took play well upfield where a great forward surge was crowned by W.E.Kyle forcing a try. It was remarked that the Welsh backs were none too happy about checking the Scottish forwards in their foot rushes. If the win was a narrow one at 1 penalty goal and 1 try (6) to nil, at least amends had been partly made for the previous disappointing season —Triple Crown to Wooden Spoon.

Ireland came to Inverleith on 28 February 1903 having suffered a rough crossing on the steamer and this may have had some effect, because the majority of their backs were not in form and their pack faded in the second half. They began well enough yet could not break a steady defence. Scotland's W.T.Forrest was his usual frightening self—wonderful at times but every now and then making a terrifying mistake only to bring off an astonishing recovery. H.H.Corley (Ireland) broke away and when faced with Forrest passed to L.M. Magee but Forrest contrived to collar Magee and the ball, and clear with a run and a kick. Then Magee, J.B.Allison and G.A.D.Harvey combined for Ireland to give H.J.Anderson an open field, however, E.D.Simson came across and tackled for Scotland. In the second half the Scottish pack had an ascendancy. M.C.Morrison and D.R.Bedell-Sivright showed up well, and from one rush and scrimmage Simson, J.Knox and J.H.Orr let J.E.Crabbie make a sprint for the corner and score. The solitary try came in the nick of time to keep Scotland by 1 try (3) to nil in the bidding for another Triple Crown.

The Scots went to Richmond on 21 March 1903 knowing that England had already been beaten by Ireland and Wales. The match proved to be an undistinguished and rather scrambling affair, Scotland winning by 1 drop goal and 2 tries (10) to 2 tries (6) but at the end of the day the visitors had once again achieved the honours. The Scottish pack, although without two of its most powerful members in Morrison and Bedell-Sivright, gave a good account of itself. Early on, a sudden English attack produced a score, countered by a fine forward rush followed by a scrimmage. It resulted in Timms dropping an excellent goal. After another rush, Simson initiated a passing run with the forwards which finished with J.D.Dallas scoring. Early in the second half A.N.Fell had a telling run but could not pass H.T.Gamlin, the English full-back, and then A.T.Brettargh (England) broke clear and though tackled by Fell, got the ball out to P.D.Kendall who was stopped short of the line by Simson, who actually overhauled him. The score was only delayed, for from a scrimmage, D.D.Dobson went over to reduce the lead to a single point. However, Scotland kept cool and when the forwards caught Gamlin with the ball, it broke to Simson who had a splendid dodging run for a solo try. Forrest again played well. Once with several opponents bearing down on him, he failed to gather the ball, fell on it, jumped up with it, evaded the attackers and then put in his clearance. The Scottish threes had colonial aspects because A.B.Timms and H.J.Orr were Australians, Fell was from New Zealand and J.S.Macdonald had a South African connection.

The season 1906–07 began in resounding fashion when Scotland encountered the touring South Africans at Hampden Park on 17 November 1906 and emerged triumphant by 2 tries (6) to nil. A record crowd of 32,000 watched a game made memorable by an historic Scottish try by K.G.MacLeod. Shortly after the interval, P.Munro broke away to his left from a scrum at the centre and when faced by the cover defence he hoisted a towering kick clear across the field to the right wing where MacLeod, going full out, caught the wet ball cleanly and outpaced the defence along the touch line to score at the corner. A.B.H.L.Purves picked up the other try following some stirring ground-work by the pack. It was a morale-boosting victory which augured well for the season.

Wales came to Inverleith on 2 February 1907 after a workmanlike win over England. They again adopted the seven-forward formation, but this failed against a good defence and a vigorous Scottish pack. Yet play was fairly even in the first half, the only score being a penalty for offside kicked by H.B.Winfield (Wales). Early in the second half, the Scottish pack took the ball right down to the line and from a line-out swift transference gave Purves the chance to hand-off a defender and run in at the corner. Shortly afterwards, Winfield courageously halted another tremendous dribbling rush but he was so injured he had to leave the field. Near the end, Purves had an effective foray, finishing with a cross kick which was picked up by D.G.

MacGregor and he passed to H.G.Monteith who scored. Wales put in a great finish; R.A.Gibbs touched down, only to be recalled for a foot in touch. MacGregor had had a fine debut; born in Pontypridd he had a Scottish father and was educated at Watson's College, Edinburgh. He was captain of Pontypridd but played so well for Watsonians on their Christmas tour at Newport that the Welsh selectors picked him as a reserve for this game only to find him amongst the opposition who, of course, had won by 2 tries (6) to 1 penalty goal (3).

Scotland seemed to have found form, an opinion confirmed when Ireland came to Inverleith on 23 February 1907 and lost by 3 goals (15) to 1 penalty goal (3). Conditions for the game were good, although the usual Inverleith breeze was in evidence. Play in the first half was quite even, both sets of backs bent on moving the ball. B.McClear (Ireland) had two fine runs halted by firm tackles and this was the occasion when he handed-off Bedell-Sivright so fiercely that the latter, who was probably the hardest forward ever to play for Scotland, was knocked out and spent quite a while recovering on the straw at the touch line! After the restart, the strength of the Scottish pack and the pace of their backs began to tell and Scotland finished worthy winners. All the home scoring was in the second half. G.A. Sanderson, A.B.H.L.Purves and G.M.Frew produced tries. The first was converted by K.G.MacLeod and the other two by I.C.Geddes.

Scotland travelled to Blackheath on 16 March 1907 for the England fixture. England held the initiative, especially as their pack was more than competent, and Scotland were not using the wind sensibly. MacLeod, however, had about six lengthy drops at goal which narrowly missed, one from halfway rebounding from an upright. In the second half both back divisions had some exciting thrusts stopped by strong defensive play, but suddenly Simson broke away from midfield to score a fine try after a long evasive run. It was noted that Bedell-Sivright kept up with him and acted as some form of shield! The Scottish pack finished powerfully and from one rush the ball was put over the line for Purves to touch down. The result was narrow but emphatic enough, 1 goal and 1 try (8) to 1 try (3), and Scotland had their fifth Triple Crown.

There were some lean years to come prior to the First World War and of the 26 matches played, including the new fixture with France in 1910, Scotland won 9 and lost 17. When that tragic era of war was over and the countries again picked up the threads of their rugby, Scotland opened with a flourish in January 1920 by beating France, then Wales and Ireland only to lose at Twickenham on 20 March 1920 before HM King George V and a record crowd of 40,000. The early twenties saw a patchwork of results, and then the 1925 International campaign opened with another remarkable flourish when Scotland beat France on 24 January 1925 in the last International to be played at Inverleith, to the tune of 2 goals and 5 tries (25) to 1 drop goal (4). A crowd of 20,000 watched the comfortable victory, although numerous critics were not happy with the Scottish forwards who had not dominated play. I.S.Smith, with four tries, and J.B.Nelson both had sound games, while G.P.S.Macpherson had a hand in practically every score. The French team was numbered and frequently packed down 3–4. The scoring sequence was as follows: A.C.Gillies scored and converted (5–0); Y.de Manoir dropped a goal (5–4). Half-time. A.C.Wallace scored but Gillies failed to convert (8–4); I.S.Smith scored and D.Drysdale converted (13–4); A.C.Wallace scored but Drysdale failed to convert (16–4); I.S.Smith scored thrice; none was converted (25–4). Of course caps were now awarded to those who played against France, thus success in all games could bring not only a Triple Crown but a Grand Slam.

There was an immediate air of purpose about this Scottish team and Wales, even at home in Swansea on 7 February 1925, looked vulnerable in the face of the onslaught. The speed and skill of the visiting backs were quite devastating and I.S.Smith again scored four tries. D.Drysdale converted one and dropped a goal. A.C.Wallace had two tries. However, the Welsh pack lifted their game over the last fifteen minutes and put in a storming finish; W.J.Hopkins, W.I.Jones and R.A.Cornish scored tries, one of which was converted by D.Parker, but Wales could not surpass the scoring power of Scotland and the final analysis comprised: 1 goal, 1 drop goal and 5 tries (24) to 1 goal, 1 penalty goal and 2 tries (14). It was an encouraging start to what was to prove an historic achievement.

Scotland then faced Ireland at Lansdowne Road on 28 February 1925, and finished up with a third satisfactory victory. As against Wales, the speed and handling of the Scottish backs were splendid. The absence of Macpherson had much to do with the comparative quietness of I.S.Smith but the return of H.Waddell outside to J.B.Nelson compensated for this. The second Scottish score was the result of great handling which started in midfield. The ball went from Nelson, Waddell, J.C.Dykes, G.G.Aitken to Wallace, who after a 30-yard run passed the ball back to Dykes and thence via J.W.Scott to D.J.MacMyn who scored under the posts. The Irish try came from a dodge by H.W.V.Stephenson. Inside the Scottish half he flung the ball in from touch, caught the throw himself and sprinted to score in the corner before a surprised defence could tackle him. As a result of this action the touch law was later altered. In the Scottish scoring A.C.Wallace crossed and D.Drysdale converted. This was followed by MacMyn's excellent try, converted by J.C.Dykes. Finally, H. Waddell dropped a goal. Apart from the Irish try, W.E.Crawford had kicked a penalty. The final scoreline was 2 goals, 1 drop goal (14) to 1 goal, 1 penalty goal (8). The stage was now set for the England match at Murrayfield, a game of immense significance with Triple Crown and Grand Slam at stake for Scotland. Meanwhile, England were undefeated, although they had a drawn game with Ireland.

Beautiful weather for the opening of the new ground at Murrayfield brought out on 21 March 1925 a record crowd of at least 70,000 who watched one of the most exciting matches ever played. The lead changed hands thrice and England's great fight to save the game during the last minutes only failed because of tremendous tackling by the Scots and the utter exhaustion of the attackers. The scoring sequence reveals the ebb and flow of this classic of rugby football. W.G.E.Luddington (England) kicked a penalty goal (0–3); J.B.Nelson scored and Drysdale converted (5–3); R.H.Hamilton-Wickes (England) scored and Luddington converted (5–8). Half-time. W.W. Wakefield (England) scored (5–11); A.C.Wallace scored and A.C. Gillies converted (10–11); H.Waddell dropped a goal (14–11). The final stage of the encounter built up into a frenzy of excitement for the vast crowd. Scotland came near to scoring in the last quarter as they trailed narrowly 10–11. Wallace was halted by a forward pass; J.W. Scott beat the full-back only to be felled by A.M.Smallwood cutting across in defence; G.G.Aitken dribbled through only to have the ball rebound wide off a goal post and H.Waddell narrowly missed with a drop-goal. The score was merely delayed, however, and all Murrayfield erupted—as it did in 1984 when J.H.Calder got his try against France—when J.B.Nelson fed his stand-off who coolly dropped a goal from the 25. With five minutes left, England made desperate efforts to score. A.M.Smallwood broke away but was floored by Drysdale; E.Myers was halted on the line by sheer force of numbers and finally L.J.Corbett broke through only to stumble and fall apparently through sheer exhaustion about a yard short of the Scottish line. Thus England had given their all but the day belonged to the wearers of the Thistle who had won by 2 goals and 1 drop goal (14) to 1 goal, 1 penalty goal and 1 try (11), and a more wonderful day and way to open the new Murrayfield could not be imagined.

In the subsequent years up to the next success in 1933 Scotland had won 14, lost 14 and drawn only one (against England at Twickenham in 1930) of the matches played. The 1932 season held no promise of what was to come because Scotland had lost to the South African tourists (3–6); Wales (0–6); Ireland (8–20) and England (3–16), whilst there was no game against France. However, rugby being the game of optimism it is, each new season brings afresh its opportunity and challenge.

Scotland went to Swansea on 4 February 1933 and had the satis-

71

faction of being victors by 1 goal, 1 penalty goal and 1 try (11) to 1 try (3). The visitors held a distinct territorial advantage in the first half and scored twice. I.S.Smith crossed with a typical run to the corner flag, then K.C.Fyfe kicked a good penalty from near the centre. Wales started the second half without D.Thomas who had broken a collar bone and fell further behind when another long run by Smith finished with K.L.T.Jackson scoring. A late revival by the depleted Welsh pack gave T.Arthur a score after a good forward rush. Scotland's H.Lind who defended well was subdued in attack, for E.C.Davey tackled viciously and never gave him room to move. After the match the SRU selection committee, convened by D.Drysdale, retired to their hotel room to pick the XV for the next game in Dublin. Although delighted with the result, the committee found points to discuss and after a while deemed it sensible to ring for some further refreshments. When a head was poked round the door the Convener said, 'Ah, the same again'. 'Oh, good!', said the face and vanished but nothing arrived and it took another approach before the drinks appeared. Suitably fortified, the Committee resumed its deliberations and eventually decided to play an unchanged team—which was just as well because one morning paper carried the news that 'the same' team had indeed been chosen!

England came to Murrayfield on 18 March 1933. The game was not a classic and a try by K.C.Fyfe was all either team could raise. However, it was fortunate for England that they exercised a definite superiority forward, for during the game both their centres went lame and some desperate tackling was needed to confine the tally to a solitary try, Scotland winning by 1 try (3) to nil. But at least Scotland were due to face Ireland in a postponed match at Lansdowne Road, knowing that they were clear contenders for the Triple Crown, albeit with rather economical scoring during the season to date!

On 24 February 1933 the Scottish team and officials had had the very discomfiting experience of being stormbound in their steamer in Dublin Bay for sixteen hours and the players were in no condition to compete on the Saturday. Thus the match had been postponed until 1 April 1933. For this game Scotland were forced to make the only change during the season when P.M.S.Gedge replaced Fyfe who had been injured in a car accident the previous day. This was a bruising match due to hard ground and fierce tackling. Lind suffered a nasty face scrape; Smith was lame for most of the match; H.D.B.Lorraine was dazed due to a heavy tackle, and Gedge broke a bone in his hand attempting a hand-off. Scotland contrived to be in the lead at the interval through a K.L.T.Jackson dropped goal, following an Irish try by M.P.Crowe. After half-time, P.F.Murray slipped over for a try to put Ireland in the lead (4–6). The Scottish pack then set-to and controlled play so well that W.R.Logan and Jackson, the only fit backs, were able to take play into the Irish 25. With some ten minutes left, Logan from a scrum threw a long pass to Lind who had just time to drop a good goal. Scotland thus won by 2 drop goals (8) to 2 tries (6). So in I.S.Smith's last season he had the satisfaction of captaining Scotland to a Triple Crown.

The intervening years between 1933 and the next Triple Crown were not rewarding in terms of results. France, of course, were out of the reckoning during most of the thirties because of transgressions, thus a Grand Slam could no longer apply. As it was, between 1934 and 1937 Scotland won only three out of thirteen matches. But amends were made in the 1938 series, a splendid purple patch in the history of Scottish Rugby.

Wales travelled to Murrayfield on 5 February 1938 and met Scotland in a closely fought contest. The match will be remembered for the dramatic penalty goal kicked in the last minutes to give Scotland a win. During the first half Scotland had an equal share of the ball and hardly deserved to be behind at the interval for R.W.Shaw was in good form, clearly undisturbed by C.W.Jones (Wales), and had one saving touch down which showed that he was the fastest man in the game over 30 yards. D.J.Macrae and R.C.S.Dick were thrustful and the latter held W.Wooller (Wales) from start to finish. Yet it was a run and good crosskick by Jones that put A.McCarley (Wales) in for the first score and the same player seized on an inaccurate pass by T.F. Dorward to get his second try. Wales, however, ran into trouble when a rib injury to M.E.Morgan forced the player to retire just before the interval. In the second half Scotland, with the numerical advantage, pressed continuously. A.H.Drummond hit the bar with a penalty. He then picked up a pass and went over only to find that the whistle had gone for a Welsh forward pass. Dorward narrowly missed with a drop before Macrae and Forrest had a good run and found W.H.Crawford up to take a scoring pass. At this stage Wooller was limping, so McCarley came out of the pack leaving six forwards to contest the scrums. This they did very well although things became rather tousy, Dorward in particular coming in for some hammering. With less than five minutes to go Drummond tried another long range penalty which dropped short but the pressure was sustained. Man after man charged at the line and Dorward seemed to have grounded the ball but the Welsh pack fell on him. There followed a maul on the line in which a Welsh forward was judged to have interfered with the ball and a penalty was awarded. There followed a nerve-racking halt to allow the weary, the maimed and the concussed to get up and get on side, whereupon Crawford kicked the goal to win the match. The score was 1 goal and 1 penalty goal (8) to 2 tries (6).

Ireland followed Wales to Murrayfield on 26 February 1938 and suffered the same fate. Scotland were full of brilliant running for Shaw, Macrae and Dick were quite explosive in attack. For Ireland G.J.Morgan had many dangerous dodging runs round the blind side, but with the exception of the sprinter F.G.Moran the backs lacked pace and also seemed over anxious to curb Shaw. The Irish forwards opened with a burst that nearly brought a score but inside fifteen minutes Shaw intercepted a pass, was through at top speed and gave J.G.S.Forrest a clear run in. T.F.Dorward dropped a goal and A.H. Drummond kicked a penalty. Shaw continued to worry the defence and found a chance to let Macrae away and give Forrest his second try. After the interval Ireland came back into the game when D.B. O'Loughlin charged down a kick and scored, and a break by Morgan put Moran in, but then a scissors move between Dick and Macrae saw the latter score. There followed a good dribbling run by Duff and Forrest which let Shaw snap up the ball and send Drummond in. With three minutes to go Morgan scored for Ireland after a fine break. The score was 2 goals, 1 drop goal, 1 penalty goal and 2 tries (23) to 1 goal and 3 tries (14).

Scotland then ventured to Twickenham on 19 March 1938 with a fierce determination to come out on top and the King and Queen and 70,000 spectators saw what was probably the most spectacular and exciting Calcutta Cup match ever played and one made memorable by a superb personal performance by R.W.Shaw, who scored two magnificent solo tries, created a third, and with the ball in his hands was a source of extreme anxiety to the English defence. Starved of the ball (the scrum count was four-one in England's favour), the Scottish forwards were splendid in the loose and get some credit for the other two tries. As for excitement a glance at the scores shows that Scotland took the lead four times, England drew level three times, fluctuations which left the spectators absolutely shattered. Scores: W.N.Renwick scored but W.H.Crawford failed to convert (3–0); G.W.Parker (England) kicked 2 penalties (3–6); W.N.Renwick scored but Crawford failed to convert (6–6); R.C.S.Dick scored but Crawford failed to convert (9–6); E.J.Unwin (England) scored but Parker failed to convert (9–9); R.W.Shaw scored but Crawford failed to convert (12–9). Half-time. F.J.Reynolds (England) dropped a goal (12–13); W.H.Crawford kicked two penalties (18–13); G.W.Parker (England) kicked a penalty (18–16); R.W.Shaw scored but Crawford failed to convert (21–16).

England made a good start and it took a touch down and good tackling to keep them out. Then a bad pass missed F.J.Reynolds and Shaw like a flash touched it ahead, picked it up and kicked ahead. Renwick ran onto the ball, also kicked ahead, got the bounce and fairly hurled himself in for a good try. Inside ten minutes Parker had kicked England into the lead only to have the Scottish forwards come back, and a crashing run by Crawford let Renwick run in again. Then the Scottish forwards on their own 25 lost a scrum but the back row broke so effectively that they got the ball back and shot up-field. P.L.Duff, Young and Crawford all made ground before the ball was suddenly passed in-field to Dick who sprinted away for a great try. Almost at once a good run by P.L.Candler (England) put E.J.Unwin in to equalise again. Just before half-time, from some loose play at half-field the ball was put out to Shaw who dummied Reynolds and cut out to the left touch line, leaving the defenders standing by his acceleration. Faced by Parker he produced a textbook right foot/left foot fast jink which left the full-back sprawling in touch and ran in for a wonderful solo try. On restarting, England pressed in spite of another fine dash by Shaw which narrowly failed and from the 25 Reynolds dropped a nice goal to put England into the lead for the last time. Soon Crawford kicked two fairly lengthy penalties for offside. Parker brought the score to 18–16 with another penalty and H.S.Sever (England) must have scored had he not collided with the goal post. With some three minutes left the ball, from a scrum near midfield on the right, came out to Shaw who shot diagonally to the left behind the English threes. With his acceleration he was clear and he finished with a five-feet dive to score far out. The kick failed but that was the virtual end. The score was 2 penalty goals and 5 tries (21) to 1 drop goal, 3 penalty goals and 1 try (16).

R.W.Shaw, who was carried off the field by his team and cheered by all, had two other memories of the afternoon. First, the bus driver bringing the Scots to the ground became confused threading his way through the enormous crowd and delivered the players at the wrong gate. Once inside they had to walk a long way round to the dressing-room through another dense crowd who, recognising them, offered a selection of comments ranging from their chance of winning to the parsimony of the SRU who apparently made their team walk to the match! Later, having showered and dressed, Shaw made his way to the tea-room, which the players shared with a section of the general public. There he was glad to sink into a vacant chair beside an elderly gentleman and to start the conversation remarked 'Pretty hard going out there today', and got the reply 'Yes, you must be glad you were not a player'.

1890—91

Wales: G.1, DG.2, T.6 (15) – Nil (0)
Ireland: G.3, DG.1, T.2 (14) – Nil (0)
England: G.2, DG.1 (9) – G.1 (3)

		W	I	E
H. J. Stevenson	Edinburgh Acads.	DG	*	*
P. R. Clauss	Oxford Univ.	T.2	T	DG
G. McGregor	Cambridge Univ.	*	T	G.2
W. Neilson	Merchiston Castle	DG	.	T
G. R. Wilson	RHSFP	.	*	.
C. E. Orr	West of Scotland	T	*	*
D. G. Anderson	London Scottish	*	.	*
W. Wotherspoon,	Cambridge Univ.	.	T.3	.
J. D. Boswell	West of Scotland	T	G.3	*
A. Dalgleish	Gala	*	*	.
W. R. Gibson,	RHSFP	.	*	*
F. W. J. Goodhue	London Scottish	T	*	*
H. T. O. Leggatt	Watsonians	T	*	*
M. C. McEwan, *Capt.*	Edinburgh Acads.	G	DG	*
I. McIntyre,	Edinburgh Wands.	*	*	*
R. G. Macmillan	London Scottish	*	.	*
G. T. Neilson	West of Scotland	*	*	*
J. E. Orr	West of Scotland	T	*	T

NOTE
The teams are set out in such a way as to show the positions occupied by the players, the order (from the top) being: full-back, wingers and centres, half-backs, forwards.

Any score by a player is registered, otherwise his participation is indicated by an asterisk (*).

In season 1924-25, J. C. Dykes played at stand-off against France and Wales, but played as a centre against Ireland.

In season 1983-84, the three replacements who came on during play, are listed.

1894–95

Wales: G.1 (5) – DG.1 (4)
Ireland: T.2 (6) – Nil (0)
England: PG.1, T.1 (6) – PG.1 (3)

		W	I	E
A. R. Smith	Oxford Univ.	*	*	*
J. J. Gowans	London Scottish	T	*	*
G. T. Campbell	London Scottish	*	T	*
W. Neilson	London Scottish	*	*	*
R. Welsh	Watsonians	*	T	*
J. W. Simpson	RHSFP	*	*	*
M. Elliot	Hawick	*	.	.
P. R. Clauss	Birkenhead Park	.	*	.
W. P. Donaldson	West of Scotland	.	.	*
W. B. Cowrie	Watsonians	*	*	*
J. H. Dods	Edinburgh Acads.	*	*	*
W. R. Gibson, *Capt.* (w)	RHSFP	*	*	*
R. G. Macmillan, *Capt.* (I, E)	London Scottish	*	*	*
G. T. Neilson	West of Scotland	*	*	PG, T
T. M. Scott	Hawick	*	*	*
W. M. C. McEwan	Edinburgh Acads.	*	.	*
J. N. Millar	West of Scotland	.	*	*
H. O. Smith	Watsonians	G	.	.
T. L. Hendry	Clydesdale	.	*	.

1900—01

Wales: G.3, T.1 (18) − G.1, T.1 (8)
Ireland: T.3 (9) − G.1 (5)
England: G.3, T.1 (18) − T.1 (3)

		W	I	E
A. W. Duncan	Edinburgh Univ.	*	*	*
W. H. Welsh	Edinburgh Univ.	*	T.2	T
A. B. Timms	Edinburgh Univ.	*	*	T
P. Turnbull	Edinburgh Acads.	T	*	*
A. N. Fell	Edinburgh Univ.	*	*	T
J. I. Gillespie	Edinburgh Acads.	G.2, T.2	T	G.3, T
F. H. Fasson	Edinburgh Univ.	*	*	.
R. M. Neill	Edinburgh Acads.	.	.	*
D. R. Bedell-Sivright	Cambridge Univ.	*	*	*
J. A. Bell	Clydesdale	*	*	*
J. M. Dykes	Glasgow HSFP	*	*	*
A. B. Flett	Edinburgh Univ.	G, T	*	*
A. Frew	Edinburgh Univ.	*	*	*
M. C. Morrison, *Capt.*	RHSFP	*	*	*
J. Ross	London Scottish	*	*	*
R. S. Stronach	Glasgow Acads.	*	.	*
F. P. Dods	Edinburgh Acads.	.	*	.

78

1902–03

Wales: PG.1, T.1 (6) – Nil (0)
Ireland: T.1 (3) – Nil (0)
England: DG.1, T.2 (10) – T.2 (6)

		W	I	E
W. T. Forrest	Hawick	*	*	*
A. N. Fell	Edinburgh Univ.	*	.	*
A. B. Timms	Edinburgh Univ.	PG	.	DG
H. J. Orr	London Scottish	*	*	*
J. E. Crabbie	Oxford Univ.	*	T	.
C. France	Kelvinside Acads.	.	*	.
A. S. Dryburgh	Edinburgh Wands.	.	*	.
J. S. Macdonald	Edinburgh Univ.	.	.	*
E. D. Simson	Edinburgh Univ.	*	*	T
J. Knox	Kelvinside Acads.	*	*	*
A. G. Cairns	Watsonians	*	*	*
J. R. C. Greenlees, *Capt.* (E)	Kelvinside Acads.	*	*	*
N. Kennedy	West of Scotland	*	*	*
W. E. Kyle	Hawick	T	*	*
W. P. Scott	West of Scotland	*	*	*
L. West	Edinburgh Univ.	*	*	*
D. R. Bedell-Sivright	Cambridge Univ.	*	*	.
M. C. Morrison, *Capt.* (W, I)	RHSFP	*	*	.
J. D. Dallas	Watsonians	.	.	T
J. Ross	London Scottish	.	.	*

1906–07

South Africa: T.2 (6) – Nil (0)

Wales: T.2 (6) – PG.1 (3)
Ireland: G.3 (15) – PG.1 (3)
England: G.1, T.1 (8) – T.1 (3)

		W	I	E
T. Sloan	Glasgow Acads.	*	.	*
D. G. Schulze	London Scottish	.	*	*
K. G. MacLeod	Cambridge Univ.	*	G	*
D. G. MacGregor	Pontypridd	*	*	*
M. W. Walter	London Scottish	*	*	.
A. B. H. L. Purves	London Scottish	T	T	T
E. D. Simson	London Scottish	*	*	T
L. L. Greig, *Capt.* (W)	United Services	*	.	.
P. Munro, *Capt.* (I, E)	London Scottish	.	*	*
D. R. Bedell-Sivright	Edinburgh Univ.	*	*	*
G. M. Frew	Glasgow HSFP	*	T	*
I. C. Geddes	London Scottish	*	G.2	G
J. C. MacCallum	Watsonians	*	*	*
G. A. Sanderson	RHSFP	*	T	*
W. P. Scott	West of Scotland	*	*	*
L. M. Spiers	Watsonians	*	*	*
H. G. Monteith	London Scottish	T	*	.
J. M. B. Scott	Edinburgh Acads.	.	.	*

1924—25

France: G.2, T.5 (25) — DG.1 (4)
Wales: G.1, DG.1, T.5 (24) — G.1, PG.1, T.2 (14)
Ireland: G.2, DG.1 (14) — G.1, PG.1 (8)
England: G.2, DG.1 (14) — G.1, PG.1, T.1 (11)

		F	W	I	E
D. Drysdale, *Capt.* (I)	Heriot's FP	G	G, DG	G	G
I. S. Smith	Oxford Univ.	T.4	T.4	*	*
G. P. S. Macpherson, *Capt.* (F, W, E)	Oxford Univ.	*	*	.	*
G. G. Aitken	Oxford Univ.	*	*	*	*
A. C. Wallace	Oxford Univ.	T.2	T.2	T	T
J. C. Dykes	Glasgow Acads.	*	*	G	.
H. Waddell	Glasgow Acads.	.	.	DG	DG
J. B. Nelson	Glasgow Acads.	*	*	*	T
D. J. MacMyn	Cambridge Univ.	*	*	T	*
J. M. Bannerman	Glasgow HSFP	*	*	*	*
J. W. Scott	Stewart's FP	*	*	*	*
J. R. Paterson	Birkenhead Park	*	*	*	*
A. C. Gillies	Carlisle	G, T	*	.	G
J. R. E. Buchanan	Exeter	*	.	*	.
J. Gilchrist	Glasgow Acads.	*	.	.	.
W. H. Stevenson	Glasgow Acads.	*	.	.	.
D. S. Davies	Hawick	.	*	*	*
J. C. H. Ireland	Glasgow HSFP	.	*	*	*
R. A. Howie	Kirkcaldy	.	*	*	*

81

1932–33

Wales: G.1, PG.1, T.1 (11) – T.1 (3)
Ireland: Postponed
England: T.1 (3) – Nil (0)
Ireland: DG.2 (8) – T.2 (6)

		W	E	I
D. I. Brown	Cambridge Univ.	*	*	*
I. S. Smith, *Capt.*	London Scottish	T	*	*
H. D. B. Lorraine	Oxford Univ.	*	*	*
H. Lind	Dunfermline	*	*	DG
K. C. Fyfe	Cambridge Univ.	G, PG	T	.
P. M. S. Gedge	Edinburgh Wands.	.	.	*
K. L. T. Jackson	Oxford Univ.	T	*	DG
W. R. Logan	Edinburgh Wands.	*	*	*
J. A. Waters	Selkirk	*	*	*
J. M. Ritchie	Watsonians	*	*	*
J. R. Thom	Watsonians	*	*	*
J. A. Beattie	Hawick	*	*	*
M. S. Stewart	Stewart's FP	*	*	*
W. B. Welsh	Hawick	*	*	*
R. Rowand	Glasgow HSFP	*	*	*
J. M. Henderson	Edinburgh Acads.	*	*	*

1937–38

Wales: G.1, PG.1 (8) – T.2 (6)
Ireland: G.2, DG.1, PG.1, T.2 (23) – G.1, T.3 (14)
England: PG.2, T.5 (21) – DG.1, PG.3, T.1 (16)

		W	I	E
G. Roberts	Watsonians	*	*	*
J. G. S. Forrest	Cambridge Univ.	*	T.2	*
D. J. Macrae	St Andrews Univ.	*	T	*
R. C. S. Dick	Guy's	*	*	T
A. H. Drummond	Kelvinside Acads.	*	PG, T	.
W. N. Renwick	London Scottish	.	.	T.2
R. W. Shaw, *Capt.*	Glasgow HSFP	*	*	T.2
T. F. Dorward	Gala	*	DG	*
J. D. Hastie	Melrose	*	*	*
W. M. Inglis	Army	*	*	*
G. B. Horsburgh	London Scottish	*	*	*
A. Roy	Waterloo	*	*	*
W. B. Young	Cambridge Univ.	*	*	*
P. L. Duff	Glasgow Acads.	*	*	*
W. H. Crawford	United Services	G, PG, T	G.2	PG.2
J. B. Borthwick	Stewart's FP	*	*	.
W. F. Blackadder	West of Scotland	.	.	*

1983—84 (see next Chapter)

New Zealand; DG.2, PG.5, T.1 (25) — G.2, PG.3, T.1 (25)

Wales: G.2, PG.1 (15) — G.1, PG.1 (9)
England: G.2, PG.2 (18) — PG.2 (6)
Ireland: G.3, PG.2, T.2 (32) — G.1, PG.1 (9)
France: G.1, PG.5 (21) — G.1, DG.1, PG.1 (12)

		W	E	I	F
P. W. Dods	Gala	G.2, PG	G.2, PG.2	G.3, PG.2 T	G, PG.5
G. R. T. Baird	Kelso	*	*	*	*
A. E. Kennedy	Watsonians	*	T	.	.
D. I. Johnston	Watsonians	*	T	*	*
S. Munro	Ayr	*	.	.	.
K. W. Robertson	Melrose	.	*	T	*
J. A. Pollock	Gosforth	.	* (R)	*	*
J. Y. Rutherford	Selkirk	*	*	*	*
R. J. Laidlaw	Jed Forest	*	*	T.2	*
I. G. Hunter	Selkirk	.	.	* (R)	.
J. Aitken, *Capt.*	Gala	T	*	*	*
C. T. Deans	Hawick	*	*	*	*
I. G. Milne	Heriot's FP	*	*	*	*
A. J. Tomes	Hawick	*	*	*	*
J. H. Calder	Stewart's-Mel. FP	*	*	*	T
I. A. M. Paxton	Selkirk	T	*	*	*
D. G. Leslie	Gala	*	*	*	*
W. Cuthbertson	Harlequins	*	*	.	.
J. R. Beattie	Glasgow Acads.	.	* (R)	.	.
A. J. Campbell	Hawick	.	.	*	*
—				Pen-T	

Replacements not used:
R. Cunningham — Bath
N. A. Rowan — Boroughmuir
D. S. Wyllie — Stewart's-Mel. FP
A. R. Irvine — Heriot's FP
S. G. Johnston — Watsonians
G. J. Callander — Kelso

9

A TRIPLE CROWN AND GRAND SLAM: SEASON 1983–84

A cold, wet Sunday at Murrayfield. A squad, coaches, background organisation. The prospect of hard work after hard games the day before—and at the end of it hot showers and a hot meal.

The stiffness wears off as the work-rate builds up. Once sweat is broken it is a cushion against the chill. Hard and intensive scrummaging; more and more weight to shift on the machine. The backs sweep from end to end on the Wanderers pitch. Moves are organised. Concentration. Intensive rucking by the forwards. The backs seem to move ever faster—penetrating. More concentration. Intensive lineout drills; high trajectory; low trajectory. Support. Again and again. Encouragement. Constructive criticism. Again and again. Avid discussion is a feature. Nothing is left to chance at a Scottish squad session. The selectors hover, anxious, involved.

Such potent preparation was typical during many a Sunday or mid-week session before and during the international championship campaign of 1983/84. There was a commitment in the Scottish camp derived from acumen, vast experience, and belief in team and self; and at the end of an extraordinary season there was a Triple Crown—after 46 years; and a Grand Slam—after 59 years. If the nation had been forced to wait for what had become the seemingly impossible—so-near-and-yet-so-far in 1955, 1961, 1962, 1973 and 1975 (five near misses in the Triple Crown)—when the ultimate victory brought heady success, perhaps it was that much sweeter. All Scotland, as well as a multitude of Scots overseas, rejoiced and were exceedingly glad; intensely proud of the young men who had worn the thistle with conviction and fervour.

Endings are more important than beginnings it is true, yet without a start there can be no finish. It may or may not be coincidence, but Scotland's near-success during the international championships of 1961 and 1962 immediately followed the initiative of the Scottish Rugby Union in pioneering the short tour, to South Africa in 1960. We were the first country to do so. Since then a vigorous policy has been pursued, with our key players having the opportunity to appear in as high a level of competition as is reasonably possible. More recently Scottish rugby men had responded enthusiastically to touring France in 1980, New Zealand in 1981 and Australia in 1982. Finally, and probably crucially, G.R.T.Baird, J.R.Beattie, J.H.Calder, C.T.Deans, R.J.Laidlaw, I.G.Milne, I.A.M.Paxton and J.Y.Rutherford experienced the cauldron of New Zealand rugby in the summer of 1983, when they were in the Lions. With them was the intrepid Jim Telfer, a players' coach in every sense. Rugby is the great leveller—up or down—and if the outcome for the British Lions in the Test series was a whitewash, the tremendous collective participation prompted John Rutherford to remark to the Scottish President on the Scots players' return at Edinburgh Airport, 'Triple Crown this year'. They were prophetic words. The seeds were sown!

What followed is now exciting history and part of the ongoing story of Scottish Rugby. The challenge of the new season came earlier than expected and was welcomed when New Zealand requested a tour to England and Scotland as a result of the Argentinians' refusal to grant visas because of New Zealand's alleged involvement in the Falklands War of 1982. The Argentinian loss of the New Zealand rugby tourists was our gain. I.A.L (Bill) Hogg, the new Secretary of the Scottish Rugby Union, successor to the long-serving John Law, found himself 'in at the deep end'. Of course the pressure was on in terms of readiness to tackle the All Blacks a mere four months after the final test against the Lions at Auckland.

The administration and the coaching structure coped admirably and Scottish rugby girded itself as the visitors flew into London in October 1983, short, it is true, of some experienced men, but always a formidable side to anticipate and engage. This became uncomfortable reality when two proud Scottish district sides, Edinburgh and the South, fell heavily to the wearers of the silver fern, and thus the burden of upholding our game was transferred to the Scottish international squad.

For sheer, sustained excitement the encounter between Scotland and New Zealand on Saturday, 12 November 1983 was a classic and the Murrayfield crowd was kept at fever pitch as Scotland clawed back repeatedly, showing a determination and tenacity which were to prove vital in games to come. The scoring sequence is revealing (Scotland first) 3–0, 3–3, 6–3, 6–7, _6–13_, 9–13, _9–16_, 12–16, 15–16, _15–22_, 18–22, 21–22, 21–25, 25–25. That the Scots three times (underlined) recovered a seven-point deficit is testimony to a side prepared to fight until the bitter end. The ferocious driving and rucking of a pack who moved as one showed that the wearers of the thistle were not going to stand on ceremony, and the support from the backs was finally highlighted when Jim Pollock dived into a beautifully flighted ball from a David Johnston kick at the north-east corner of Murrayfield, to the exultant roar of a delighted crowd. If Scotland had had 'the rub of the green' and New Zealand the try count of 3–1, the new electronic scoreboard still carried the legend for all the world to see, 'Scotland 25, New Zealand 25'. A point had been made and honour restored. The Scottish Lions had made full use of that collective participation! In theory the stage was set for a promising international season. The very commendable draw had provided a platform.

However, fate decreed that events were not quite straightforward, when, following a very promising victory at Melrose by Scotland B over Ireland B by 22 points to 13 on 3 December, in the first Scottish trial in three years, at the beginning of January 1984, the Whites comprehensively outplayed and beat an apparently complacent Blues XV to the extent of a 4–nil try count. The cat was amongst the pigeons with a vengeance! With such a disconcerting result and with the Welsh game at Cardiff a mere fortnight away on 21 January 1984, there was some very serious and concise thinking by the selectors, who pinned their faith in a judicious blend of vast experience and the evidence of the trial. So the die was cast in Scotland's bid for success in the championship.

If optimism for an exacting task had taken a knock as a result of the trial there was a measure of encouragement from a famous win at Cardiff two years previously, when Scotland had defeated Wales by the remarkable margin of 34 points to 18, a first success there after some nine matches—in fact, twenty years of waiting! A long time again—but the feat had been accomplished. Surely the trial reverse would sting numerous players into strong reaction in the International arena.

Intense conditioning and supreme motivation had had their effect; the atmosphere in the Scottish dressing-room was electric in the long minutes before the team pounded out on to the turf of Cardiff Arms Park. They breathed dedication and defiance; it was no place for the faint hearted!

With the match under way before the familiar, knowledgeable, partisan but sporting Welsh supporters, and the Scottish faithful, the first scrum exuded pressure, and within minutes the referee was sorting out some 'teething troubles'. These dispensed with, the game developed as a tremendously exciting contest with neither side able to score for a fiercely fought half-hour, the crowd being kept in a state of sustained tension. The Scottish forwards were in rare fettle, and despite their powerful, controlled aggression they had conceded nothing in the way of penalties until 'going over the top' spawned a Welsh penalty which opened the account, this not far short of half-time. Into injury minutes the Scots stole the lead with a beautifully constructed short penalty ploy to the right of the posts, and near the Welsh 22, which baffled the defence and Iain Paxton dived spectacularly for a try which was converted by Peter Dods. Yet, opinion in the stadium amid the Scots was that a mere 6–3 interval lead was scant return for all their forward dominance.

The red jerseys had to come back. It was the National Stadium and pride was at stake! So back they came and the Scots were forced to soak up pressure. When a score materialised it was a good Welsh try far out. They had the lead, and the conversion initiated 'Bread of Heaven' which wafted around the ground, subsequently stifled only by Peter Dods as he stroked over a penalty to draw the score.

Then came the moment of uplift for the Scots on the field, throughout the great stadium, and around television sets at home. Well into the last quarter of the game brilliant forward play paved the way for a line-out in the Welsh corner and indirectly from it Jim Aitken, propelled by David Leslie, slammed through a wall of red jerseys for a real captain's try to the left of the posts. Peter Dods' conversion in the seventieth minute was the end of the scoring but not the end of the Welsh efforts, for the Scots lived dangerously, yet with tenacity, under continuous assault until the end.

Here was another aspect of rugby history in a season in which the making of history was a feature. Not since the second decade of the century, in 1925 and 1927, had Scotland been victors in consecutive games in Wales. Curiously enough, the 1925 match at Swansea had been during the year when a Grand Slam was achieved. Perhaps it was the hand of fate influencing the trend of events.

The 15–9 win at the expense of Wales had brought the Scottish points total for two matches to 40—albeit with only 3 tries—and the platform resulting from the New Zealand match had now become a springboard for the 100th fixture against England on 4 February 1984. Mentally and physically the players were well placed. Psychologically, the away win in a first game is probably ideal in any international campaign, then Murrayfield with the fervent supporters of the day can work wonders in incentive for men representing their country on that sacred ground. With such a prospect, the work-rate at the squad session on 29 January was impressive. But if there were thoughts of a Triple Crown in some quarters they had no part in the build-up for the Scottish squad. It was for the 'next game' only, for in international rugby each game is a 'one off'; it cannot be otherwise with each national team so well prepared. Yet there was a stimulus at the thought of the 100th game against the 'auld enemy' and the fact that Scotland had won the first fixture away back in 1871; also, there was the coveted Calcutta Cup at stake. Of course the cherished trophy would not have far to go in that it had been wrested from the English at Twickenham in 1983, the previous victory there being in 1971, a long time ago yet again.

Unfortunately, Steve Munro had been injured and he was replaced by Keith Robertson. Otherwise the selected team itself was identical to the side which had produced the goods at Cardiff.

Both teams were greeted by the Murrayfield crowd with a warm acclaim which belied a cold, grey February afternoon, the yellow Lions rampant supporters flags contrasting the overcast sky. As always the staff under Jim Thain, the Head Groundsman, had the playing surface in immaculate appearance, but it was no fault of theirs that underfoot it was treacherous from incessant drizzle. However, the weather was not enough to dampen the enthusiasm of a host of bright-eyed 8–10-year-old boys who had the unforgettable thrill of treading the hallowed turf in a series of games of the fashionable (and very important) mini-rugby prior to the international itself and as part of the celebrations for the 100th match. Then they retired to reserved seats to witness Scotland's continuing campaign.

That John Rutherford was 'on song' with his kicking became abundantly clear early on in the game when he teased and tantalised the English defence, a softening-up process that had the desired effect. On the other hand the Scots appeared to have some kind of 'death wish' as they gave away penalties with a disconcerting regularity. Had the attempts at goal by England's Dusty Hare also been 'on song', much of Rutherford's authoritative kicking would have been nullified. However, 'fortune favoured the brave' and the blue jerseys dictated events in the set-pieces and open play, climaxing eventually in the 29th minute with a near-traditional 'Feet, Scotland, Feet' rush that would have gladdened the heart of J.M. Bannerman. A resultant line-out on the left eventually provided loose ball to the right of the posts at the north end, the English centres amazingly over-ran the ball and Iain Paxton, ever-present, probed it towards the line. Then the class footballing skills of David Johnston enabled him to dribble and thrust past the shredded defence for a first try. The confident Peter Dods converted, thus Scotland had the opening spoils.

Minutes before half-time Dusty Hare at last found the target with his fifth attempt and so the score stood at 6–3—as it had done at Cardiff. Was it to be a good omen? Doubts would have been understandable when the stalwart grafter Bill Cuthbertson left the field with a groin strain which, sadly was to put him out for what was to come at Lansdowne Road. The experienced and versatile John Beattie then came on and wisely the selectors elected to make a straight change rather than put Iain Paxton to lock, where he had played in the

89

Calcutta Cup success of 1983 at Twickenham. No, Calder, Leslie and Paxton were going too splendidly to risk anything! Such judgement was justified when the unit, thriving from the dominance of the front five had a big part in the second score, moments after half-time. It was Jim Calder who finally screened the ball on the west touchline in the English 22 at the clock-end, gleaned possession for the charging Alan Tomes, and in a twinkling John Rutherford had laid bare the defence to put a triumphant Euan Kennedy through beside the right-hand post. It was one to be relished in the replay on television! Peter Dods' conversion was a mere formality and now the Scottish morale was high, with the capacity crowd beginning to sense a Scottish victory. At 12–3 England had to score twice. This they failed to do although Hare, having found his line, contributed a solitary penalty goal in the second half. At 12–6 the Scots appeared to have the Calcutta Cup within their sights and with the clock at forty-eight minutes Dods added 3 points from another penalty. England attacks were unproductive, while their line suffered at least one near-miss from an astute Roy Laidlaw chip-kick. But unluckily Euan Kennedy, the big-hearted centre, limped off after a collision with Dusty Hare. Keith Robertson moved to centre and Jim Pollock, who had been in an unbeaten team for his three appearances for Scotland, came on for his fourth cap.

In the dying moments Dods added to his major points contribution with a penalty and, suddenly, Jim Aitken and his men were swamped by a great flood of jubilant supporters. The 100th match and the cherished cup now mirrored a triumph in Scottish rugby history, the margin being 18 points to 6. The 40 points had now become 58, with five tries scored in the last three games.

There followed two very successful and purposeful Sundays for Scottish rugby. On the first, their Calcutta Cup revelries behind them, the Scottish squad worked with a will under coaches Jim and Colin Telfer for the 'next game'. On the second Sunday, 18 February 1984, a brave and resourceful Scotland B took on a powerful and intimidating France B side at Albi and won a bruising match by 13 points to 10. They could not have given a better incentive to their senior men in what was, to all intents and purposes, a bid for the mythical yet meaningful Triple Crown.

Hordes of Scottish supporters made the trip across the Irish Sea to Dublin's fair city and they travelled with high hopes. The atmosphere in Dublin is special at an international week-end; perhaps it would be a better place than most in which to celebrate a Triple Crown!

In the Scottish camp there was the reality of facing an Irish team at Lansdowne Road with their backs to the wall in a less-than-successful season, and of complacency there was none; a grim determination and near-emotional commitment were nearer the facts.

What happened is now woven into the complex tapestry of Scottish rugby as a purple patch as real and as colourful as one could wish, yet with the half-time score of 22 points to nil—and for Scotland at that!—there was surely near-incredulity that it could be happening so convincingly and so smoothly.

Roy Laidlaw, that india-rubber competitor, had started a near-avalanche of scoring after Alister Campbell, who had replaced the injured Bill Cuthbertson at lock to win his first cap, had made a significant drive from a line-out near the Irish line. Laidlaw went blind, suddenly checked inside and beat four defenders in an unstoppable dash after only four minutes of play. Peter Dods was right on target with the conversion. Ireland could not break out and were inclined to give away penalties rather in the manner of Scotland against England. Unlike Dusty Hare, Dods did not miss. Before a quarter of an hour had elapsed he had two kicks which took the Scottish total to 12 points.

The front row of Jim Aitken, Colin Deans and Iain Milne was again providing a sure base in scrummaging, splendidly supported by Alan Tomes and Alister Campbell, thus the number eight and flankers were able to play havoc in the Irish ranks. The assault continued and the next score was controversial when the Scots won and drove their scrum for a push-over try. As the splintering scrum pivoted left Willie Duggan, the Irish Captain, who had broken behind the hindmost foot—and his own goal line—chose to dive into the Scottish scrum in the field of play as the Scottish pack held the ball, pushed and poised for the score. Referee Fred Howard (England) signalled a penalty try which attracted much comment from the Irish supporters in the packed stands and terraces of Lansdowne Road, and Dods converted amid the din. Suddenly, and unbelievably, the score was 18 points to nil! There was a gem still to come. The blue jerseys continued to swarm around the Irish 22-metre line. Another scrum on the right provided an inviting blind side and a beautifully struck controlled ball from Colin Deans enabled Laidlaw to take off. This time there was no check inside, and the scrum-half bored through desperate and despairing tackles in a diagonal drive for a try right out of the top drawer. Could it be true? Scotland facing Ireland in a Triple Crown decider and 22 points up at the interval!

Attempted Irish retribution had to come. They were not going to give in so easily. The Scots, however, had lost Roy Laidlaw with a head knock which, happily, in the longer term was not serious. He was replaced by fellow-Borderer Gordon Hunter, who had a ferocious baptism of fire from the Irish pack. When their try did come it was finely executed and worth the 6 points after Michael Kiernan had crossed the Scotland line. It added to an earlier penalty goal which illustrated the Irish pressure, but the 9 points were all they could muster.

Eventually, and finally, Scotland set the seal on the match and, praise be, the Triple Crown. Hunter had ventured more into the game as he gained in confidence and he indulged in some effective spoiling, although his telling contribution had still to happen. First, David Johnston had shown his quite astonishing acceleration and pace only to find Roger Baird closely marked, and a chance evaporated. Then, in subsequent play moments later, Hunter set off on a wide, flat run after line-out possession from Alister Campbell, found his club-mate John Rutherford at his elbow for a short pass, and decisively Keith Robertson shot through the remnants of the green jerseys for a splendid try to the right of the posts—close enough for Peter Dods to improve on it. And then the words 'Scotland, Scotland' wafted round the ground, chanted by the thousands over with their team. They knew that the match was theirs to rejoice over.

It was the same Dods who added the trimmings in a move which epitomised all the hard work done at Murrayfield during the preceding months. The forwards had yet again provided good ball and Rutherford produced a searing break which split the defence. The play swept left with superb and beautiful running and passing by Robertson and Baird, and ultimately and fittingly it was the full-back who fixed perfectly on to Roger Baird's well-flighted and unselfish pass. If the try was too far out to convert no matter, for the final margin was 32 points to 9—a clear-cut victory!

Thus Scotland took the Triple Crown with, at the end of each game, a more than satisfactory margin of victory, summed up overall with 65 points for and 24 against. There were two tries against Wales, two against England and five against Ireland—and nine tries in a successful bid for the Triple Crown cannot be bad! The fact that a mere two tries were inflicted on this Scottish side can only be a tribute to a gritty and devoted defence. So there was much to celebrate after 4.30 p.m. on Saturday, 3 March 1984!

The release of tension; the boundless joy written over the face of each Scottish player; hands round shoulders in acclaim and rugby fellowship; the upraised arms of jubilation—the ultimate expression of many a secret hope—for any man who pulls on a thistled navy blue jersey will think privately of a clean sweep in an International Championship. Here was a dream come true! An object not much mentioned had been fulfilled.

That momentous Saturday night the Shelbourne Hotel, traditionally the post-match entertainment centre, was the scene of thanksgiving and joyous celebration. Packed crowds in the foyer gave an ecstatic welcome under the television lights to smiling Scottish players. The Irish, always so generous in attitude, gave the Scots unstinting praise and the teams' dinner was one of rejoicing yet all kept in perspective. Later that night the Scottish squad made a successful take-over bid for the BBC Television Sportscene programme and, most importantly, were able to share their well-mannered revelry with the countless thousands watching at home. What had been achieved had touched the hearts of the nation and there was intense pride as well as warm gratitude as Jim Aitken's 'choir' sang 'Scotland the Brave' and 'Flower of Scotland' under the bright lights in the Shelbourne and before an unseen but rapturous audience over the Irish Sea.

Through the heady elation of the Triple Crown conquest there came the glimmer of the possibility of another triumph, although the French had scored the same total of 32 points in defeating England on the same day and, clearly, they would be dangerous opposition even at Murrayfield on Saturday, 17 March 1984. It was, however, observed that they had not won in Edinburgh since 1978.

A confident, though in no way complacent, Scottish squad went through the preliminaries on the Sunday prior to the Grand Slam challenge, Jim and Colin Telfer dwelling on the realities of facing the French. The following Thursday night, the squad settled into the comfortable and familiar Braid Hills Hotel and began the work on their build-up which came to its climax as the team took to the field ready for battle.

With Roy Laidlaw again fit, the fifteen was identical to that which faced Ireland originally and Jim Aitken's team ran out to an ovation the like of which had never before been witnessed at the Scottish Rugby Union's headquarters. The Murrayfield stands and terraces resounded to the acclaim of the packed thousands welcoming their Triple Crown heroes.

The French, undaunted by the display of fervour, showed typical dynamism and flair from the kick-off, which was a probing jab for the open side wing. Such unorthodoxy set them up and, for an agonising twenty minutes, the Scottish line was threatened by all manner of thrusts in typical French fashion. That they did not cross was as much due to dour defence as it was to that indefinable 'rub of the green' in minor but, in the final analysis, significant French errors of judgement.

Admittedly Scotland had raised the first points with a Peter Dods penalty goal in the third minute, but then came a siege on the slender lead, and hair-raising incidents with the ball alive and bouncing in the Scottish in-goal area. Jerome Gallion, the adventurous French scrum-half, eventually did the damage and surged over on the blind side at the north end by the new East Stand. Jean Patrick Lescarboura, a powerful stand-off, converted.

The game was becoming a turmoil of intensity, the Scots stoicism and tough determination contrasting the French effervescence and gradually developing frustration at their own failure to score further. But, seen from the West Stand, the game was disconcerting in that it was all happening to the left, before the north terracing—at the Scots end. Only isolated forays by Scottish individuals eased the pressure and half-time was a welcome relief. For the French there was the disappointment of being ahead by only 6 points to 3—remarkably, the same interval score as in the Scotland v Wales and England fixtures, except that the Scots were on the credit side then.

Portents for the next forty minutes were not good on the evidence, and no doubt there was the thought running through the mind of many a Scot that at least we did have the Triple Crown. Perhaps, after all, the clean sweep would have been merely a bonus.

The giving away of penalties in a manner even more prolific than that of the Scots against the English had punctuated the French play even in the first half and thereafter they frequently conceded 10 metres for dissent with the referee. This did no harm to Scotland's cause and to many in the crowd there seemed a distinct possibility that the French were going to be victims of their own temperament as well as through Scottish pressure. Neither side threatened a try–the French, surprisingly, resorting to kicking and the Scots unable to wrest any initiative. Lescarboura increased the lead to 6 points with a seemingly inevitable penalty, making the score 9–3, which, at the time, looked enough to last. Then Dods equalised through two penalty goals the second of which was made considerably easier by the French arguing with the referee and conceding 10 metres. Scots hopes were then raised.

Meanwhile, there had been a misfortune to Jerome Gallion when the normally sturdy scrum-half collided with David Leslie and came off second best. Although stretchered off he reappeared later at night. He had been replaced by Pierre Berbizier.

A soaring, towering drop-goal from the boot of the persistent Lescarboura, a memorable affair like that of Peter Kininmonth against Wales in 1951, put the Tricolours in the lead. But it was one of few final forays by France and their dejection began to show, just as the discipline, courage and character of all the Scots prevailed towards the end. The same area of the field was the scene of prolonged French discomfiture in the second half as it had been for the Scots in the first. Certainly the French were ahead by 12 points to 9, but the pressure was on. Peter Dods with one eye virtually closed by a collision early in the game placed his fourth penalty to bring about the draw again and then came the famous turning-point with minutes to go. It was the

94

1947. France v Scotland. A. W. Black (Edin. Univ.), C. H. Gadney (England) Referee, G. L. Cawkwell (Oxford
iv.), J. H. Orr (Edin. City Police), A. G. M. Watt (Edin. Acads.), J. M. Hunter (Camb. Univ.), I. C. Henderson*
in. Acads.), C. R. Bruce (Glas. Acads.), K. I. Geddes (LS) *Captain*, I. J. M. Lumsden (Bath & Watsonians),
I. D. Elliot (Edin. Acads.), T. P. L. McGlashan (RHSFP), T. G. H. Jackson (Army), C. W. Drummond (Melrose),
D. Maclennan (Watsonians), D. W. Deas (Heriot's FP), D. S. Kerr (SRU) Touch Judge.
This was the first post-war International for which caps were awarded. The player marked * was a pre-war cap.)

1951. Scotland v Wales. *Back row*: D. M. Scott (Langholm), D. M. Rose (Jed-Forest), N. G. R. Mair (Edin. Univ.),
VI. Inglis (Edin. Acads.), D. A. Sloan (Edin. Acads.), R. C. Taylor (Kelvinside-West), M. J. Dowling (Ireland)
eree. *Seated*: R. L. Wilson (Gala), R. Gemmill (Glas. HSFP), A. Cameron (Glas. HSFP), P. W. Kininmonth
hmond) *Captain*, W. I. D. Elliot (Edin. Acads.), J. C. Dawson (Glas. Acads.), I. A. Ross (Hillhead HSFP). *In front*:
ordon (Edin. Wrs.), I. H. M. Thomson (Heriot's FP).
A memorable win which preceded the terrible run of losses. P. W. Kininmonth's drop goal from the touch line
an historic kick.)

56. 1955. Scotland *v* Wales. *Back row*: C. W. Drummond (sru) Touch Judge, A. R. Smith (Camb. Univ.),
T. Elliot (Gala), W. S. Glen (Edin. Wrs.), J. W. Y. Kemp (Glas. hsfp), R. G. Charters (Hawick), J. T. Docherty (G[
hsfp) M. J. Dowling (Ireland) Referee. *Second row*: M. K. Elgie (ls), E. J. S. Michie (Aber. Univ.),
J. T. Greenwood (Dunfermline), A. Cameron (Glas. hsfp) *Captain*, H. F. McLeod (Hawick), A. Robson (Hawic[
J. A. Nichol (rhsfp). *In front*: J. S. Swan (ls), W. K. L. Relph (Stewart's Coll. fp).
(The win which ended the terrible run of losses. A. R. Smith's solo try up the Stand touch line was memorable

57. 1891. England *v* Scotland. A Triple Crown year. *Back*: G. T. Neilson (wos), J. D. Boswell (wos & Fet.-Lor[
J. E. Orr (wos), H. T. O. Leggatt (Watsonians), W. R. Gibson (rhsfp), R. G. MacMillan (ls). *Middle*: F. W. Good[
(ls), H. J. Stevenson (Edin. Acads.), M. C. McEwan (Edin. Acads.) *Captain*, C. E. Orr (wos & Fet.-Lor.), I. McInty[
(Wrs. & Fet.-Lor.). *Front*: G. McGregor (Camb. Univ. & Wrs.), D. G. Anderson (ls), P. R. Clauss (Oxford Univ. 8[
Fet.-Lor.), W. Neilson (Merchiston).

1895. Scotland v Wales. A Triple Crown Year. *Back row*: G. T. Neilson (WOS), J. J. Gowans (LS), J. H. Dods (Edin. ads.), W. B. Cownie (Watsonians), A. R. Smith (Oxford Univ.), R. Welsh (Watsonians), W. M. C. McEwan (Edin. ads.). *Middle*: H. O. Smith (Watsonians), R. G. Macmillan (LS), W. R. Gibson (RHSFP) *Captain*, J. W. Simpson (SFP), T. Scott (Hawick). *Front row*: G. T. Campbell (LS), W. Neilson (LS), M. Elliot (Hawick).

1901. Scotland v England. A Triple Crown Year. *Back row*: W. H. Welsh (Edin. Univ.), A. B. Flett (Edin. Univ.), W. Duncan (Edin. Univ.), R. S. Stronach (Glas. Acads.), A. Phipps-Turnbull (Edin. Acads.), J. A. Bell ydesdale), A. Frew (Edin. Univ.), J. M. Dykes (Glas. HSFP). *Seated*: J. I. Gillespie (Edin. Acads.), R. Bedell-Sivright (Fet.-Lor.), M. C. Morrison (RHSFP) *Captain*, A. N. Fell (Edin. Univ.), A. B. Timms (Edin. iv.). *At front*: J. Ross (LS), R. M. Neill (Edin. Acads.). The XV included six from Edinburgh University.)

60. 1903. Scotland *v* Ireland. A Triple Crown year. *Back*: C. W. France (Kelvinside Acads.), W. E. Kyle (Hawic L. West (Edin. Univ.), J. R. C. Greenlees (Kelvinside Acads.), A. G. Cairns (Watsonians), N. Kennedy (wos). *Mide* J. Knox (Kelvinside Acads.), E. D. Simson (Edin. Univ.), D. R. Bedell-Sivright (Camb. Univ.), M. C. Morrison (rhsfp) *Captain*, H. J. Orr (ls), W. T. Forrest (Hawick), W. P. Scott (wos). *Front*: J. E. Crabbie (Edin. Acads.), A. S. Drybrough (Edin. Wrs.).

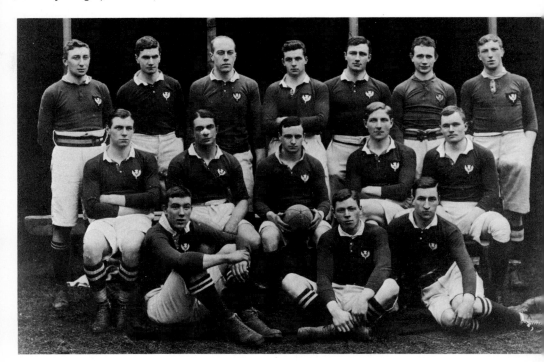

61. 1907. England *v* Scotland. A Triple Crown year. *Back row*: G. A. Sanderson (rhsfp), D. G. Schulze (ls), I. C. Geddes (ls), J. M. B. Scott (Edin. Acads.), G. M. Frew (Glas. hsfp), J. C. MacCallum (Watsonians), L. M. Spe (Watsonians). *Seated*: K. G. Macleod (Fet.-Lor.), D. R. Bodell-Sivright (Edin. Univ.), P. Munro (ls) *Captain*, W. P. Scott (wos), E. D. Simson (ls). *Front*: A. B. H. L. Purves (ls), D. G. McGregor (Watsonians), T. Sloan (Gl Acads.).

1925. Scotland v England. A Triple Crown and a Grand Slam Year. *Back row*: D. J. MacMyn (Camb. Univ.),
W. Scott (Stewart's Coll. FP), A. C. Gillies (Watsonians & Carlisle), J. C. H. Ireland (Glas. HSFP), R. Howie
(Kirkcaldy), I. S. Smith (Oxford Univ.). *Front row*: G. G. Aitken (Oxford Univ.), D. S. Davies (Hawick),
J. M. Bannerman (Glas. HSFP), G. P. S. Macpherson (Oxford Univ.) *Captain*, D. Drysdale (Heriot's FP), A. C. Wallace
(Oxford Univ.), H. Waddell (Glas. Acads.). *Front*: J. B. Nelson (Glas. Acads.), J. R. Paterson (Birkenhead Park).
This was the opening match at Murrayfield. The three quarters were the famous four from Oxford University.)

1933. Ireland v Scotland. A Triple Crown Year. *Back row*: K. L. T. Jackson (Oxford Univ.), J. R. Thom
(Watsonians), J. M. Ritchie (Watsonians), J. M. Henderson (Edin. Acads.), H. D. B. Lorraine (Oxford Univ.),
J. Brown (Camb. Univ.), B. S. Cumberlege (England) Referee. *Seated*: W. R. Logan (Edin. Wrs.), R. Rowland
(Glas. HSFP), W. B. Welsh (Hawick), I. S. Smith (LS) *Captain*, J. Beattie (Hawick), M. S. Stewart (Stewart's Coll. FP),
A. Waters (Selkirk). *Front*: P. M. S. Gedge (Edin. Wrs.), H. Lind (Dunfermline).
This match had been postponed from February. Except for P. M. S. Gedge who came in at the last minute for
C. Fyfe, the team played unchanged throughout the season.)

64. 1938. England v Scotland. A Triple Crown Year. *Back row*: W. N. Renwick (L S), J. D. Hastie (Melrose), W. F. Blackadder (W O S), W. H. Crawford (Utd. Services), J. S. Forrest (Camb. Univ.), A. Roy (Waterloo), W. B. Young (Camb. Univ.), I. David (Wales) Referee. *Seated*: D. J. Macrae (St Andrews Univ.), R. C. S. Dick (Guy Hospital), R. W. Shaw (Glas. H S F P) *Captain*, P. L. Duff (Glas. Acads.), G. B. Horsburgh (L S), W. M. Inglis (Camb Univ.). *At front*: G. Roberts (Watsonians), T. F. Dorward (Gala).

(A match made memorable by the play of R. W. Shaw.)

65. 1984. Scotland's players and replacements in a Triple Crown and Grand Slam Year. *Back row*: R. Cunningh (Bath) replacement, N. A. Rowan (Boroughmuir) Replacement, A. R. Irvine (Heriot's F P) Replacement, A. J. Campbell (Hawick), A. J. Tomes (Hawick), W. Cuthbertson (Harlequins), G. J. Callander (Kelso) Replaceme D. S. Wyllie (Stew.-Mel. F P) Replacement, S. G. Johnston (Watsonians) Replacement. *Middle*: P. W. Dods (Ga I. G. Hunter (Selkirk), K. W. Robertson (Melrose), S. Munro (Ayr), J. A. Pollock (Gosforth), I. A. M. Paxton (Selki A. E. Kennedy (Watsonians), J. R. Beattie (Glas. Acads.), D. G. Leslie (Gala), I. G. Milne (Heriot's F P), D. I. Johnsto (Watsonians), G. R. T. Baird (Kelso). *Front*: J. W. Telfer (Hon. Coach), J. Y. Rutherford (Selkirk), R. J. Laidlaw (Jed-Forest), I. A. A. MacGregor (Selection Convener), J. Aitken (Gala) *Captain*, A. Robson (President), C. T. Dea (Hawick), J. H. Calder (Stew.-Mel. F P), C. M. Telfer (Hon. Assistant Coach).

6. 1984. City Chambers, Edinburgh. The Lord Provost receives the Grand Slam group. *L. to r.*: C. M. Telfer (SRU),
. R. Irvine, C. T. Deans, J. Y. Rutherford, R. J. Laidlaw, J. W. Telfer (SRU), J. H. Calder, A. Robson (President),
. Morgan (The Lord Provost), I. A. M. Paxton, W. Cuthbertson, J. Aitken (Captain), G. M. McGuinness,
. W. Robertson, S. Munro, P. W. Dods, I. G. Hunter.

7. 1984. Holyrood Palace Garden Party. A group of Border rugby men attend the annual Garden Party. *L. to r.*:
. Gray (South Coach), J. Aitken (Gala), P. W. Dods (Gala), R. J. Laidlaw (Jed-Forest), J. Y. Rutherford (Selkirk),
. W. Robertson (Melrose), C. T. Deans (Hawick), J. W. Telfer (Scotland Coach).

68. 1984. Wales *v* Scotland. Iain Paxton, in full flight, about to score the first try.

69. 1984. Wales *v* Scotland. Iain Paxton watches admiringly as his captain, Jim Aitken, goes over the Welsh line score the match-winning try.

70. 1984. Scotland v England. Euan Kennedy scores the second Scottish try—and the Scots are on their way toward winning the Triple Crown. Roger Baird (11) shows his delight.

71. 1984. Ireland v Scotland. Keith Robertson goes over to score a try despite a tackle from Ireland's Trevor Ringland. Winning this match gave Scotland the Triple Crown.

72. 1984. Scotland *v* France. A determined Roy Laidlaw goes for a loose ball whilst his captain, Jim Aitken, and Jim Calder look on anxiously.

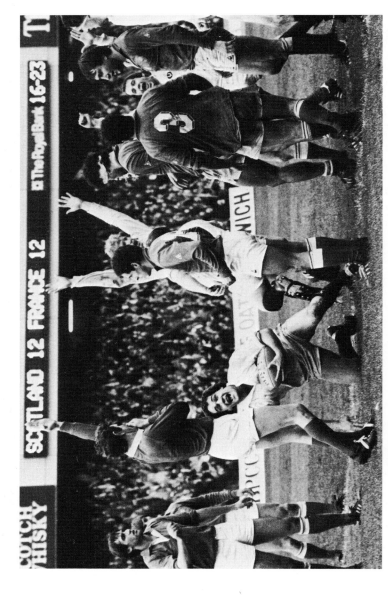

73. 1984. Scotland *v* France. The famous turning point. Jim Calder's joy is unmistakable at having scored the try which gave Scotland the lead. This win earned the Scots the 'Grand Slam'.

74. 1983. Scotland v Wales. Bill Cuthbertson shows characteristic determination as he commits an opponent to the tackle. Peter Dods lends a hand. Iain Milne and Jim Aitken about to give support.

75. 1983. Scotland v Barbarians. Roy Laidlaw drives through watched approvingly by Colin Deans and Jim Aitken.

76. 1983. Scotland v Barbarians. E. G. Tobias and W. G. Davies close in on David Johnston.

77. 1982. Wales v Scotland. Jim Renwick accelerates away for a memorable score and a famous win.

78. 1981. Scotland *v* Romania. Roy Laidlaw swings the ball away despite the close attention of an opponent.

79. 1980. Ireland *v* Scotland. John Rutherford breaks into a typical swerving run closely supported by John Beattie.

80. 1980. Scotland *v* France. Roy Laidlaw clears the ball safely following a line-out.

81. 1974. Scotland *v* France. A typical Andy Irvine thrust out of defence.

incident chosen for a commemorative painting, commissioned at a later date by the Royal Bank of Scotland, who had sponsored Scotland's home Internationals, to recognise the historic achievement of the Grand Slam. Jim Calder, who dived through a line-out for a telling try, is seen in the delirious moment, and around him in the painting, the exuberant faces of those involved in the Triple Crown and Grand Slam.

The try had stemmed from a penetrating diagonal kick by John Rutherford which forced the line-out a mere metre from the French line below the north end of the West Stand, and Colin Deans' long throw appeared to deflect off a French arm, leaving Calder's reflex action to do the rest. All Murrayfield erupted as Peter Dods improved the try—18 points to 12 and time running out! Finally, Serge Blanco the French full-back, who had had a discomfiting afternoon, followed up his own kick and late-tackled Peter Dods after his act of counter-kicking. Dods retaliated in the best possible way with an additional penalty goal, making the final score 21–12 in Scotland's favour. Then, in a last admirable gesture, Jim Aitken elected to run a kickable penalty and so ended the match with an appropriate flourish. Possibly he would think back to his proud moment of the Calcutta Cup win at Twickenham in 1983 when he commented at the teams' dinner after the game, 'They say that winning isn't everything, but it beats the hell out of being second!' All Scotland would have echoed him that night of the Grand Slam.

As it was, the first spontaneous celebration became the invasion of the pitch as thousands of flag-waving young people from the enclosure swept irresistibly forward towards their heroes and, momentarily, many of the team were lost in the milling throng. The crowd lingered as if reluctant to give up the magic of the moment. In the dressing-room the Lord Provost of Edinburgh, Tom Morgan, appeared with a gigantic bottle of champagne—a marvellous piece of anticipation! Could there ever have been more delirium in a rugby dressing-room?

The lofty pinnacle of Triple Crown and Grand Slam achievement had at long last been scaled again and was now the recognition of what a fine group of young men had done for their country and its rugby. Tribute was paid at the teams' dinner that night. The wives, fiancées and girlfriends, who had given their support to their men, joined in the dance revelries to follow.

Recognition and acknowledgement came from the Secretary of State for Scotland, Edinburgh District Council, the Borders Regional Council and the BBC, all of whom gave generous receptions to team and committee, while congratulatory messages in remarkable variety poured in from world-wide rugby sources. The Scottish Rugby Union held a dinner dance in the North British Hotel on Saturday, 28 April 1984, for all players, committee-men, officials and staff of Headquarters, and their partners. It was the rugby family expression of fulfillment, joy and gratitude; a far cry from a cold, wet Sunday at Murrayfield!

Adam Robson
President, sru, 1983–84

Appendix 1

SRU ANNUAL DIARY

« 1873–74 »

President: Dr J. Chiene (Edinburgh Academicals)
Vice-President: H. Gibson (Merchistonians)

The thirteen-man Committee met only once—to select a team to represent Scotland and also to nominate members to serve on a sub-committee to discuss with the RFU details of qualification for inclusion in the team.

FIRST BALANCE SHEET 1873–74

Entry money and subscriptions: 8 Clubs	£10. 8. 0
Inter-City Gate money: Edinburgh	33. 0. 6
Inter-City Gate money: Glasgow	25. 0. 0
Donations towards London expenses	42. 1. 0
	£110. 9. 6
London expenses (England v Scotland)	£89. 0. 6
Ground fee to Edin. Acads. for first Inter-City	5. 0. 0
Postages, Adverts., Printing etc.	5.15. 6
Surplus for year—Balance due by Treasurer	10.13. 6
	£110. 9. 6

The Entry money was £1.1.0 and the subscription was 5s.

« 1874–75 »

President: A. Harvey (Glasgow Academicals)
Vice-President: H. Cheyne (Edinburgh Academicals)

The following clubs were admitted to membership of the SFU: Edinburgh Institution FP, Paisley and Glasgow St Vincent. However, Craigmount School was refused membership because no club, as distinct from the school, existed.

A motion to reduce the membership of the Committee from thirteen to nine was withdrawn. It was judged to be important that all member clubs be represented on that body.

President: B. Hall Blyth (Merchistonians)
Vice-President: R. McClure (West of Scotland)

Stirlingshire were admitted to membership of the SFU. It was intimated that the Warriston club had been disbanded.

The validity of picking up a rolling ball (Rule 12) was again discussed. However, a remit of the question to the member clubs left it unchanged.

The RFU changed Rule 7 to give a try a scoring value. By the month of December, this had been accepted and antedated to the beginning of the Scottish season.

A request to the RFU to play fifteen-a-side in the International match came too late in the season to be homologated.

One of the two Inter-City matches was now termed East v West to allow for a wider choice of players.

It was decided that in the International match in London, the Scottish XX should play six instead of seven behind the scrum ('. . . as upon all former occasions.'). 'The usual allowance of £5 . . .' was made to each player.

« 1876–77 »

President: W. H. Kidston (West of Scotland)
Vice-President: A. Buchanan (Royal High School FP)

The following clubs were admitted to membership: Dundee Abertay (Broughty Ferry), Dundee Red Cross, Aberdeen Rangers, Dumfries Rangers, Carlton, Clackmannan County, and Edinburgh Collegiate FP. This brought the membership total to 21.

The Constitution was altered to allow a Committee comprising three office-bearers plus four others—two each from the Eastern and Western districts.

Once again a request was made to the RFU to play XVs and, on this occasion, the suggestion was accepted. As a result, the England v Ireland match, at the Oval in February 1877, was the first to be played with XVs. Two weeks later Scotland played Ireland in a XV-a-side match in Belfast. This game was otherwise notable for the fact that Scotland was first to play a single full back.

« 1877–78 »

President: Dr J. Chiene (Edinburgh Academicals)
Vice-President: G. R. Fleming (Glasgow Academicals)

Two clubs were admitted to membership: Southern (Glasgow) and Watsonians. Two clubs were intimated as having been disbanded: Edinburgh Collegiate FP and Dundee.

A Saturday fixture was offered to the Northern Football Union of Ireland. This was declined because of dissension between the Belfast and Dublin Unions.

« 1878–79 »

President: G. R. Fleming (Glasgow Academicals)
Vice-President: Hon. J. W. Moncreiff (Edinburgh Academicals)

The Perth Wanderers and North British (Edinburgh) clubs were admitted to membership.

The annual membership subscription was increased to one guinea.

There was now a single Irish Football Union which accepted a fixture in Belfast.

The first match for the Calcutta Cup was played at Raeburn Place.

« 1879–80 »

President: A. Buchanan (Royal High School FP)
Vice-President: H. W. Little (West of Scotland)

Greenock Wanderers, Thurso, St George (Edinburgh), Cronstadt (Leith) and London Scottish were all admitted to membership. It was announced that the following clubs had disbanded: Clackmannan County, Carlton and St Vincent.

Permission was granted for Dundee Red Cross to change its name to Dundee Institution FP.

Proceedings were instigated against two clubs for non-payment of the annual subscription: Abertay (who were thought to have disbanded) and St Andrews University.

« 1880–81 »

President: D. H. Watson (Glasgow Academicals)
Vice-President: J. Reid (Edinburgh Wanderers)

Galashiels, Melrose and Earlston were all admitted to membership, whilst Edinburgh Collegiate FP were re-admitted. The Stirlingshire club had disbanded.

The Constitution of the Committee was altered to allow for three office-bearers plus six others—three each from the Eastern and Western districts.

A request was made to the RFU to play the International on a Saturday instead of a Monday.

A North v South fixture was begun.

Controversy erupted before the Irish game over the captaining of the Scottish XV.

« 1881–82 »

President: A. G. Petrie (Royal High School FP)
Vice-President: W. Cross (Glasgow Academicals)

Clubs admitted to membership were Greenock Regent and Fettesian-Lorettonians.

A request from the Welsh Union for a fixture was declined for 1881–82 but was projected for the following season.

It was reported that the President of the RFU had, at their AGM, made some particularly scathing comments about the standard of Scottish umpiring at the last Scotland v England game. Not surprisingly, the Scottish Committee was deeply offended and some extremely acrimonious correspondence between the two Unions ensued before the matter was settled. One important outcome was that, for the first time, a neutral referee (from Ireland) was appointed to officiate at the next Calcutta Cup match.

« 1882–83 »

President: W. Cross (Glasgow Academicals)
Vice-President: J. H. S. Graham (Edinburgh Academicals)

The following clubs were admitted to membership: Roxburgh County and 1st Lanarkshire Rifle Volunteers.

It was agreed that an official ruling on the practice of 'heeling out' was not practicable, but the general opinion was that this mode of play was contrary to the principles of sound football.

« 1883–84 »

President: J. H. S. Graham (Edinburgh Academicals)
Vice-President: M. Cross (Glasgow Academicals)

The clubs admitted to membership were: Craigielea, Larchfield Academicals, Wayfarers and Aberdeen University.

The game against Ireland was transferred from Glasgow to Edinburgh. It was anticipated that the expected larger attendance would boost the rather slender funds of the Union.

A disputed English try (following a knock-back by a Scot) in the match at Blackheath triggered off a disagreement which was to have far-reaching consequences in the game of rugby.

« 1884–85 »

President: M. Cross (Glasgow Academicals)
Vice-President: N. T. Brewis (Edinburgh Institution FP)

Dundee High School FP, Dundee Panmure and Brechin were admitted to membership.

At the AGM. discussion of the dispute with the RFU following the previous season's incident in the game at Blackheath, the following motion was agreed to: 'That the recent Match in March . . . may either be held null, or a draw, or be satisfactorily settled by reference; that the independence of the Scottish Union be fully recognised, and arrangements made for the settlement of future disputes by reference; and that when these points are settled the Secretary shall either issue or accept a challenge for the ensuing season.'

The meeting also agreed to print the Rules of the Game as played by the SFU.

« 1885–86 »

President: N. T. Brewis (Edinburgh Institution FP)
Vice-President: J. S. Carrick (Glasgow Academicals)

Blairlodgians, Clarendon, Nondescripts, Kirkcaldy and Hawick & Wilton were all admitted to membership. Roxburgh County and Larchfield Academicals were disbanded.

Southern was allowed to alter its name to Clydesdale.

« 1886—87 »

President: J.S.Carrick (Glasgow Academicals)
Vice-President: W.S.Brown (Edinburgh Institution FP)

A motion, proposed by J.A.Smith (Royal High School FP) that, in future, a summary of the annual financial report should be issued with the circular calling the AGM was carried.

The SFU refused to accept a scoring system, introduced by the RFU, which included a scoring value for a penalty goal. The matter was referred to the IB (which body had already decided that International matches be played under the RFU rules of 1885).

At this point in time, SFU Minutes are minimal and all but vanish. This was almost certainly because of the increasing ill-health of the Honorary Secretary and Treasurer, J.A.Gardner, whose early and tragic death occurred in September 1887, a mere three weeks before the AGM.

« 1887—88 »

President: W.S.Brown (Edinburgh Institution FP)
Vice-President: Dr R.B.Young (Glasgow University)

Admitted to membership were: Hawick, Langholm, Portobello, Stewartonians and Veterinary College. During the season, Cupar and Kelvinside Academicals were admitted.

No SFU Minutes exist for the period between the AGMs of 1886 and 1887, but the daily and sporting newspapers reported at length at that time.

At the AGM a motion was put forward, unsuccessfully, that a team selection committee be appointed, consisting of the President, Vice-President and two past players—one each from East and West. A further motion that the Honorary Secretary and Treasurer should have no voting power was also defeated.

A first investment of funds was made: £150 at 4½ per cent in the National Bank of India.

Following the England *v* Scotland game at Blackheath, the dispute between the IB and the RFU remained unresolved. As a result, no International matches were played between England and member-countries of the IB. The situation was well set out in a manifesto issued by the IB in September 1888.

« 1888—89 »

President: Dr R.B.Young (Glasgow University)
Vice-President: A.R.Don Wauchope (Fettesian-Lorettonians)

The following clubs were admitted to membership: Kelso, Peebles County and St Cuthbert (Hawick). However, later in the season, Kelso declined to take up membership.

A motion to have the choice of the six members of Committee not confined to the Eastern and Western districts was rejected.

The New Zealand Native touring team requested a fixture but, this was not taken up.

The Committee interviewed three Hawick players who had taken part in a rugby tour of Australia organised by two cricket professionals, Shaw and Shrewsbury. The players' statements on allegations of professionalism were accepted as being satisfactory—unless direct evidence to the contrary came forward.

101

Representative teams were sent to Aberdeen and St Andrews to encourage the development of the game in these areas.

Rough play had been causing problems and a report by the Honorary Secretary was published. Referees were empowered to send players off.

Mr W.S.Lang (Edinburgh University) generously offered a Silver Cup for competition. The offer was respectfully declined because it was thought that '. . . such competitions were injurious to the welfare and purity of the game'.

There was evidence of some disagreement over the terms of the renting of Raeburn Place.

The final proof of the IB Laws was accepted. It was agreed that they came into force for all games on 1 November 1889.

Again, this season, no International games were played against England.

« 1889–90 »

President: A.R.Don Wauchope (Fettesian-Lorettonians)
Vice-President: J.G.Mitchell (West of Scotland)

Australasian (Edinburgh), Jed-Forest and Walkerburn were all admitted to membership, whilst the name of Midland County appears in the accounts. The Portobello club changed its name to Grange.

Two further members were added to the Committee: one each from the South and North districts. It was decided that all eight representative members should be past players.

The new IB Laws were accepted and it was agreed that referees should indicate a 'fair catch' by blowing their whistle.

The Union gave the Hawick club permission to insure their members and an apposite Rule was incorporated into the SFU Regulations.

The game of rugby started to flourish and a Constitution for the North of Scotland Union was approved. The SFU agreed to pay excursion fares to clubs travelling to play in the north, whilst North Committee members were allowed travelling expenses for SFU meetings.

A request to formulate a set of bye-laws for the Schools' Inter-City matches was declined, but the Committee asked the schools to submit their own set for consideration and possible approval.

There was an ongoing dialogue with member clubs in settling points of Law and other disputes. A complaint from an English referee led to the suspension of the Langholm club until November 1890.

Initial steps to procure a permanent ground for the Union were taken. An approach was made to Fettes College for the lease of ground between the College and Comely Bank, but this was refused.

No further progress had been made in the dispute with the RFU, and in December 1889, the Scottish Committee decided to ask the IB to put the matter to arbitration. The IB acceded to the request, and the resulting award by the two appointed arbitrators, in April 1890, was accepted by the four Unions. Following this, the RFU joined the IB, which was then given authority to rule on questions and rulings pertaining to International matters. These points settled, the matches with England were resumed.

President: J.G.Mitchell (West of Scotland)
Vice-President: T.Ainslie (Edinburgh Institution FP)

The Northern Counties Football Union were admitted to membership.

The new IB rules, recently accepted, were issued for use by member clubs.

Jed-Forest appealed, unsuccessfully, against a penalty try awarded to Hawick by a referee. The Jed-forest club were reprimanded for leaving the field of play before the referee had whistled for 'no side'.

The Union took responsibility for the Edinburgh v South and the Glasgow v North games, including expenses and gate receipts. Subsequently, the same undertaking was given for the East v West game, which came to be regarded as an International Trial match.

Further discussions were held with Edinburgh Academical Cricket Club over the use of Raeburn Place as a field for International rugby matches. However, by the end of the season, it had been decided definitely to acquire suitable land and own a ground which could be used for all Union matches.

An appeal against the validity of a 'field-goal' was dismissed: its scoring value was set at 3 points.

« 1891–92 »

President: T.Ainslie (Edinburgh Institution FP)
Vice-President: D.S.Morton (West of Scotland)

The following clubs were admitted to membership: Aberdeen Nomads, Dundee High School FP, George Heriot's School FP and also the South of Scotland Football Union. St Cuthberts (Hawick) were disbanded.

The Committee was empowered (a) to invest Union Funds without liability; (b) to co-opt should any vacancy occur; (c) to regulate the selection of teams for all games played under the auspices of the SFU.

It was decided to change the date of the AGM to be held in Edinburgh on the second Thursday in October.

The Honorary Secretary and Treasurer was allocated an allowance amounting to £25 towards clerical assistance.

The following IB amendments to the Laws of the Game were accepted:

1. A try to be awarded 2 points; a goal from a try, 5 points; a penalty goal, 3 points; any other goal, 4 points.

2. A player may lift a ball at any time except (a) in a scrummage; (b) from the ground after a tackle.

3. The dead-ball line to be limited to 25 yards.

It was agreed that J.Marsh, an Englishman at Edinburgh University, who had played for Scotland on two occasions in 1889 (against Ireland and Wales), would still be eligible for selection. Ironically, Marsh, then resident in Swinton, was selected for the England XV and played against Ireland!

It was resolved that, for the past season and in the future, International caps should be presented by the Union.

President: D.S.Morton (West of Scotland)
Vice-President: L.M.Balfour (Edinburgh Academicals)

The Aberdeen Thistle club were admitted to membership.

Northern Counties FU were re-admitted after having been omitted from the list of members because of non-payment of their subscription for 1891–92.

The latest set of Laws issued by the IB was adopted. For the first time the Laws included a definition of a rugby ball.

During the season the IB was asked to consider the proposal that a referee be allowed to blow his whistle for an infringement without an appeal having been made by a player. At a special meeting held to confirm this point, Scottish clubs had been almost unanimous in their opposition, but the Committee declared that the referee could do so by mutual consent of both captains. Another point debated was a proposal that a penalty be available for feet up in the scrummage.

It was recorded that the match *v* England at Raeburn Place in 1892 had produced record gate takings of £1,309. It was decided to erect a temporary stand to hold 2,000 people in time for the game *v* Wales.

A Cities *v* Anglo-Scots game was arranged.

The subject of rough play was a cause of concern, '. . . helped by the practice of wearing shinguards concealed under the stockings . . .'. Clubs were informed '. . . that no player is allowed to wear shinguards or other similar protection, unless worn outside the stockings'.

A testimonial to their retiring Honorary Secretary was proposed by the Welsh RU, but this was held to be a matter for individual members and not for the Committee as a body.

Travelling and hotel expenses for players and Committee members were fixed.

« 1893–94 »

President: L.M.Balfour-Melville (Edinburgh Academicals)
Vice-President: W.E.Maclagan (London Scottish)

Aberdeen Grammar School FP, Kelso and Partickhill (Glasgow) were admitted to membership. The following clubs withdrew: Cupar, Edinburgh Collegiate FP and Grange. Aberdeen Thistle were granted permission to change their name to Aberdeenshire.

At the AGM, some critical comments were made about the Union's regulation on the wearing of shinguards. This led to a General Meeting being called, in November 1893, to either challenge or ratify the Committee's assumption of overall authority. In the event, there was passed a motion which '. . . recognised the power of the Committee to pass any Resolution which in their opinion tends to the encouragement of Rugby Football in Scotland, so long as the written Bye-Laws of the Union or Laws of the Game are not altered, and to enforce the same until the said Resolution is disapproved by a General Meeting convened in terms of Bye-Law 10 . . .'. The Committee's views on their recently acquired powers were expertly set out in a statement which accompanied the notice calling the meeting. The episode leaves one in little doubt that a new, yet mature and determined, sense of authority was manifesting itself.

The IB announced the following changes to their rules: 1. Feet-up in the scrummage is to be penalised. 2. The abolition of appeals to the Referee is recommended. 3. The value of a try to be 3 points. 4. The Referee may nominate on which side the ball is to be put into the scrummage.

The disagreements with the Edinburgh Academical Cricket Club over the use of Raeburn Place became more obvious.

It is recorded that, in October 1893, whilst refereeing the Stewart's FP v Melrose match, J.A.Smith '. . . used his whistle . . . without appeal, which is the first instance in this country of a referee having absolute control of a game . . .'. Later in the season, the same authoritative gentleman refereed a Gala v Hunslet match and suffered so much abuse from the English captain that the matter was referred to the RFU, which body insisted on an apology being sent to the referee.

« 1894—95 »

President: W.E.Maclagan (London Scottish)
Vice-President: M.C.McEwan (Edinburgh Academicals)

Clyne Mitchell & Co. (Aberdeen), Hall, Russell & Co. (Aberdeen), Selkirk and Stirlingshire were all admitted to membership and Kirkcaldy were re-admitted. Australasians and the South of Scotland FU were disbanded.

The Committee structure was changed to become the three office-bearers plus eight past players—the latter to comprise three from Edinburgh, two from Glasgow, two from the Southern District and one from the Northern District.

One member of the Committee demitted office, on request, because he was connected with the press.

It was decided that, in future, the Union accounts be audited by a non-Committee member.

The IB empowered referees in International matches to blow their whistle with or without appeals from players. This important event marked the point in time when the umpires became touch judges, leaving the referee in sole control.

The Edinburgh Academical Cricket Club resolved, with great reluctance, not to let Raeburn Place for any Union matches. The SFU minuted their regret of the interruption of their association with Raeburn Place, which had continued for so many years.

Serious charges made by the referee against Gala on the occasion of their match with Watsonians were carefully investigated and found proven. It was, therefore, unanimously resolved: 1. That no Union club be allowed to play at Galashiels until March 1895. 2. That the Gala captain be severely censured and ordered to apologise or be suspended *sine die*.

« 1895—96 »

President: W.E.Maclagan (London Scottish)
Vice-President: D.G.Findlay (West of Scotland)

M.C.McEwan, the previous year's Vice-President having gone abroad, W.E. Maclagan agreed to accept office for a second year.

The following clubs were admitted to membership: Forfar County, Glasgow High School FP and Newport (on Tay).

The RFU had suspended all their clubs which had joined the new Northern Union and, in support, the SFU decided that '. . . the Union shall recognise

105

suspensions by the National Unions of England, Ireland and Wales'. They later warned the Scottish clubs to check the standing of any 'foreign clubs' before accepting a fixture with them.

A Glasgow motion seeking to restore their Committee representation to three failed.

The lack of a suitable ground was troubling the Committee and a sub-committee was set up to study the possible acquisition, for the Union, of a field on a site known to the Honorary Secretary. The game against England was to be played at Old Hampden Park, Glasgow (later re-named Cathkin Park when owned by Third Lanark FC). The Trial and District matches would be played on the grounds of Merchiston Castle School and the Royal High School FP Club at Newington. A request from Melrose to have an International match was refused. Powderhall, in Edinburgh, was booked for use in 1897.

The IB Laws now gave the referee full powers to control a game. Two touch judges with flags would indicate when the ball went out of play and, if requested, would assist the referee when kicks at goal were taken.

« 1896–97 »

President: D. G. Findlay (West of Scotland)
Vice-President: R. D. Rainie (Edinburgh Wanderers)

Clubs admitted to membership were: Celts, Glasgow Technical College and Strathesk. Perthshire and Hall, Russell & Co. withdrew from membership, whilst Forfar County resigned at the end of the season.

A Special General Meeting was called and it was agreed that the proposed new Union Field at Inverleith be largely financed by an issue of Debentures.

Discussion took place about the control of seven-a-side competitions, but the Union decided that no further action be taken unless the clubs involved so desired.

Jed-Forest was refused permission to make a grant from club funds to a player who had a leg broken in a game.

The Gala case was concluded and the Union issued a comprehensive summary of the affair to the member clubs, explaining the final decision taken to suspend several members of the Gala Club.

The Welsh RU resigned from the IB over the Gould affair, and as a result, the matches against Scotland and Ireland were cancelled (their game against England had already been played).

« 1897–98 »

President: R. D. Rainie (Edinburgh Wanderers)
Vice-President: J. D. Boswell (West of Scotland)

A start was made to work on the new field at Inverleith. Debentures were issued to meet part of the cost. Leith Caledonian CC were granted a summer lease for the area.

«1898–99 »

President: J. D. Boswell (West of Scotland)
Vice-President: I. MacIntyre (Fettesian-Lorettonians)

The Ayr, Bearsden, Kilmarnock and Paisley Craigielea clubs were admitted to membership.

106

The game v Wales, scheduled for January, was postponed because of inclement weather. This meant that the Inverleith ground was opened with the match against Ireland on 18 February 1899.

The cost of £140 to provide a permanent Telegraph Office at Inverleith proved to be prohibitive, and the matter was dropped.

The price of Stand and Enclosure tickets was set at five shillings (25p). Tickets were to be sold in one shop in Edinburgh and one in Glasgow.

The St Mirren FC ground in Paisley was used for the South v North match.

A copy of a further IB circular letter on the new Rules was sent to all clubs.

Special modifications to the Rules were permitted to enable schools to cut down the possibility of dangerous play. These included the allowing of a referee in a school match, after a first offence of rough or foul play or misconduct, to award a 'free kick' or order off the offending player. If a second offence was committed, the player had to be ordered off.

At a meeting of the IB, the Welsh representative claimed that he had information that professionalism existed in Scotland. This was at once challenged, and at the next meeting the charge was unreservedly withdrawn.

« 1899–1900 »

President: Ian MacIntyre (Fettesian-Lorettonians)
Vice-President: R. G. MacMillan (Merchistonians)

Perth Rugby Club were admitted to membership whilst Celts were removed.

West delegates again failed in a bid to have the Committee structure amended—but only by the Chairman's casting vote being used to retain the *status quo*.

Inverleith was let, free of charge, to the SAAA for the Inter-Scholastic games.

It was decided that each member of the Committee would receive two complimentary tickets for International games. Members of the XV would receive one each.

The Vice-President resigned following a dispute about Committee members' travelling expenses. His resignation was later withdrawn, but this withdrawal was accepted only after due apology had been made firstly to the Committee and, later, to the AGM.

A new sequence of international fixtures was laid down by the IB.

« 1900–01 »

President: R. G. MacMillan (Merchistonians)
Vice-President: G. T. Neilson (West of Scotland)

The Brunstane and Morningside clubs were admitted to membership.

After voicing objections to various comments made at previous meetings, the Honorary Secretary received apologies from both the President and the Glasgow representative.

A motion that the Inter-City match should be played on alternate years in Glasgow and Edinburgh was defeated.

Edinburgh Wanderers were given a conditional lease of the Inverleith ground for their home games.

Following an unauthorised trip to Germany by a scratch Scottish team, a request, from a German source, for a SFU XV to play a match against a German XV on the Glasgow Exhibition ground at Gilmorehill was turned down.

The Committee, although unable themselves to offer any financial aid to a visiting Canadian team, encouraged member clubs to help make the trip a success.

The Melrose club and their captain received heavy suspensions following their behaviour in a match against Royal High School FP.

Clubs were reminded that the Union had first call on their players. This followed an incident in which a Gala player opted to play for his club rather than the South XV. The player was questioned about his decision and had his explanation accepted, albeit rather grudgingly.

A decision was made that, for the season, Greenock Wanderers players should be eligible for selection for both the Glasgow and South West teams.

An important change in terminology took place when it was agreed that, in future, the English term 'half-back' would be used instead of the Scottish 'quarter-back'.

The IB ruled that stoppage of a game because of injury should not exceed three minutes.

« 1901–02 »

President: G. T. Neilson (West of Scotland)
Vice-President: Rev. R. S. Davidson (Perthshire)

The following clubs were admitted to membership: Cupar, 1st Lanark Rifle Volunteers, Lenzie, Melville and Old Spierians.

A further small piece of ground at Inverleith was purchased. This allowed for the erection of a reporters' box and telephone office. Later, the *Evening Dispatch* was given permission to install its own private line.

It was agreed that Past Presidents be permitted to attend all General and Committee meetings to which they were invited—but without having a vote.

Use of the Inverleith ground was granted to the Scottish Women's Hockey Association, without charge, for their game v Ireland. Use of the ground was also granted to two athletics bodies.

Gilmorehill was named for the next Inter-City match.

The fixtures for the proposed Canadian trip were announced.

A request to take a scratch club side to Paris at Christmas was turned down.

The Cluny club proposed that a Junior League be formed in the East.

It was decided that Union funds were sound enough to enable repayment of £600 of Debentures to be made.

The Honorary Secretary complained of having difficulty with certain international players who either neglected or refused to pay for their jersey. He was authorised to do his best to extract payment but, if unsuccessful, to pay the account from Union funds.

« 1902–03 »

President: Rev. R. S. Davidson (Perthshire)
Vice-President: R. C. Greig (Glasgow Academicals)

The Cluny (Edinburgh) and Renfrew clubs were admitted to membership.

The success of the visit of the Canadian tourists was recorded and a contribution from Union funds was made to those clubs which had entertained the visitors.

The SWHA was again granted use of Inverleith for its match v England, but on this occasion a rental fee amounting to 20 per cent of the net gate receipts was imposed. At a later date, a similar request from the men's Hockey Association was turned down!

108

A.E.Sellars, groundsman at Inverleith, asked for an issue of free coal to combat the dampness of the cottage he occupied at the ground. The matter was held over pending the report of a builder appointed to make an inspection.

Concern was expressed about the rough manner of play by the Welsh forwards. A decision was made to place the matter before the IB in general terms. This body later urged referees to be firm in their judgement of such matters.

The possibility of a visit by a New Zealand team was raised by the RFU. It was agreed that a date should be made available but that further consideration should be given as to whether or not a National team would play against the visitors.

« 1903—04 »

President: R.C.Greig (Glasgow Academicals)
Vice-President: J.W.Simpson (Royal High School FP)

The Newington and Trinity clubs were admitted to membership.

A proposal by the West that one representative, from the South West District, be added to the Committee was narrowly defeated.

Clubs were urged to start their matches punctually at the advertised time, with play continuing for 40 minutes each way, thus conforming to International conditions.

Some essential repairs were carried out to the groundsman's cottage—but he did not get the free coal he had requested!

Requests for the use of Inverleith, made by two Hockey Associations, were refused, but use of the dressing-rooms was granted to some athletics bodies.

A further repayment of Debentures was made.

A Gala club member was reported as having played for the Heart of Midlothian FC. However, no action was taken when it transpired that no payment had been made—not even for travelling expenses.

The teams for the games v Wales and v Ireland travelled overnight on the Thursday to ensure they had a full day's rest before each game was played.

The Committee declined to recognise officially a proposed tour to New South Wales.

The action of the SFU in advising their members not to play against any team which included G.Boots, who had signed Northern Union forms, was questioned by the Welsh RU.

New Zealand again requested a tour in season 1903—04 which would include international matches with each country. The Committee agreed to assist such a tour but felt that no satisfactory date could be found for season 1903—04. It was obvious that the guarantee asked for could not be met by a club game, but the Committee agreed to hand over the total gate receipts after deduction of expenses.

Later, the IB ruled that the tour should take place in season 1905—06 and the SFU accepted 18 November 1905 for their fixture.

« 1904—05 »

President: J.W.Simpson (Royal High School FP)
Vice-President: W.Neilson (London Scottish)

The Dunfermline, Lismore, Old Larchfieldians and Stirling High School FP were admitted to membership.

109

Another motion to include a Committee representative from the South West District failed. Following this, the Committee was asked to investigate the structure with a view to adjusting the inequality of the representation of the Eastern and Western Districts.

The retiral of M.C.Morrison (Royal High School FP) was noted and appreciation expressed for his outstanding service and captaincy over the previous six years.

The remaining Debentures, with the exception of one standing in the name of the Honorary Secretary, were paid off.

It was decided that the South XV should be selected by the two Committee members from the South, with powers to co-opt.

The elected North representative, having moved to Glasgow, resigned and was replaced.

A resolution was passed stating that 'No player . . . shall be permitted to take payment for an article upon Rugby Football'.

Concern over payments being made to players taking part in Sevens Tournaments, brought forth the resolution that future tournaments would be under the jurisdiction of the Union, whose permission to take part would be required by clubs.

A proposed constitution for the Midlands Counties Union was approved.

An enquiry was received from the RFU, seeking the SFU views about a possible tour by a South Africa team in 1906–07. It was decided that such a visit would be acceptable, but it was made clear that a great deal would depend on the financial result of the New Zealand match. If, however, the Cape authorities were prepared to take the risk, then the Committee would agree to the tour taking place.

« 1905–06 »

President: W. Neilson (London Scottish)
Vice-President: J. T. Tulloch (Kelvinside Academicals)

Clubs admitted to membership were Hillhead High School FP, Priestfield (Edinburgh), Queen's Cross (Aberdeen) and Robert Gordon's College FP.

As requested at the previous AGM, the Committee presented a Report on 'Committee Representation'. This reiterated the belief that the Committee was large enough to fulfil its basic function of conducting the business of the Union and also to keep in view the requirements of any particular District so that its players would have every chance of receiving justice in Trial matches.

The South clubs were permitted to start a league with a Challenge Cup. Later, the Union provided 75 per cent of the cost of the Cup.

A request from the Hawick club to hold a benefit match for an injured player was rejected as being quite impossible.

It was decreed that only teams entered by their club secretary could take part in Sevens tournaments. No prizes, other than medals or badges, were to be allowed, although this restriction was relaxed for the current season because clubs had already bought their prizes.

Permission was granted to the Clydesdale club to play in Bordeaux.

Against the Committee's wishes, Dr A. N. Fell, already capped seven times for Scotland, withdrew from the XV selected to play against New Zealand. Having sought the advice of several members of the team who had already played for England against the tourists, the Committee chose to play a third half-back instead of four backs.

110

The SFU remained concerned about the RFU's financial agreements with the New Zealand authorities. It would seem that relationships with the visitors were somewhat cool, because their manager wrote declining the offer of any entertainment. Theatre tickets which the Committee had obtained for the Friday evening were not used, but use was made of a team photographer who had been laid on.

The RFU continued to make arrangements for the forthcoming South Africa tour.

The SFU offered the same financial terms as for the New Zealand games, but again showed their concern by stating that they must be entirely satisfied as to the method in which the tour was to be conducted. They did not feel justified in once more handing over money to a visiting team without knowing beforehand what was to become of it.

The New South Wales RU circularised their suggestions for the control of the game:

1. It was now time to constitute an Imperial Board to control the game.

2. This Board would contain representatives from the four home Unions, New Zealand, New South Wales, Queensland, Griqualand West, Nova Scotia, Transvaal, Western Province, British Columbia and any other to be admitted, under the Presidency of the RFU President.

The IB and, indeed, some of the home Unions, refused to consider this proposal. It maintained that it (the IB) must be the controlling body of the game in this country.

« 1906–07 »

President: J. T. Tulloch (Kelvinside Academicals)
Vice-President: Dr A. B. Flett (Edinburgh University)

The Bishopbriggs and Cambuslang clubs were admitted as members.

At the AGM, J. A. Smith, Honorary Secretary, commenting on the refusal to meet any guarantee to the New Zealand tourists, pointed out that the Union was faced with a Debenture Debt of £3,800 as well as a Bond of £2,800 on the field and so did not think it advisable to place the Debenture holders under any guarantee.

Yet again, a motion seeking to augment the West representation on the Committee failed.

The Honorary Secretary was instructed to ignore requests for stand tickets from past officials and former international players. Such requests were thought to be 'unfair to the public'.

It was noted that a member club had played a Sunday match in France. This produced a stern circular forbidding Sunday play anywhere and added that '... the Committee regret that there should be any necessity for giving this intimation'.

The Pontypridd club was refused permission to present a gift to their new Scottish cap, D. G. MacGregor. Later, MacGregor, who also played for Newport, was reminded that he must not play with or against any team that included G. Boots.

A request to the SFU, by the Union des Sociétés Françaises des Sports Athlétiques, that each Union should recognise the other's jurisdiction over Rugby football in their respective countries was refused. The Committee thought that nothing would be gained by entering into such an agreement.

The New South Wales RU again suggested the formation of an Imperial

111

Rugby Board, but the SFU reiterated its previous refusal to accept such a body. Later, the Union declined to support a proposed visit to the UK by a NSW team and also a proposed British tour to New Zealand in 1908.

The IB were approached by the Olympic Games authorities, but felt that it would be impossible for the Unions to take any official part in the Games.

« 1907–08 »

President: Dr A.B.Flett (Edinburgh University)
Vice-President: D.Y.Cassels (West of Scotland)

Bellahouston Academicals, Falkirk, Madras College FP and Uddingston were all admitted to membership. Also admitted were the newly-constituted Edinburgh and District RFU and the Western District RFU.

Another motion to alter the structure of the Committee failed to get the necessary two-thirds majority.

At the AGM, the Honorary Treasurer reported that the South Africa authorities had received £1,100 from the games played in Scotland. The accounts for that tour were examined and found to be acceptable. It was agreed to ask for a similar financial statement on the New Zealand tour.

It was agreed to support a proposed tour to South Africa in 1909 provided there was no visit from a Colonial team in 1908.

A request by C.F.Rutherford, Paris, for an international match or a visit by a strong Scottish club was set aside until it was seen how the French XV fared against England and Wales that season.

A request that a Sevens tournament be permitted at the Edinburgh National Exhibition was refused.

A Clydesdale player who had accepted an invitation to go on tour to New Zealand was suspended. The matter was closed by his withdrawal from the tour.

A sub-committee was set up to look into the question of dividing the country into Districts.

The IB was asked to legislate on a decision by the referee in the game v Wales in which the Welsh full-back, when tackled, flung the ball into touch, thus preventing a possible score for Scotland. After hearing from the referee, the appeal for a penalty try was dismissed.

The New South Wales visit was still being proposed. The SFU, whilst prepared to attend a meeting, deemed it inadvisable to have a visit the following season and so decided not to seek any fixtures.

The New South Wales, the New Zealand and the Queensland Unions continued to press for the establishment of an Imperial Board, but the IB and the Home Unions did not alter their view.

« 1908–09 »

President: D.Y.Cassels (West of Scotland)
Vice-President: A.S.Blair (Fettesian-Lorettonians)

The Cartha and Selkirk clubs were admitted.

A motion, submitted by the Committee, to change the structure of the Committee was passed. The new representation became: Edinburgh, two; Glasgow, two; South, one; North, one; London, one. The Border clubs voted against the new proposal, stating that one member was not sufficient to oversee the supervision of such a scattered district as the South.

The Treasurer's Report revealed that the Union was now free of debt, the Bond and Debentures having been paid off. In order to settle some queries raised by the Union auditor, the Committee minuted that the Treasurer had full control over the issue of complimentary tickets, the payment of hotel bills and other Union expenditure.

Following further correspondence with C.F.Rutherford in Paris, a first international game with France was arranged to be played in Scotland in January 1910.

London Scottish asked that the Union should not consider any men playing in London who did not associate with their club. The Committee, whilst expressing sympathy, would not accept this.

The SFU co-operated with other sporting bodies in having recreation grounds made exempt from tax as proposed in a new Finance Bill.

A request from Los Angeles for fixtures and guarantees for a Pacific Coast team tour was turned down.

« 1909–10 »

President: A.S.Blair (Fettesian-Lorettonians)
Vice-President: C.J.N.Fleming (Melrose)

The Southern District RFU were admitted to membership.

J. A. Smith recommended that the Union should consider appointing a paid Treasurer to cope with the increased work in looking after its financial affairs.

The groundsman, A.E.Sellars, had his allowances increased to £80 p.a. plus free house and gas.

A Glasgow University player who had played for a Northern Union club was suspended. The University's querying of the Union's authority to take such action was firmly and swiftly answered.

The behaviour of Border spectators came under fire with the result that the Hawick club were forbidden to play within 10 miles of Mansfield Park during the month of March. Selkirk and Melrose also received stern warnings.

Gala asked if they might receive a loan to enable them to acquire a new field.

A request by Melrose to stage a match for the benefit of an old player, was refused. However, they were permitted to collect subscriptions for the purpose.

The private offer of the presentation of a cup for the Selkirk Junior Sevens competition was deemed inadvisable, but the Committee suggested that it might provide a cup for all such junior sports.

For the game against France at Inverleith, Scotland agreed to play in white jerseys in order that the visitors could use their own uniform of blue jerseys. The price of stand tickets was set at three shillings. Later, Lord Rosebery was thanked for the hospitality he had extended to the visitors. It was agreed to play the next match in Paris on Monday, 2 January 1911, that date being a public holiday, when a decent gate might be expected.

It was agreed to support the tour to South Africa in 1910. The team, chosen by a committee of four, one from each Union, would be the guests of the SA Union. The manager, W.Cail of the RFU, was later given permission to send home a Scot who, through injury, was unable to play in any of the matches.

The IB produced several alterations to the Laws of the Game. It also agreed to a change in its Constitution whereby the English representation was reduced from six to four, thus allowing a majority to the representatives of the other Unions.

113

« 1910–11 »

President: C.J.N.Fleming (Melrose)
Vice-President: W.A.Walls (Glasgow Academicals)

The Old Spierians and Rosyth clubs were admitted to membership.

Dunfermline were refused permission to join the Edinburgh and District Union.

A.D.Flett, CA, became, as Treasurer, the first paid official of the Union with a salary of £50 p.a., but he had no vote in any Committee meeting. The investments of the Union were put in the names of three trustees: D.Y.Cassels, A.S.Blair and J.A.Smith.

It was agreed that, for International games, portions of the stand be reserved for London, North of Scotland and South of Scotland, and that each player in a match receive tickets for two seats instead of one.

Agreement was reached to redesignate the Cities v Rest Trial match to be known as Blue v White.

During the season the South played Monmouth County at Hawick. Other Union business included a reaffirmation that the SFU South representative on the Border League Committee was entitled to a vote. The Union presented a cup (costing five guineas) to Selkirk for the Border Junior Sevens competition and it was agreed that the Gala club be given a loan of £200 towards the cost of a new field.

The principle that the Union's representatives on the IB were the President and the Hon. Secretary was abandoned for the sake of continuity. A.S.Blair and J.A.Smith were appointed. The IB resolved that no player was eligible to play for a country until he had resided for two years in that country, but a player born abroad was eligible to play for the country of birth of either parent.

The allowable expenses for visiting touring teams, who must come as guests, were tentatively agreed. These included third-class fares, all medical attention, first-class hotel accommodation, laundry, and a drink at meals only. It was decided that a Tour Manager be appointed.

« 1911–12 »

President: W.A.Walls (Glasgow Academicals)
Vice-President: J.D.Dallas (Watsonians)

The following clubs were admitted to membership: Drumchapel, East of Scotland (Dundee), Robert Gordon's College FP, Kilmarnock, Old Larch-fieldians and Uddingston.

The Western District Union became defunct and an ensuing blank fixture was filled by Edinburgh and District Union playing Aberdeen University.

It was announced that the Gala club had repaid the loan made to them. Emphasis was put on the point that Gala had not been allocated a grant but that it had been a business transaction whereby a loan had been made upon securities offered.

Ground improvements included the replacing of the wooden front of the stand by a steel and concrete structure. A standing platform, which could be lifted and stored, was purchased for use at Hamilton Crescent.

It was recorded that, for all Trial matches, numbered jerseys would be supplied to the players, who would also be given the option of dining together after the match. For the first time the halves in the Trial were designated as stand-off and scrum-half and A.W.Gunn and J.Hume (both RHSFP) became

114

the first caps to be picked for these positions.

Messrs J.C.Stewart were defunct and Messrs R.W.Forsyth's offer to sell match tickets was accepted. Dissatisfaction over the distribution of stand tickets was aired at a Special General Meeting, which recommended that the Committee give preference to: (a) old and present Caps; (b) old and present Committee members; (c) clubs; (d) schools. It was suggested that only a restricted number should be given to any one individual.

The Home Unions agreed to having a South Africa tour in Britain during 1912–13 and the financial arrangements proposed by the RFU were approved.

« 1912–13 »

President: J.D.Dallas (Watsonians)
Vice-President: Dr J.R.C.Greenlees
(Kelvinside Academicals and Fettesian-Lorettonians)

The Kelso club were admitted to membership whilst Old Larchfieldians resigned. The Newington club were dissolved because of difficulty over a ground. The Bruntsfield club, who had been co-tenants with Newington on the Edinburgh Polo Club field, asked for financial assistance toward the rental of the field. This led to an unsuccessful attempt by the Union to rent the same field for use by Junior clubs. This was the field that was later to become Murrayfield.

Selkirk were awarded a loan of £230 toward the cost of erection of a stand.

An annual South v Cumberland match was initiated.

An adverse report by a referee on the conduct of the Hawick spectators led to a decision that the price of admission to Mansfield Park be raised to sixpence (2½p), with a further sixpence for entry to the stand.

With the Inter-University match a month away, the Oxford University club barred their players from accepting a place in the Scotland v South Africa match. The SFU objected and letters to the RFU and Oxford University resulted in the edict being cancelled.

Again it was minuted that players would be numbered in all Trial games. Press privileges were withdrawn from two Edinburgh newspapers which had offended a player by making untrue statements about the reasons for his withdrawal from a Trial. An apology was eventually given and the Union made it known that they would always defend their players against any unjust charges brought against them.

A New South Wales request for a visit by a touring team was regarded favourably by the Home Unions.

In November 1912 the *Scottish Referee* carried an advertisement which read: 'The Stade Bordelais, Rugby Champions of France, wish a good Stand-off Half [left-half] for their team. A good business situation will be found in Bordeaux for a capable player.' This was regarded as an act of professionalism and the French Rugby authorities were alerted. That body at once thoroughly investigated the matter, suspended the club committee concerned, dismissed the club coach and banned the club president and one other member for life. Glasgow Academicals, the club which had brought the advertisement to the Committee's notice, were reminded that their projected fixture with the Stade Bordelais must be cancelled.

At the end of the International match in Paris, the English referee, whose strictness and decisions had greatly incensed the spectators, had to be protected by the police and mounted soldiers as he left the field. After

115

receiving the referee's report, the IB warned that no further games would be played in Paris if sufficient security to referees and players was not ensured. The SFU, after several meetings and thorough investigation, cancelled the next French fixture so that the serious nature of their behaviour might be brought home to the spectators. The Union also expressed their sympathy with the French Committee and players, who had done what they could to protect the referee.

« 1913–14 »

President: Dr J.R.C.Greenlees
(Kelvinside Academicals and Fettesian-Lorettonians)
Vice-President: T.Scott (Langholm)

The Bye-Laws were altered to permit the Past Presidents for the three immediately-preceding years to be members of the Committee, but they were not entitled to take part in team selection.

Following medical advice, J.A.Smith expressed a wish to demit office and a sub-committee was set up to prepare Constitutional changes which involved the employment of a paid secretary.

Glasgow Academicals were pressing a suggestion that District Representatives should be responsible to the District clubs. Selkirk were given permission to play a match to provide funds for the Town Band, who gave their services free to the club. Hawick were given a loan of £240 towards the erection of a new pavilion.

A Schools' International between Scotland and Wales was considered to be undesirable.

A change of hotel for Union meetings followed the receipt of a bill considered to be unacceptable.

Following on a query from D.G.Anderson in Buenos Aires, it was agreed that former International players should have the right to wear a silver thistle on a blazer which, for preference, should be dark blue.

The IB decreed that the employment of a paid trainer or coach was contrary to the principles of amateur rugby. A proposal that players in an International should be numbered was passed over because of the strong opposition from certain members of the Board.

In early August the RFU wrote proposing a tour to Australia and New Zealand during the summer of 1915. It was considered injudicious to proceed with such a scheme because of the existing state of National affairs. In any case the Committee recorded that they would not permit any of their players to visit New Zealand! At the same time the SFU made a contribution of £500 to the National Relief Fund and advised the clubs to continue playing as long as this did not interfere with National duties. However, by September, most clubs had closed down and the Home Unions agreed to cancel all Representative matches.

« 1914–15 »

President: T.Scott (Langholm)
Vice-President: J.M.Dykes (Glasgow High School FP)

Dr J.R.C.Greenlees could not be in the Chair, having already left for France. It was also minuted that, after 27 years, this would be the last meeting at which the Honorary Secretary, J.A.Smith, would attend in that capacity.

116

The Meeting debated and passed the new Constitution before electing the new Committee. The date of the AGM was now changed to the first Friday in May. A circular to the clubs revealed that, after only two months of war, 24 clubs with a total of 817 players, had 638 of these in the armed forces as well as 304 non-playing members. It was also noted that two International players, R.F. Simson and Dr J.L. Huggan, had been killed and that C.M. Usher was a prisoner of war.

THE WAR YEARS

Only two Minutes are evident during the period of 1915–18.

In March 1915 seven of the Committee met and decided to circularise the clubs to inform them that no annual subscription would be asked for the coming year. Repayment was made of the remaining Debenture standing in the name of J.A. Smith. A sub-committee consisting of J.M. Dykes, J.D. Dallas, J.A. Smith and A.D. Flett was appointed to deal with any business that might arise.

In August 1916 five of the Committee met and approved the Treasurer's Accounts for 1915–16. It was decided that, during A.D. Flett's absence on military duties, J.A. Smith would act in his place, thus confirming the situation that had existed since the previous year. The names of 18 International players killed in action were recorded. Two Committee members, J.M. Usher (in 1915) and J.H. Lindsay (also in 1915), had fallen. A.D. Flett fell in 1917.

The break enforced by the War marked the end of a period of some 50 years of development not only in the Laws and style of playing the game but also in the composition of its governing bodies. From 1873 to 1886 the Union Committee consisted of three office-bearers supported by active players of International or high club standard, a composition well suited to arrange fixtures, discuss changes in the Laws and select teams. From 1886 onwards the emergence of the IB, the demands made by an increasing number of clubs for decisions, grants and reprimands, saw the composition quite quickly change to contain older non-players who, however, still came mainly from the same prosperous backgrounds of Public Schools or Universities but were now fully established in their professions. Such men, with their Victorian or Edwardian backgrounds, were determined to preserve the amateur status of their game and they were guided (one might almost say, led) by that seemingly permanent member, J.A. Smith, whose authority after some 24 years in office was truly formidable.

THE RESTART

The first post-war Committee Meeting took place in January 1919. The two vacancies were filled but the post of Secretary-Treasurer was passed to a sub-committee for consideration.

Dates proposed by the RFU for the resumption of International matches in 1919–20 were accepted and it was also agreed to resume the French fixture. A New Zealand request for a fixture was answered, but no indication of the decision reached is observed in the Minute. Some suggested alterations to the Laws (by NZ), designed to make the game '. . . more open to spectacular play' were firmly rejected because it was considered that the game was fast enough and that the policy should be to seek to look after the interests of the players

117

and not those of the spectators.

The Army Sports Control Board was granted use of Inverleith (which had been used for military games during the War), but no Union assistance would be offered if Northern Union players were selected. Actually, two fully-amateur matches were played, v Canada and New Zealand. The Union co-operated fully and received £471 as its share of the 'gates'.

The groundsman's wage was raised to £150 p.a. Gala was given permission to stage a Sevens competition for a cup. Leith Caledonian Cricket Club was granted a further lease of Inverleith.

A second list of 13 International players, killed in action, was recorded.

« 1919–20 »

President: T. Scott (Langholm)
Vice-President: J.M. Dykes (Glasgow High School FP)

The Border clubs once again raised the question of increased representation on the Committee.

The broad principles of the allocation of International tickets and expenses of Committee members travelling to Trial and other matches were set out.

The Glasgow clubs pressed for the English match to be played in Glasgow using an Association Football ground as venue. This, eventually, was not granted. The wooden structure of the enclosure seats at Inverleith was replaced by metal framework.

Edinburgh Wanderers had their lease of Inverleith renewed. Royal High School FP were granted use of the ground for a Sevens tournament in aid of their War Memorial Funds and it was also used for a Heriot's FP v Edinburgh University match in aid of the Funds of the Edinburgh Royal Infirmary.

Hawick, having the opportunity of acquiring its field at Mansfield Park, was granted an extension of its Union loan.

A former Association Football player and Highland Games competitor had been appointed as a sports coach in an Aberdeen school. It was agreed that the status of the pupils in his care would not be affected. It was also agreed that schoolboys playing under Northern Union rules in England remain amateurs.

The IB, after debating the control of rugby in the Army, ended their meeting with a recommendation to the Unions that no champagne or expensive wines should be used meantime at International Dinners.

A French request for admission to the IB was held over until more information was obtained about the administration of the game in France.

« 1920–21 »

President: J.M. Dykes (Glasgow High School FP)
Vice-President: T. Anderson (Glasgow Academicals)

Clubs admitted to membership were Allan Glen's School FP, Craigard, Dundee High School FP, Dunfermline, Lenzie and Walkerburn.

During the season help was given to form a club in the Howe of Fife area. Dunfermline High School, having started playing rugby during the season, was given a grant towards the expenses of a field.

Two estimates, both over £20,000, for the erection of a stand on the east side of Inverleith were rejected as being too costly. Much repainting was done, the state of the woodwork causing concern. A second row of enclosure seats was installed, the centre seats being reserved for schoolboys.

For the English match two military bands were engaged. This being the fiftieth anniversary of the first Scotland v England match, all survivors of the 1871 match were invited as guests. Six were able to accept the invitation. The stand tickets were set at 10 shillings (50p) and the clubs received an allocation.

A Glasgow request that Hampden Park be used for the English match was turned down.

The groundsman's wage was raised to £200 p.a. An estimate of £1,998 was accepted for the erection of a War Memorial Arch at Inverleith.

The former Royal High School FP field at Corstorphine was leased for the use of local Junior clubs. Boroughmuir Higher Grade School was given permission to use the pavilion and one pitch free of charge on Saturday mornings, while Clarendon CC was given use of the field in the summer.

Edinburgh Institution FP was given permission to use Inverleith for a Sevens tournament in aid of its School Memorial Fund. A Glasgow request for the resumption of a Junior Inter-City match was agreed to. A further request for a meeting of referees to discuss the Laws was also agreed.

A Kelso player whose motor cycle broke down, hired a car to complete his journey to Inverleith for the Trial. His request for travelling expenses was refused '. . . as it was plainly his duty to wire his inability to play on such an occasion'. He was, however, granted £3 towards the cost of the repair bill!

The Minutes record the receipt of the following letter: 'La Fédération Française de Rugby sur le rapport de ses représentants. Attendu que la réception réservée à ses délégués fut non seulement cordiale mais affectueuse. Que la vieille Fédération Écossaise a sportivement, et avec la delicatesse la plus parfaite, offert à sa jeune soeur Française aide et appui. Addresse à l'unanimité à la Scottish Football Union ses affectueux remerciements avec l'assurance de son entier dévouement.'

The Committee decided that temporary residence in the country did not qualify a player for consideration for the International team. The IB decided that France should not be admitted to membership of the Board. An English request that players in an International be numbered was left as a matter for each Union to decide.

« 1921–22 »

President: J.M.Dykes (Glasgow High School FP)
Vice-President: H.S.Dixon (London Scottish)

T.Anderson declined nomination for the post of President for business reasons and J.M.Dykes was re-elected.

Clubs admitted to membership were: Cambuslang, Craigielea, Earlston, Edinburgh Borderers, Howe of Fife, RAF Leuchars and University College, Dundee.

A proposal to start rugby in Inverness-shire and Ross-shire was approved. The purchase by the City of a field at Corstorphine (Edinburgh), much to the openly expressed indignation of J.A.Smith, meant that it was lost for use by the Union.

Glasgow University were given permission to play in France; proper accounts were to be produced and no Sunday games to be played. Greenock Wanderers sought a substantial grant to acquire a field at Fort Matilda, and Melrose and Glasgow High School FP asked for grants to build stands. Edinburgh University were given permission to use Inverleith for their match v Oxford University.

W. W. Mabon resigned from the Committee to allow J. Macgill, now resident in Edinburgh, to take his place on the Emergency Committee. J. A. Smith was chosen to represent the Union on the RFU Centenary Committee.

« 1922–23 »

President: H. S. Dixon (London Scottish)
Vice-President: R. T. Neilson (West of Scotland)

The following clubs were admitted: Ardrossan, Bearsden, Highland, Peebles, Royal Technical College (Glasgow), Southern (Glasgow), Stewartry, Uddingston and Wigtownshire.

The Committee took over the selection of all teams and no selection sub-committee was nominated. They also decided to take control of the 'Official Match Programme'.

Negotiations with the Fettes Trust for the purchase of ground to the east of Inverleith broke down because of the high cost. However, the Edinburgh Polo Club ground at Murrayfield became available and was immediately purchased, possession being taken in November. The area was at once used by Junior clubs and Boroughmuir Secondary School while Murrayfield CC were granted a summer lease. Inverleith was used for two Sevens tournaments: that of Edinburgh Secondary Schools and one run by Edinburgh and District Union in aid of the Royal Infirmary Funds (later to become known as the 'Infirmary Sevens').

During the year many requests for loans were received, including one from Musselburgh Grammar School which had made rugby its main sport. Some clubs, like Cambuslang and Hillhead High School FP were turned down. A loan to Glasgow High School FP was granted, while Greenock Wanderers, strengthened by the promise of a Union loan, were able to acquire their field by their own efforts.

The Duke of York accepted an invitation to attend the game v England. For this match the Pipe Band of Queen Victoria School, Dunblane, was engaged.

The SFU was averse to sending a team to the Dominions in 1924, but decided to accept the decision of the IB if it was thought that the game in South Africa would benefit from such a visit. The Oxford Scots v Cambridge Scots match was resuscitated.

J. A. Smith and J. M. Dykes were invited to join the board of a newspaper called Rugger. The offer was refused, since no member of the Committee could accept such a position.

« 1923–24 »

President: R. T. Neilson (West of Scotland)
Vice-President: Sir R. C. Mackenzie (Glasgow Academicals)

Dumfries, Ross County and Western clubs were proposed for admission, but progress in the matter was halted by a motion asking for the whole question of Union membership to be examined.

During the season J. M. Tennent resigned from the Committee and was replaced by W. L. Russell (Glasgow Academicals). Following the death of D. Y. Cassels, R. T. Neilson became a Trustee.

The method of allocation of International tickets was still a source of worry

120

and the matter was referred to a sub-committee. Agreement was reached with the City, who, initially, had wished to continue the line of Roseburn Street through the intended site of the pitch at Murrayfield.

It was decided that the period 1 May to 14 September should be a close season for rugby. A field at St Machar, Aberdeen, was acquired by the Union and would be used, initially, by the Aberdeenshire RFC. A Welsh proposal to initiate a Welsh-Scottish Secondary and Public Schools' International fixture was not entertained.

A request from the BBC for the names of men who could talk on rugby football for broadcasting purposes was not acceded to. The IB agreed to join in a Conference with the Unions of the Dominions but expressed the wish that all delegates should be direct representatives from their Unions. It was also suggested that delegates from France might also be invited to attend.

« 1924–25 »

President: Sir R.C.Mackenzie (Glasgow Academicals)
Vice-President: R.Welsh (Watsonians)

At the AGM several changes were made to the Bye-Laws:
1. The title of the Union was changed to 'The Scottish Rugby Union'.
2. To reduce the pressure of business on the Committee, decentralisation was begun by establishing five District Unions who would handle most of the routine local questions. This new organisation was, apparently, behind the decisions to refuse admission to the Union of the Moray and Perthshire clubs.
3. The number of Special Representatives was increased to six.

The contract for the initial work on the new ground at Murrayfield had gone to Sir Robert McAlpine & Sons, Glasgow, whilst a competition for the design of a grandstand was won by R.F.Sherar, Edinburgh. To finance the project the Committee gained authorisation to issue Debentures of £100 at 4% p.a. up to a total of £75,000 and within a month, finding themselves oversubscribed, made a first issue of 267 Debentures.

Queries about the future of the Inverleith ground, from Edinburgh Institution FP club and the George Heriot's Trust, were set aside as being too premature. Later, Edinburgh Wanderers were given a further lease of the ground for 1925–26. A lease was taken of the Royal (Dick) Veterinary College ground at Duddingston for the use of Junior clubs.

Hawick were permitted to accept a cup for their Sevens, presented by D. Patterson. The Midlands DRU was permitted to accept cups for its League and Sevens winners.

The IB rejected the idea of an Imperial Board, but advocated the formation of a Conference at intervals of not less than three years. The IB also decided that '... it was contrary to the spirit of amateur Rugby Football that teams should be assembled at a centre during a period prior to a match for the purpose of a change of air and training'.

« 1925–26 »

President: R.Welsh (Watsonians)
Vice-President: J.A.Smith (Royal High School FP)

Yet again a motion to increase the South representation on the Committee failed.

The date of the AGM was altered to the third week in May. The Secretary was authorised to employ a clerkess-typist.

A. Wemyss was contacted over articles on rugby appearing in a weekly newspaper and it was decided to add a note in the Bye-Laws: 'No member of the Committee or member of a club under the jurisdiction of this Union is permitted to write any article to the public press on Rugby Football'.

The Inter-City game was postponed because of frost. Following this, it was decided to put straw down on the playing surface at Murrayfield and to transfer the game there if necessary.

Three Edinburgh clubs were given the use of Inverleith for special fixtures. The Merchant Company made an offer to purchase that ground. The Military Band were granted £3.10s (£3.50) to replace sheet music ruined by the rain at the Irish match. Electric lighting was installed in the press gallery at the back of the stand.

Kelso and Selkirk were given permission to accept cups for their Sevens. The Irish RU raised the question of numbering players in International games, but the SRU decided on no change meantime. They also decided that they should not recognise suspensions on rugby players made by the AAA or kindred bodies.

« 1926–27 »

President: J. A. Smith (Royal High School FP)
Vice-President: Col. M. M. Duncan (Fettesian-Lorettonians)

Another motion by the South to increase their Committee representation failed. It was decided to set up any sub-committees felt necessary to deal with the business of the Union. The Calcutta RFC enquired if it was eligible for Union membership but this was not considered possible.

The ground and stand (but not the War Memorial) at Inverleith were sold to the Merchant Company Education Board for £8,000. A house for the grounds-man (A. E. Sellars) was built at the NE corner of Murrayfield.

An action raised by a spectator, injured while leaving Murrayfield after the first English match at Murrayfield, was successfully defended, but, thereafter, the Union advised their clubs to ensure that they carried adequate insurance against Third Party risks. The BBC was given permission to broadcast the English match on radio.

A request from a Quebec source for the Union to recognise and finance a Scottish tour in Canada was considered to be too costly for the time being.

It was reiterated that players should be presented with their first International jersey by the Union and a replacement if torn. However, the player thereafter would be responsible for any other needed. This was aimed at discouraging the practice of exchanging jerseys with opposing players at the end of a match. Three members of the Scottish team who missed the return boat from Dublin after the Irish game were eventually allowed the added expenses thereby incurred, along with a firm warning that such incidents were most undesirable and not expected of players of their standing. Permission was given for Scottish players to be included in a group to tour Argentina.

A request from C. B. Cochran to stage a professional lawn tennis match involving Mlle Suzanne Lenglen, at Murrayfield, was not acceded to. The Committee approved the use of the IB redraft of the Laws, but added the suggestion that no alterations should be made for a period of three years.

There had been an objection to the proposal that only three forwards could form the front row of the scrum, but to assist the RFU to control some local trouble, this was accepted for a three-year trial. (Looking ahead, this restriction was allowed to remain in 1930.) However, there was objection to the decision that '. . . in all matches between clubs of different Unions the game should be played under the IB Rules', maintaining that the IB had no power to insist on such a Resolution.

<h2 style="text-align:center">« 1927–28 »</h2>

President: Col. M. M. Duncan (Fettesian-Lorettonians)
Vice-President: D. McCowan (West of Scotland)

During the season, the Vice-President received a knighthood. At the AGM it was agreed that the forty years' service on the Committee of J. A. Smith, the retiring President, should be recognised by commissioning a portrait to be hung in the Committee Room at Murrayfield. An Executive Committee for immediate Union business and a Field Committee was appointed. J. A. Smith, re-elected as a Special Representative, was on both Committees.

The ground to the west of Murrayfield, bounded by the Water of Leith, was purchased and the cost of erecting two access bridges across the river was shared with the City. A further area was later acquired to serve as a car park. Edinburgh Wanderers were granted the use of a pitch in this area, at Damhead, running parallel to the railway.

It is surprising to note that a motion, in Committee, to award caps for the New South Wales and French matches failed to get a seconder. Apparently it was still held that caps were only awarded for games against the Home Countries.

The BBC was given permission to broadcast all International matches played at Murrayfield. The Infirmary Sevens were played at Murrayfield during the season. Langholm received permission to present a shield at their Sevens. Musselburgh were granted £100 to help replace their access bridge across the Esk which had been carried away by a flood.

The New South Wales tourists, who had been allocated £600 by the Home Countries Touring Board to allow a return via Canada, requested a further £400 for the trip. This was firmly rejected by the Board, which was considerably disturbed to learn that the tourists had ignored its ruling that a visiting team should be the guests of the host countries. It came to light that a separate agreement had been made with the French authorities whereby the tourists received a sum of £1,600 from matches played in France en route to the UK. The Board regarded this '. . . as contrary to the spirit in which these tours are arranged', a view later supported by the IB, who repeated the firm monetary arrangements to be observed by touring teams.

<h2 style="text-align:center">« 1928–29 »</h2>

President: Sir D. McCowan (West of Scotland)
Vice-President: Sir A. G. G. Asher (Fettesian-Lorettonians)

The accounts showed that the expenditure on Murrayfield to date was £160,571. Six new pitches had been laid out there and an assistant groundsman had been employed. The British Rugby Club (Paris) asked for affiliation to the Union, but this was refused on Constitutional grounds.

A Committee motion to have a Selection Sub-Committee of five was defeated. The Committee did not agree to have a representative on a committee to select players for a NZ tour as '... it is entirely under the auspices of the RFU'—but they expressed their willingness to answer enquiries about any of their players considered for the tour.

« 1929–30 »

President: Sir A.G.G. Asher (Fettesian-Lorettonians)
Vice-President: Dr A. Balfour (London Scottish)

The President, because of poor health, was ordered abroad during the season. The Vice-President was created KCMG during the season. The retiring President presented a clock for use at Murrayfield to the Union whilst, later, J.A. Smith presented a scoreboard. The death was noted of the oldest Past President, W.H. Kidston (1876–77).

It was agreed to take part in a Memorial Match for the late Sir G. Rowland Hill, a distinguished former President and Honorary Secretary of the RFU. The groundsman, A.E. Sellars, was warmly thanked for his untiring efforts, which allowed the Irish match to be played.

The provision of a suitable tie for International players was undertaken. Langholm were given permission to accept a cup for their Sevens. The BBC was again permitted to cover the matches at Murrayfield but was refused permission to erect a permanent hut.

The IB favoured a tour in Canada but would not accept offers to tour in Argentina and Japan.

« 1930–31 »

President: Sir A. Balfour, KCMG, CB (London Scottish)/
J.C. Sturrock (Royal High School FP)
Vice-President: J.C. Sturrock (Royal High School FP)/
J.D. Dallas (Watsonians)

During the season, the Union suffered devastating blows with the untimely deaths of three of their leading administrators: Sir A.G.G. Asher, Sir A. Balfour and J.A. Smith. The resulting vacant posts of President and Vice-President were filled by J.C. Sturrock and J.D. Dallas, respectively.

Murrayfield was proudly resplendent in the new season by displaying and using to good effect the new scoreboard gifted by J.A. Smith and the flag and flagstaff presented to the Union by Sheriff Watt, KC.

The business of the Union included a motion, in Committee, to form a Selection Sub-Committee. This was defeated. The new car park was brought into use during the season.

A scarcity of referees caused some concern and member clubs were asked to seek out suitable members to undertake this most onerous of tasks. Still on refereeing, guidelines as to the procedure to be followed, after the sending off of a player, were set out in detail.

At one point during the season, an eyebrow-raising complaint was received from Edinburgh Academicals FC stating that two of its members had been approached by Border clubs seeking their services. This despite the fact that the players in question had no connection whatsoever with the clubs concerned.

More eyebrow-raising was the order of the day with the growing concern over the control and conduct of the game in France. The four Home Countries convened a conference at which it was mutually agreed to suspend relations with France at the end of the season.

« 1931–32 »

President: J.C.Sturrock (Royal High School FP)
Vice-President: J.C.Findlay (London Scottish and West of Scotland)

Stewartry RFC disbanded during the season. At the AGM a motion to establish a Selection Committee failed. During the season a Finance Sub-Committee was formed.

The SRU joined with other sporting bodies in a successful attempt to gain exemption from a proposed Finance Bill which would impose a tax on Land Values. The Minute notes that there were 127 rugby clubs in the country, of which 62 were members of the Union.

Economies connected with the handling of International matches were agreed in view of tax and rates payments exceeding £3,000. Improvements to the heating arrangements at Murrayfield were passed. The cost of a schoolboy ticket for Murrayfield Internationals was raised to one shilling (5p).

Langholm and Dumfries were permitted to play for a long-lost medal (dating from 1880) which had been recovered. The ban on players writing about rugby for the press was extended to include broadcasting. Two Aberdeen members and two well-known International players were suspended because of their published articles. The BBC continued to broadcast from Murrayfield, but a request to discuss a choice of commentator was declined.

The Aberdeen FC ground at Pittodrie was used for the North v South Africa match. The French Ambassador made an approach to have relations with French rugby resumed. The four Home Countries agreed to adopt the Laws as framed by the IB and further decided to join a Rugby Football Commission set up to discuss the Laws of the Game as played throughout the British Empire. The IB received an acceptance from New Zealand of a tour in 1936–37. A request from Japan for a tour was not favoured.

« 1932–33 »

President: J.C.Findlay (London Scottish and West of Scotland)
Vice-President: J.Macgill (Glasgow Academicals)

Following on recommendations passed at the AGM, the Committee agreed to set up a Selection Committee of five and also agreed that players should now be numbered in Trials and International matches. It was decided to redeem all the outstanding 4 per cent Debentures and to offer a new issue at 3 per cent.

There was much activity on the International scene. An Italian Rugby Federation had been formed and contacted the IB suggesting the formation of a wider Board of Control, but this was rejected as unworkable and undesirable. The NZ and NSW Boards declined to enter the proposed RF Commission, so the idea was shelved. A NZ proposal to permit replacements for injured players was not accepted. The IB decided that the time had not yet come to resume relations with France. The IB also decided to recommend that the Home Unions should appoint a panel of suitable referees for their International matches and issued a circular dealing with the difficulties of getting the ball into a scrum.

125

« 1933–34 »

President: J.Macgill (Glasgow Academicals)
Vice-President: M.C.Morrison (Royal High School FP)

Members for five sub-committees were appointed viz.: Executive, Field, Finance, Ticket Allocation and Selection. Under certain conditions members of Committee were permitted to have first-class sleeper accommodation.

Following a visit to France, R.T.Neilson gave a report on the state of the game there, and later, the IB regretted that relations with France could still not be resumed. Two Border players were expelled for taking part in Northern Union Trials.

« 1934–35 »

President: M.C.Morrison (Royal High School FP)
Vice-President: W.P.Scott (West of Scotland)

Planned major alterations to the stand were passed: (i) two end extensions to seat a further 7,000; (ii) two main dressing-rooms to be refloored; (iii) the Committee rooms to be improved. A telephone, ex-directory, was installed in the Secretary's home. An offer was made to rent the Scotstoun Show Ground.

Edinburgh Wanderers were allowed the use of the main pitch at Murrayfield on selected dates, but always at the discretion of the groundsman. Gala requested that the suspension, placed on four of its players in 1896, be lifted, but it was decided to retain the *status quo*.

Several South players were reprimanded for taking part in an out-of-season Sevens tournament at Bonchester. Two other Border players were suspended *sine die* for apparent contact with Northern Union clubs. A request from the Canadian RU for a tour was refused, but Edinburgh University was given permission to play four matches in the USA.

« 1935–36 »

President: W.P.Scott (West of Scotland)
Vice-President: A.A.Lawrie (Edinburgh Wanderers and
Fettesian-Lorettonians)

Clubs were invited to support the Thank-Offering Fund to commemorate the King's Jubilee, the proceeds from which were to be devoted to Youth Welfare. Four doctors were named 'To look after the medical services' in the various District matches. The assessed rental for the Murrayfield ground was set at £1,950.

New Zealand played in Scotland and were sent a cable, at the end of their tour, wishing them God speed and a happy tour in Canada. It was agreed to support a proposed tour to South Africa in 1938.

« 1936–37 »

President: A.A.Lawrie (Edinburgh Wanderers and Fettesian-Lorettonians)
Vice-President: Dr W.H.Welsh (Merchistonians)

The deaths were noted of three ex-Presidents: A.S.Blair, D.S.Morton and Sir D.McCowan. A.S.Blair's appointment as the Union's Law Agent was passed on to his son, A.W.Blair.

Edinburgh Institution FP changed its name to Melville College FP. St

Above. 82. 1974. Scotland *v* England. Andy Irvine scores a spectacular try for his country, frustrating the defensive efforts of two English opponents.
Left. 83. 1973. England *v* Scotland. A ballet-like situation at a line-out with Peter Brown and an embattled Alistair McHarg in contention for the ball.

84. 1971. Scotland *v* England. Centenary Match. The opening try of the match scored by John Frame within 13 seconds of the kick-off. This was the extra match *v* England to mark the centenary of the first match in 1871.

85. 1971. Scotland *v* England. Centenary Match. Peter Brown scores in unusual fashion just before half-time. Sandy Carmichael looks on anxiously to confirm the score.

86. 1971. Scotland *v* England. Centenary Match. Chris Rea scores the last try with an emphatic gesture with John Frame registering his delight.

87. 1967. England *v* Scotland. R. E. Webb is tackled by one Scot with David Rollo about to take a hand. Billy Hunter and Ian McCrae are in the background.

88. 1967. England *v* Scotland. Ian McCrae gets the ball away with a splendid copybook dive-pass.

89. 1962. Wales *v* Scotland. A famous try which registered Scotland's first win in Wales since 1927. Ron Glasgow scores, closely observed by Stan Coughtrie (9) and Mike Campbell-Lamerton.

90. 1962. Ireland *v* Scotland. Arthur Smith about to cross the Irish line.

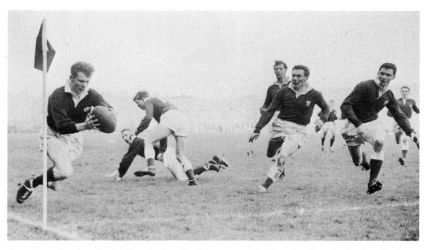

91. 1961. Scotland *v* Wales. Arthur Smith scores. Ken Scotland made the break, drew
the full back and the Scotland winger scored in the corner.

92. 1957. Scotland *v* Ireland. J. W. Kyle loses the ball to a smother-tackle by Ken Scotland. Adam Robson is back to help. This game was played in near-blizzard conditions which continued throughout the match.

93. 1956. Wales *v* Scotland. Adam Robson is not the full back although wearing the no. 15 jersey. Hamish Kemp is the other Scot in this tableau. Both players went on to become President of the Scottish Rugby Union.

94. 1955. France *v* Scotland. A determined Grant Weatherstone faces up to a challenge from A. Boniface.

95. 1955. Scotland *v* Wales. Jimmy Nichol prepares to pass from Scottish possession. Adam Robson gets ready to break away.

96. 1951. France *v* Scotland. F. O. Turnbull about to hand-off an opponent with Douglas Elliot in close support.

97. 1953. Scotland *v* Ireland. Ken Spence thrusts forward on the break. Shortly after this he was badly injured. Doug Smith, currently Vice-President of the Union, is on the extreme right.

Top. 98. 1951. Scotland *v* South Africa. A line-out in that devastating match. However, here, Bob Wilson (in white) has the ball in infrequent Scottish set-piece possession. *Bottom.* 99. 1949. England *v* Scotland. An acrobatic pass by Dally Allardyce the Scottish scrum-half.

100. 1948. Scotland v England. T. G. H. Jackson, the burly Scottish wing, moves the ball forward by means of a grubber kick to keep up the momentum of the attack.

101. 1938. England v Scotland. A match made memorable by a sustained personal performance from Wilson Shaw. Here he is scoring his first try after a 40-yard run towards the left corner flag. An initial dummy and his acceleration moved him clear of the defence and a final side-step left the full back sprawling on the touch-line.

102. 1938. England v Scotland. A scrum breaks up and, although the ball is not in evidence, it would appear that England have possession. Bill Crawford tackles the English scrum-half. The dress of the referee contrasts with that of the present-day officials.

103. 1938. Scotland v Wales. Duncan Macrae splits the Welsh defence supported by R. C. S. Dick and Wilson Shaw.

104. 1937. Scotland *v* England. Ken Marshall, facing his own line, safely gathers an awkward kick ahead by an opponent.

105. 1935. Scotland *v* New Zealand. Jeff Forrest (12) brings down his man. The other Scots are K. C. Fyfe, W. R. Logan, W. A. Burnett, R. W. Shaw and J. M. Kerr.

106. 1934. England v Scotland. J. L. Cotter makes a break and looks for support.

107. 1931. Wales v Scotland. George Wood has the ball and, despite his nearness to touch, keeps it in play. Amongst the forwards can be seen J. W. Allan, J. A. Beattie, A. W. Walker, D. Crichton-Miller and J. S. Wilson.

108. 1927. Scotland *v* New South Wales. Max Simmers evades E. E. Ford. H. D. Greenlees comes across in support.

109. 1925. Scotland *v* England. R. A. Howie jumps for the ball. D. S. Davies and J. W. Scott are behind him. The England players were numbered, no. 5 being J. S. Tucker.

110. 1925. Scotland *v* England. A. C. Wallace, although tackled by the full-back, scores in the corner. The touch judge, well placed to give a decision, was R. Welsh, Vice-President of the SRU. The density of the crowd at this opening match at Murrayfield is obvious.

111. 1924. Scotland *v* Ireland. Spot the ball? Dan Drysdale gets his kick away in spite of an unorthodox tackle. Herbert Waddell and Ian Smith are close at hand. Amongst others, Willie Bryce and John Bannerman watch the flight of the ball.

112. 1920. Scotland *v* Wales. G. L. Pattullo, the full back (identified by his club stockings), makes a tackle with A. W. Angus in support.

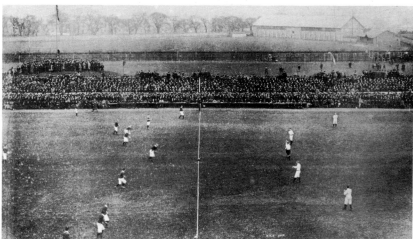

113. 1892. Scotland *v* England. Prominent in the left background is the former archery mound which was removed in 1947. In the background, the Grange cricket field was the area used by the Edinburgh Wanderers and Edinburgh University clubs.

Andrews University absorbed University College, Dundee, whose name was dropped from the roll of member clubs. Another access bridge to the car park was built and a new issue of Debentures was issued to finance all the recent alterations to the stand and ground. The seating capacity of the stand was given as 15,228. It was decided to remove the War Memorial Arch from Inverleith to a suitable position at Murrayfield.

Scottish clubs did not support an IB move to reduce the value of a drop goal to 3 points. The Home Countries Board was asked to debate the question of the broadcast of International matches.

The name of a Scottish referee was withdrawn from the Panel because he reversed his decision to send a player off in an International match. The RFU wrote protesting that only Irish referees were being selected for the Calcutta Cup games.

« 1937–38 »

President: A. A. Lawrie (Edinburgh Wanderers and Fettesian-Lorettonians)
Vice-President: Dr W. H. Welsh (Merchistonians)

At the suggestion of the Committee, the President, being deeply involved in the arrangements for the wing stand additions, was invited to take office for a further year and was re-elected.

At the AGM a revised set of Bye-Laws was approved. These contained conditions to be met by new applicants for membership of the Union: (i) the maximum number of clubs to be 70; (ii) new applicants must have been members of their District Union for at least 12 years; held tenure of a ground with adequate playing facilities; have a playing membership of at least 60 during the 6 previous seasons and have at least 2 teams playing a minimum of 14 games per season. It was agreed that the Midlands District should have a representative on the Committee.

The following clubs were admitted (the first new members admitted since 1922–23): Perthshire and Hutchesons' Grammar School FP. Old Larchfieldians, being defunct, was removed from the roll.

Murrayfield Ice Rink and Sports Stadium Ltd sought to feu a portion of the car park area, but the Committee was not in favour of the application. It was decided to build a Committee Box in the stand.

Ayr RFC was permitted to present a Cup at its Sevens. A request from the River Plate RU to have a team sent out was refused because of the coming heavy programme. A request from the Chicago Club, Illinois, to tour in Britain was passed to the Home Countries Board. An itinerary for the Australian tour in 1939–40 was issued by the Home Countries Tour Committee.

« 1938–39 »

President: Dr W. H. Welsh (Merchistonians)
Vice-President: P. Munro, MP (London Scottish)

Bearsden RFC announced its resignation from the Union. The Midlands DU was represented on the Union Committee. The Wigtownshire club was given permission to transfer from the South-West to the Glasgow and District RU. D. K. Duff was appointed Official Consultant Engineer and Architect to the Union. Edinburgh Wanderers were granted permission to erect training lights at their own expense.

A request from the Heart of Midlothian FC for the use of Murrayfield for

127

certain important fixtures was not entertained. It was decided that an existing surplus from the Edinburgh and District Union Sevens at Dam Head should be shared by the existing clubs who had participated in such Tournaments.

Because of the political situation Edinburgh University was refused permission to play three matches in Germany and a proposed annual match between the University students of France and Scotland was not considered since the Home Countries had again refused to resume fixtures with the FFR. However, a Home Countries University tour to New Zealand in 1940 was agreed to.

« 1939–40 »

President: P.Munro, MP (London Scottish)
Vice-President: Dr H.O.Smith (Watsonians)

Boroughmuir was admitted to membership of the Union.

Edinburgh University was advised not to take part in the proposed tour of New Zealand in view of the worsening political situation. It was agreed to resume relations with France and an offer was made to play a match in Paris on 1 January 1940.

The outbreak of the War in September 1939 caused the abandonment of the Australian tour, the team returning home without a game being played. The Committee at once decided: (a) that all fixtures should be considered as cancelled; (b) games which could be arranged should be played; (c) contributions to the Union should be remitted; (d) Murrayfield should be offered to the authorities for national purposes and clubs were recommended to follow suit. In fact Murrayfield ground and offices were commandeered by the Military authorities.

It was decided that no SRU XV could play against Service teams fielding Rugby League players.

« 1940–41 »

President: P.Munro, MP (London Scottish)
Vice-President: Dr H.O.Smith (Watsonians)

The death of J.C.Sturrock was recorded. At the AGM the Committee, in view of the prevailing War conditions, proposed that the Bye-Laws be changed to allow the affairs of the Union to be administered by the existing Committee and to dispense with General Meetings until the termination of the National Emergency. This was accepted.

With no income from clubs or matches, there was a substantial deficit for the year and it was agreed that the payment of the interest on Debentures should be postponed.

THE WAR YEARS

Between May 1940 and May 1945 the Minute Book has only two entries. The first, in June 1943, notes the deaths of J.D.Dallas, A.A.Lawrie, G.C.Muir and W.Laidlaw but makes no reference to the death of the President, Pat Munro, who died in May 1942. The other Minute reveals that Murrayfield had been released back to the Union by the War Department and that a Services game, Scotland v England, would be played there in March 1945.

128

In 1945–46, the deaths of M.C.Morrison, R.T.Neilson and R.D.Rainie were recorded. Vacancies on the Committee were filled by J.M.Mackenzie, W.A. McKinnon and R.J.Hogg.

The State of Emergency was now regarded as terminated. The District Unions were encouraged to restart the game during the coming season and matches were arranged and played against, England, Wales, Ireland and a NZ Army XV. The proceeds from the last-mentioned match were handed over to NZ War Charities. No caps were awarded for those games. A French fixture was held over till the following season.

Edinburgh University was permitted to tour in the South of France but a request for permission to send a team to Prague was not granted. The AGM was arranged for May 1946 at which the original Bye-Laws would be restored.

« 1946–47 »

President: Dr H.O.Smith (Watsonians)
Vice-President: R.L.Scott (Hawick)

Edinburgh Borderers, not without dissent, were allowed to change their name to Trinity Borderers. The Secretary-Treasurer, H.M.Simson, coping valiantly with an overload of work, asked that an assistant be appointed. The Head Groundsman, A. E. Sellars, was presented with a cheque for 100 guineas (£105) in recognition of his fifty years' service to the Union.

The aftermath of the war was still casting shadows over the population; clothes rationing was still in force and an allocation of clothing coupons was made to the District Unions to assist their member clubs in the purchase of rugby kits.

A Hospitality Sub-committee was set up.

The French fixture was resumed. It was agreed to award caps for this match and decided that, in future, this practice was to be observed and a cap awarded to any man who played for Scotland. Centre stand prices were fixed at 15 shillings (75p) and ground admittance at two shillings and sixpence (12½p).

An original Union instruction to clubs to confine playing matches to Saturdays or public holidays was, after a meeting with the Secretary of State for Scotland, amended to allow play on mid-week evenings. Several requests from clubs seeking help in restarting after the war were sympathetically considered, but a request from one club to be allowed to run a football pool was not granted. George Heriot's School FP received permission to provide a Cup for their Under-20 Sevens.

Heart of Midlothian FC, faced with the possibility of meeting Hibernian FC in the final of the Scottish Cup, asked and received permission for the use of Murrayfield for the final. In the event, however, that confrontation did not materialise. Arrangements were announced for the 1947–48 Australian tour. It was mentioned that the anticipated costs would be £23,770 compared with the £12,584 cost of the 1935–36 NZ tour.

President: R.L.Scott (Hawick)
Vice-President: J.M.Mackenzie (Fettesian-Lorettonians)

F.A.Wright, CA (Edinburgh Academicals) was appointed Treasurer and Assistant Secretary with the consideration that he might succeed to the combined post of Secretary-Treasurer. Those District Unions housing Australian Tour games were asked to appoint a local doctor and a dentist to attend the matches in their area.

It was decided that the Debenture payments should be brought up to date and that various Union salaries should be increased. Dumfries RFC were allowed to change from the South to the Glasgow and District Union.

A request for an Edinburgh XV to visit France was refused because of the National Emergency. Edinburgh and Glasgow Universities were permitted to entertain a tour from Paris University.

Another allocation of clothing coupons was made to the District Unions. Two lots of food parcels from the Otago RFU were accepted with gratitude and distributed to the players taking part in the Final Trial and the English game.

The half-backs, selected for the opening French match, requested permission to arrive and practice together on the Thursday before the game. Permission was refused, but all players selected were informed that a practice would be arranged for the Friday for those who chose to turn up. It was agreed that, following the Irish game in Dublin, the Scottish party should fly back to Edinburgh.

Permission was given to the Lord Provost of Edinburgh to hold Highland Games at Murrayfield. However, a request from Scottish Speedway to lay down a dirt track around the main pitch was not considered.

Kelso were given permission to present a cup at their Sevens. The close season was set as 1 May to 31 August. A request regarding affiliation, from the Union de Rugby Chile, received a courteous refusal. It was intimated that South Africa, New Zealand and Australia were to be admitted to the IB with one seat each while England's representation was reduced to two. It was not yet agreed to admit France.

The deaths of A.R.Don Wauchope and J.D.Boswell were noted.

President: J.M.Mackenzie (Fettesian-Lorettonians)
Vice-President: J.N.Shaw (Edinburgh Academicals)

Musselburgh RFC were admitted to membership of the Union. Trinity Borderers were allowed to return to their original title, i.e. Edinburgh Borderers.

The President, *ex officio*, was to be a member of all sub-committees. The insurance on Murrayfield was increased to £90,000. A loudspeaker and telephone service was installed at the ground. With the deepest regret, the death was recorded of A.E.Sellars, the Head Groundsman for over 50 years. Eventually, the post was given to his son, T.S.Sellars. The Edinburgh and District Union was given permission to play Northumberland RU and the Paris-Edinburgh match was approved, but with many conditions attached.

The Committee agreed to support the setting up of a Home Countries Tours Committee. Among other changes in the Laws, it was agreed to reduce the value of a drop goal from 4 points to 3 points.

The deaths of W.P.Scott and C.J.N.Fleming were recorded.

« 1949–50 »

President: J. N. Shaw (Edinburgh Academicals)
Vice-President: J. C. H. Ireland (Glasgow High School FP)

At the AGM, a change in the Bye-Laws increased the South representation on the Committee to two. Messrs Simson and Wright drew the Committee's attention to the difficulties created by the Union affairs being handled by two part-time officials and, eventually, it was decided that: (a) the Union should eventually have its own office at Murrayfield and have one full-time official, with the title of Secretary-Treasurer; (b) this combined office to be offered to F. A. Wright after the retiral of H. M. Simson. Mr Simson would retire on pension after a period of two years. For the time being, an office in Coates Crescent was purchased so that both the Secretary and Treasurer would be housed in the same building.

It was laid down that the name of the South Club, when playing matches, should be 'Scottish Borders'. Edinburgh Wanderers were given permission to install training lights at the back of the stand at Murrayfield.

It was noted that Referees must be members of a club under the jurisdiction of one of the Home Unions. A South proposal to establish a Scottish Schools RU, with a view to making Schoolboy Internationals more fully representative, did not meet with approval. A detailed scheme for the distribution of International tickets was formulated. Food parcels continued to arrive from New Zealand and were balloted out to clubs.

« 1950–51 »

President: J. C. H. Ireland (Glasgow High School FP)
Vice-President: D. Drysdale (London Scottish)

Clubs admitted to membership were Trinity Academicals and Aberdeen Wanderers.

A Ladies' Room was opened in the stand using what had formerly been the Secretary's area. A new Committee badge was produced; each member purchased his own. A sub-committee found itself discussing many proposed changes in the Laws and ended its remit by recommending a return to the former practice of making alterations only at three-year intervals.

The War Memorial Arch was cleaned up and a simple additional script added for the 1939–45 War losses.

The President was authorised to spend £30 on the entertainment of the players in Paris. Some discussion arose over a new scrummage rule and, eventually, it was reluctantly agreed to select a scrum which could pack down as 3-4-1. A new Instructional Film on the game, sponsored by the Home Unions, was now available.

The Minutes noted that a new Ice Rink, built on the Car Park area, would shortly be opening. The deaths of R. L. Scott and R. C. Greig were noted.

« 1951–52 »

President: D. Drysdale (London Scottish)
Vice-President: F. J. C. Moffat (Watsonians)

H. M. Simson, WS, was entertained upon his retiral after 30 years' service to the Union. The death of J. G. Y. Buchanan, the long-serving Chief Steward, was noted. It was decided that the duties of that Office should now be handled primarily by the Secretary. The death of Dr J. R. C. Greenlees was also recorded.

Clubs admitted to membership were Harris Academy FP and Royal (Dick) Veterinary College. The Perthshire club were allowed to amalgamate with the Perth Academicals club.

In spite of strong pressure from the BBC, permission to televise the English match was refused. It was apparent that the RFU had suffered a loss in 'gates' when allowing matches to be televised. During this season, first mention was made of the possible installation of undersoil heating for the main pitch. It was decided not to proceed with the project because of the heavy initial expense involved.

A start was made to halve the size of the standing steps of the embankment. The tennis courts, being uneconomical, were removed and the area used as an additional Car Park.

United College FC were refused permission to tour in Sweden, the Swedish RU being unknown and not affiliated to any Home Union. West of Scotland were given permission to tour France but were advised that because they were trying to raise funds to obtain a playing-field, a more useful purpose would be served by playing a match at home. The tour did not materialise.

The Ticket Allocation Sub-committee reported heavy over-application for all Stand tickets. It was decided to have all photographs of previous International teams reduced to uniform size, bound in suitable volumes and kept in the Committee Room. Meetings were arranged with headmasters to discuss methods of furthering the interests of the game amongst young players.

« 1952–53 »

President: F. J. C. Moffat (Watsonians)
Vice-President: M. A. Allan (Glasgow Academicals)

Leith Academicals and Old Grammarians were admitted to membership of the Union.

The AGM discussed at length a proposal from two Edinburgh clubs suggesting that a basic change in the composition of the Selection Committee was advisable, but, eventually, a vote showed that no such change was desired. Championship conditions in France continued to concern the Home Unions and the SRU, while noting that two original choices for the French XV against Scotland had been withdrawn, had to query the retention of a third player who was suspected of having played professionally. No further alteration was made, but the player concerned was not chosen again.

In lighter mood, the Committee discussed the question of the Scottish team and Committee perhaps visiting the 'Folies Bergères', on the Friday evening before the match. Since it was felt that '. . . the "Folies Bergères" was an emotional type of entertainment . . .' it was agreed that an arrangement should be made for the party to attend a musical comedy of a light nature which finished about 10.30 pm! In the event it was too late to change; the 'Folies Bergères' were visited—and Scotland lost 5–11.

The Committee accepted that the New Zealand tourists would be accompanied by an Official Press Representative, but stuck firmly to its custom that no Press representatives be permitted to attend any official social function. Allocation of stand tickets continued to be a worry, the demand always exceeding the supply.

The BBC continued to press for live television coverage of International Matches. The RFU was seen to be in favour but the other Home Unions had reservations. An invitation to Scotland to take part in a Tournament in Bucharest, made by the Romanian Rugby Federation, was declined. A cup offered by the Lord Provost of Edinburgh for the Edinburgh Clubs Sevens was accepted.

The deaths were recorded of Dr A.T.Sloan and H.S.Dixon.

« 1953–54 »

President: M.A.Allan (Glasgow Academicals)
Vice-President: J.M.Bannerman (Glasgow High School FP)

In view of the impending retiral of F.A.Wright, J.Law was appointed as Joint Secretary and Treasurer during the year and the property at 6 Coates Crescent was purchased for the use of the Union. It was decided to inaugurate an Inter-District competition, such matches to be played on a Saturday. A new agreement was reached with the BBC whereby the New Zealand match would be televised live.

The Watsonians and Heriot's FP clubs were invited to play a special match at Murrayfield to provide evidence on new scrummage Laws which were to be introduced. The production and distribution of the match programmes was put in the hands of Programme Production Ltd.

« 1954–55 »

President: J.M.Bannerman (Glasgow High School FP)
Vice-President: R.M.Meldrum (Royal High School FP)

F.A.Wright had now retired from the offices of Secretary and Treasurer. D.A.Thom withdrew, on principle, from the Selection Committee because of a decision to adhere to the selection of a 3-2-3 scrum formation.

There was continued discussion amongst the Home Unions on the subject of live television for International matches. The SRU, although now permitting a limited amount, was still very cautious about full coverage being made during the matches.

The Romanian Rugby Federation again invited Scotland to play Romania in Bucharest. After discussion the offer was courteously declined, one factor being the heavy International programme that lay ahead. Another request from the New Zealand Union for a Scottish visit was passed to the Tours Committee. Improvements were made to the dressing-room showers and plans were approved for a new Committee Room suite in the stand.

It was agreed in principle that it was wrong for players to stand down from playing in club matches on Saturdays prior to International matches. A Schools' Liaison Sub-committee was initiated and a Rugby Coaching Course set up.

A journalist, who had been paid for rugby articles but who no longer wrote about the game, was given permission to play for his club. It was agreed to take part in a Four Home Nations match in Dublin to assist in the cost of renovating the stand at Lansdowne Road.

The death of the oldest ex-President, the Rev. R.S.Davidson, was noted.

« 1955—56 »

President: R.M.Meldrum (Royal High School FP)
Vice-President: W.M.Simmers (Glasgow Academicals)

Jordanhill School FP were admitted to membership.

A motion at the AGM to elect two Past Presidents to the Committee failed. The playing of Inter-District matches on Saturdays was put before the Districts because the Edinburgh clubs strongly disapproved. After the opinions of the other Districts were made known, however, no change was made.

Hitherto the SRU had, as a matter of principle, taken no fee for any match featured on radio or television, but it was agreed that, henceforth the sum offered by the BBC would be accepted. The positioning and cost of the proposed new Committee suite was still under consideration, but the necessary electric cable to provide adequate heating for the dressing-rooms was installed.

A request from West of Scotland FC for financial aid to purchase their proposed new field could not be met in view of the financial burden still carried by the Union on its Debentures. A satisfactory Schools' Coaching Course was carried out at Fettes College.

Glasgow University were allowed to accept the Cunningham Cup for an Inter-University competition. Note was taken of an approaching tour by the South African Universities.

The possibility of a tour in Canada was regarded favourably, but a suggestion from the Italian Rugby Federation that Scotland should take part in a rugby tournament in the Rome Olympics in 1960 was rejected.

The death of J.M.Dykes was noted.

« 1956—57 »

President: W.M.Simmers (Glasgow Academicals)
Vice-President: R.J.Hogg (Gala)

Morgan Academy FP were admitted to membership.

At the AGM a considerable number of amendments to the Bye-Laws was proposed by Edinburgh Academicals, supported by other Edinburgh clubs. Discussion on these proposals was halted by the passing of an amendment which referred the subject of a review on the Bye-Laws to a specially selected Sub-committee.

The new Committee suite was now completed. Finance was causing concern and a sub-committee was set up to consider conditions for issuing a new kind of Debenture. At the AGM it was agreed to retain the practice of playing the Inter-District games on a Saturday.

Agreement was again reached on the arrangements, dates and fees for the broadcasting and televising of Scottish matches. The success of placing BBC cameras under the roof of the West Stand was noted. Designs for an International player's blazer complete with badge, and also for a Committee tie, were accepted.

134

President: R. J. Hogg (Gala)
Vice-President: Dr D. J. MacMyn (London Scottish)

Jordanhill Training College were admitted as a member of the Union.

The proposals of the Sub-committee on amendments to the Bye-Laws were passed at the AGM. These included: (a) the deletion of the maximum of 70 member clubs in the Union; (b) District representatives were now to be elected by clubs voting at their own District Election Meetings; (c) no member of the Committee or member of a club under the jurisdiction of the Union was to be permitted to write any article to the press on Rugby Football, '. . . except by special permission of the Committee no member . . . shall be permitted to Broadcast on Radio or Television on Rugby Football'; (d) the Committee was given the power to co-opt not more than two Past Presidents . . . whose services might be useful.

The new Debenture Scheme was carried out successfully. The English match, in March 1958, was honoured by the presence of HM Queen Elizabeth. Touch judges in International matches were now to be chosen from active first-class referees.

An Edinburgh club member was suspended *sine die* for having accepted a fee for taking part in a television programme on Rugby. An invitation from the Fédération Belge de Rugby to take part in a Rugby tournament in the World Fair in Brussels was declined.

President: Dr D. J. MacMyn (London Scottish)
Vice-President: R. K. Cuthbertson (Edinburgh Academicals)

Clarkston RFC were admitted to membership of the Union.

The Centenary of Edinburgh Academicals FC was referred to at the AGM.

The gift, from two Aberdeen brothers, of a silver quaich, to be used at the Calcutta Cup Dinner, was noted with appreciation. It was decided not to offer the use of Murrayfield for the Empire Games.

The possibility of erecting floodlighting at Murrayfield was investigated but found to be too expensive. The Committee, with the knowledge that the Welsh match had only been saved by the extensive use of coke braziers, considered the use of under-soil heating such as existed at the Everton FC ground. Whilst the subject was still under investigation, the Committee was greatly gratified to receive an offer from C. A. Hepburn to install such a system entirely at his own expense. Needless to say, his offer was accepted and the system was ready for use before the start of the new season.

It was decided that clubs might be offered some financial support for specific purposes such as the provision of new grounds, pavilions or stands or for improvements to their existing accommodation. Terms were now agreed with the BBC to televise five matches. An offer by the Army to erect two Bailey Bridges across the Water of Leith, to ease the traffic leaving the Car Park area, was accepted.

It was decided that a surgeon as well as a doctor should be invited to attend matches at Murrayfield. It was also decided not to allow marquees to be erected for the sale of alcohol inside the grounds.

Some far-reaching changes were made in the Laws which allowed a catch to be fumbled; the lifting of a dead ball without first playing it with the foot; and for a player taking a placed kick at goal to place the ball himself.

Support was agreed for a Four Nations Game to celebrate the 50th year of play at Twickenham. A.W.Wilson was appointed Manager of the British Isles Touring Team to Australia and New Zealand.

The death was recorded of F.A.Wright, the Union Auditor and former Secretary and Treasurer.

« 1959–60 »

President: R.K.Cuthbertson (Edinburgh Academicals)
Vice-President: D.S.Kerr (Heriot's FP)

An invitation from South Africa to undertake a short tour was accepted. It was agreed to play an International match against South Africa, followed by two provincial games. This was the first example of a short tour by any country.

After representations had been made by several clubs, it was decided that clubs could seek permission to play football on Sundays outside the UK. H.Waddell and R.W.Shaw were given permission to broadcast at their discretion when they were in New Zealand on IB business. The price of Stand tickets was raised to £1.

The deaths of J.C.Findlay and W.Neilson were noted.

« 1960–61 »

President: D.S.Kerr (Heriot's FP)
Vice-President: R.M.Ledingham (Aberdeen Grammar School FP)

Madras College FP were admitted to the Union.

The efficiency and benefit of the new undersoil heating was commented on. Projects for the future included: (a) a covered enclosure at the north end of the field; (b) floodlighting; (c) another stand over the terracing facing the existing stand; (d) a permanent PA system; (e) a new junior club dressing-room; (f) a players' tea-room.

The Edinburgh Wanderers club were given permission to erect a small stand alongside their pitch.

Membership of the Union was extended to include Affiliate, Ex-Officio and Honorary Members. The Affiliate Members included Debenture Holders and Rugby-playing Schools in Scotland. West of Scotland and other clubs were promised substantial loans for ground and accommodation improvements. A Schools' Liaison Committee was now functioning.

An invitation to tour in Canada was seriously considered. The IB recommended a uniform manner of numbering International Teams. Glasgow and District Union was permitted to run a knock-out competition.

« 1961–62 »

President: R.M.Ledingham (Aberdeen Grammar School FP)
Vice-President: A.R.Stewart (Jed-Forest)

The Aberdeen Academicals club were admitted to membership.

At the AGM mention was made of the much-improved financial situation of the Union. This was largely due to the completion of much restoration and repair work and improvements carried out at Murrayfield since the end of the War. Appreciative references were made to the great work done at Inverleith and Murrayfield by the two groundsmen, A.E.Sellars and T.S.Sellars. Their efforts had been instrumental in ensuring that no matches had been cancelled during their spell of duty.

There was continued investigation into the possibility of building another stand, installing floodlighting and PA systems. Eventually the stand project was set aside; a PA system was installed and floodlighting at Hughenden proposed.

The BBC were proposing to televise a club match, but this was not agreed to. Radio Television Française was given permission to cover the French match. A request from Edinburgh Corporation to erect a swimming pool in part of the Car Park area was turned down.

The introduction in several areas of Colts XVs was noted. The itinerary for a Canadian tour in the UK was approved and note was taken of a request from the University of British Columbia to undertake a tour in 1963–64.

« 1962–63 »

President: A. R. Stewart (Jed-Forest)
Vice-President: H. Waddell (Glasgow Academicals)

The rentals paid by the clubs using the pitches at Murrayfield were raised. Clubs were warned not to make their fixture cards available to Pools firms. It was urged that stronger action be taken against the activities of Rugby League scouts.

The Canadian visit took place, but it was marred by poor weather conditions and the absence of several of their best players. Later, the Committee accepted an invitation for a Scottish tour of five matches in Canada during May 1964. Tours, at club level, by San Isidro AC and the University of British Columbia were accepted. London Scottish were permitted to play games in France and Holland.

It was finally decided to proceed with the installation of floodlighting at Hughenden and cash was given to improve the existing system at Kelso, where eventually two South matches were played. Messrs Pillans & Wilson were given the contract to produce the programmes for the International matches.

The position of journalists who wrote on rugby matters was discussed, but eventually no change in their exclusion from membership of a club was accepted. The Harlem Globetrotters were given the use of Murrayfield.

There was the annual discussion on the choice of Home Country Internationals which the BBC were to screen. A silver quaich was presented to the Treasurer of the Welsh RU in recognition of his work on reduction of tax to the Unions.

It was agreed that clubs should experiment with the suggested Law which restricted the kicking of the ball directly into touch. The question of a rotation of the dates of the Home Countries Internationals was now being pursued. Scotland wished only to retain the third week in March for the England match. Congratulations were offered to A. R. Smith elected Captain of the British Isles Touring Team to South Africa.

The death of Sir J. M. Mackenzie was noted.

President: H. Waddell (Glasgow Academicals)
Vice-President: W. R. Logan (Edinburgh Wanderers)

Broughton FP were admitted to membership.

At the AGM, deep appreciation was expressed at the success of the electric blanket, which allowed 12 matches to be played at Murrayfield during the extremely severe spell of frost which halted rugby for almost three months. It was decided to move the Union offices from Coates Crescent to premises to be built inside the stand at Murrayfield.

The Committee considered a suggestion that a National Club Championship should be established. This was rejected as being contrary to the policy of the Union and, in any case, it was felt that there were already too many fixtures.

It was agreed that a Press conference should be held to announce Teams and answer relevant questions. The Canadian tour, managed by C. W. Drummond and H. S. P. Monro, had been highly successful, but comment was made on a need for better refereeing. It had not been possible to halt at Bermuda to play a match there.

No objection was raised to a proposed visit by the University of Toronto. Messrs Rowans announced the cessation of publication of their annual *Rugby Guide*. The Committee noted with pleasure the conferring of the OBE on H. F. McLeod.

President: W. R. Logan (Edinburgh Wanderers)
Vice-President: D. A. Thom (London Scottish)

The Union offices were now established at Murrayfield. A proposal, in Committee, to have two Vice-Presidents, so that longer Committee experience might be gained, was not accepted, although the point was noted.

A BBC suggestion that Scotland should vary its normal 'strip' to aid identification of the players in the Irish match was discussed but not accepted. The price of stand tickets was to be increased to 25 Shillings (£1.25).

Some considerable discussion took place over the future engagement or replacement of T. S. Sellars, the groundsman, who had reached the age of 65 during the season. It was noted that loans to clubs had reached a total of £20,000, still normally interest free.

A decision on the provision of floodlighting at a ground in Edinburgh was held over. Jehovah's Witnesses were granted use of the ground at Murrayfield for a two-day meeting.

A plaque was approved in recognition of the gift of the under-soil heating from C. A. Hepburn. The first definite steps were made with the RFU to celebrate their Centenary and that of the first International match in 1871.

A considerable number of new Laws relating to scrummages, line-outs and penalty kicks were made by the IB. Later, the Committee agreed to propose to the IB that no major changes be made in the Laws during the next decade. The arrangements for a short tour by South Africa to Ireland and Scotland were settled.

« 1965–66 »

President: D. A. Thom (London Scottish)
Vice-President: M. S. Stewart (Stewart's FP)

The possibility of providing a house for the Secretary at Murrayfield was investigated. It was decided to erect a new scoring-box. The provision of a tea-room for International players had been so successful that steps were taken to find a larger area inside the pavilion for a new tea-room. The former office accommodation in Coates Crescent was sold during the season.

A coaching course for schoolmasters, held at Fettes College, was very successful. During the season, the future of Schools' rugby was discussed at length and, eventually, it was agreed to encourage the establishment of a Schoolboys' International against England during a holiday period.

Messrs R. W. Forsyth were given financial and secretarial help to continue the publication of their annual *Rugby Record*. A recommendation by the Finance Sub-committee that the investment of the Union funds should be put into the hands of a recognised firm was agreed to. There were now many applications before the Committee for loans from clubs seeking to improve their ground amenities and it was essential to have the Union's finances firmly controlled. Full insurance coverage was now arranged for the travel of the team members, reserves, touch judge and Secretary.

Selkirk were advised not to employ a pavilion attendant who had been a former Rugby League player. The Anglo-Scots v Scottish Select Trial was arranged to be played at Crystal Palace. London Scottish were given permission to play both a Dutch and a Californian touring team. Edinburgh and District was also allowed to entertain Dutch tourists.

There was the annual discussion with the BBC over their television coverage of International matches and club matches which was clearly increasing. The Home Countries agreed that their Panel referees should be invited to referee prominent fixtures outside their own country and also that French referees should be invited to take charge of matches at Provincial and District level.

England, who were making extensive preparations to celebrate their Union's Centenary, agreed to play a second fixture against Scotland in 1971, in Edinburgh, to celebrate the Centenary of the first International at Raeburn Place in 1871. The SRU noted the approach of their own Centenary and eventually invited Messrs R. Ironside and A. M. C. Thorburn to prepare a History of the Union.

The payment of £2,500 by a commercial firm to the Welsh Youth RU was strongly disapproved. A Scottish club was refused permission to affix an advertising board to their stand although the payment at normal rates for an advertisement in the club's official programme was allowed.

The death was recorded of the late Secretary, H. M. Simson.

« 1966–67 »

President: M. S. Stewart (Stewart's FP)
Vice-President: R. Tod (Edinburgh Academicals)

The Centenaries of the West of Scotland, Glasgow Academicals and Edinburgh University clubs were noted at the AGM. At the same meeting, two motions were defeated: (a) that an official Club Championship be initiated not later than the beginning of the 1968–69 season; (b) that an independent committee be set up to examine the present-day structure of Scottish rugby.

The plan to build a house at Murrayfield for the Secretáry was abandoned and a house at Murrayfield Gardens, to be administered by the Field Committee, was purchased for his use.

Steel goalposts were purchased for the main pitch at Murrayfield. Dr Charles Hepburn offered to bear the entire cost of installing an up-to-date floodlighting system for Murrayfield. The offer was received with pleasure, but many reservations were voiced about the project.

The Inter-City match was transferred to Murrayfield because of frost in Glasgow. It was noted that loans to clubs now totalled £24,000 with a further £12,500 promised.

A new International players' tea room was opened in the stand. A request from Edinburgh Wanderers to have its rooms improved was not granted and there was a suggestion that the club might consider a move from Murrayfield. The after-match official Dinners were moved to the MacRobert Pavilion at Ingliston.

The Scottish Schools' RU was now established and the SRU, in recognising its existence, produced a comprehensive Constitutional Agreement of Control. A Scotland v England Schools' International match was arranged to be played at Murrayfield in April 1967. St Louis RFC, Missouri, and two Argentine clubs were given permission to seek fixtures in Scotland.

In spite of the political difficulties, an invitation to the Scottish Borders club to have a short tour in South Africa was accepted and proved very successful. It was noted that the Orkney (Kirkwall) RFC had been established.

Full coverage by the BBC radio and TV was now accepted. The Midlands District RU was encouraged to make a tour in Lancashire.

It was agreed to take part in a Four Nations game at Twickenham as part of the RFU Centenary celebrations. The rotation of International fixtures was raised again and the SRU, although still reluctant to give up the March date for the English match, decided to accept the proposed schedule.

Full interchange of referees now existed and M. Bernard Marie from France officiated at the North and Midlands v Edinburgh match at Dundee. Pleasure was noted at the conferring of the OBE upon A. I. Dickie, the former referee, and at the appointment of M. J. Campbell-Lamerton as Captain of the BI touring team.

« 1967–68 »

President: R. Tod (Edinburgh Academicals)
Vice-President: W. Nicholson (West of Scotland)

The Alloa and Dundee University clubs were admitted to membership.

J. Thain took over as Head Groundsman upon the retiral of T. S. Sellars. A part-time assistant at Murrayfield was appointed to relieve work on the Secretary and District Secretaries. A new score box came into operation.

The Trustees of the Middlesex Sevens offered £500 to any Trust Fund set up to assist a schoolboy who was seriously injured in a school game. Later, the SRU decided to establish their own Fund to cover such deserving cases. A donation of £1,000 was made towards the running of the forthcoming Commonwealth Games in Edinburgh.

Loans to clubs had reached £34,500. An offer by a brewery firm to act as guarantors for a loan sought by Alloa RFC was held to be against the IB ruling.

Clubs were asked to use the experimental change in Law 27 relating to kicking to touch on the full from within the kicker's half of the field, but later reports showed a lack of interest by the clubs. It was agreed that the system for fixtures on numbered Saturdays should operate from season 1970–71.

An International player who had published a book *Improve Your Rugby*, before submitting proofs to the SRU, was asked for an explanation and reminded that his amateur status would be affected if he retained any of the proceeds.

A short tour by Australia to Ireland and Scotland was accepted as was an invitation for a short tour in Argentina. The Committee discussed the development in other countries of the coaching of International and other teams.

Television fees were used to give grants to full SRU member clubs and certain District Union clubs. The principle of rotation of International matches was accepted to start in 1973–74. For the first time, a discussion took place regarding replacements for injured players in International matches.

A. W. Wilson presented the Union with the gift of a Maori war canoe which he had received when Manager of the BI touring team in New Zealand.

The elevation of J. M. Bannerman to the peerage was recorded.

« 1968–69 »

President: W. Nicholson (West of Scotland)
Vice-President: G. G. Crerar (Glasgow Academicals)

A Coaching Sub-committee was set up. Later, it was complimented on the issue of its *Coaching News*. Players were asked to assemble by 3 pm on the Thursday before an International. The SRU, however, were disturbed at the coaching sessions adopted elsewhere although the IB decided that squad sessions were acceptable.

The inclusion of the Anglo-Scots in the Inter-District tournament was discussed but held over. The designs for a Scottish touring tie and badges for blazer and jersey were approved. The Scottish Schools' RU also passed a design for a badge for its jerseys.

A scheme for reports by clubs on referees was to be instituted. Dr C. A. Hepburn was still interested in providing floodlighting at Murrayfield.

H. F. McLeod, who had started a sport outfitters business, was advised that he could not sell rugby boots bearing his name, so he re-labelled it as the Abbot boot—that being his nickname when on tour with the BI team. Edinburgh Wanderers sought permission to build a clubhouse of its own inside Murrayfield but received a fairly stern refusal.

It was decided to have ball boys on duty at Internationals. It was also agreed that the price of centre stand tickets should be increased to thirty shillings (£1.50), but that for end-stand seats should be reduced to £1. It was decided not to nominate a Public Relations Officer but press conferences should be called when matters of importance had been agreed on.

The Member clubs were to receive a fifty per cent increase in their share from television income. The Union had now some £50,000 out on loan to clubs. The IB brought in the new touch law in Law 27 and permitted up to two replacements for injured players in Internationals. Such replacement players were to receive caps if they took part in the game. The IB also began to look at metric system measurements in the Laws.

The deaths were recorded of R. M. Ledingham, D. S. Kerr and Lord Bannerman.

« 1969–70 »

President: G.G.Crerar (Glasgow Academicals)
Vice-President: R.W.Shaw (Glasgow High School FP)

Perthshire Academicals club changed their name to Perthshire RFC. At the AGM a motion was passed that the Committee investigate the introduction of a system of competitive club rugby in Scotland. Accordingly, throughout the season, a sub-committee maintained continual contact with District Unions and clubs in all regions and were in a position to table an appropriate motion at the next AGM.

The possibility of installing floodlighting at Murrayfield was investigated, but the project had to be abandoned when, in June 1970, Dr Hepburn advised the SRU that, because of other commitments and the state of the stock market, he had to withdraw his offer of financing the project.

The idea of appointing a coach for the International XV was seriously debated but held over meantime. The President, the Scottish Captain (F.A.L. Laidlaw) and D.M.D.Rollo were all permitted to appear in television programmes.

The South African match at Murrayfield successfully took place despite demonstrations. The Committee, however, was perturbed at being faced with an invoice from the Police Force which was some £1,100 greater than that for a normal attendance. The Universities and Colleges were given an allocation out of the BBC fee.

A successful tour to Argentina was carried out. The itinerary of a short tour to Australia was settled. The Barbarians played a Scottish XV at Murrayfield, the proceeds going to the Commonwealth Games Fund.

The IB issued a revised and simplified set of Laws. The restricted kicking to touch was now accepted. The IB recommended the formation of a Five Countries Committee which would include France, which country, incidentally, was very keen to start B International matches.

Two Four Nations matches were agreed; the first for the SRU Centenary in 1973 at Murrayfield and the second for the Irish RFU Centenary in 1975 at Lansdowne Road.

Dr D.W.C.Smith was appointed Manager for the BI tour to New Zealand in 1971.

« 1970–71 »

President: R.W.Shaw (Glasgow High School FP)
Vice-President: A.H.Brown (Heriot's FP)

Dumfries were admitted to membership.

At the AGM, the Committee was authorised to produce a scheme to initiate League rugby in Scotland. The clubs were invited to subscribe to the newly-formed Benevolent Fund for Disabled Players. The Edinburgh and District Union gave the sum of £2,100, which represented their surplus from previous Sevens tournaments at Murrayfield.

A request that clubs be allowed to play on Sundays in England and at home was not granted. Proposed B matches with France were to be accepted but no full caps were to be given.

Some form of National Sevens tournament at Murrayfield was considered but laid aside in view of the heavy programme in the approaching Centenary year. A suggestion from the Edinburgh and District Union that their Com-

142

mittee members be allowed to attend the SRU AGM without vote was rejected.

The new Meadowbank Stadium was used to stage the Edinburgh v Anglo-Scots game under the floodlights. It was decided that loans to clubs should be frozen at the present level, but loans for the purchase of ground would certainly be considered.

There was still opposition in Committee to having a coach for the International team, but eventually W. Dickinson of Jordanhill was invited to assist the Captain during training.

The Centenary of the 1871 International was duly celebrated as follows: (a) a granite memorial stone, the gift of an Aberdeen man, was set up at Raeburn Place and unveiled by Miss Buchanan, the daughter of Angus Buchanan who scored the first try in the 1871 match. This event took place at a special cocktail party held in a marquee at the ground; (b) a special Scotland v England game, for which caps were awarded, was held at Murrayfield on the actual date, 28 March, of the original match. The game was honoured by the presence of HRH Prince Charles and the Prime Minister. An historical booklet on the 1871 match was published. The two compilers, Messrs Ironside and Thorburn, were each presented with a suitably inscribed silver quaich.

« 1971–72 »

President: A. H. Brown (Heriot's FP)
Vice-President: A. W. Wilson (Dunfermline)

The following clubs were admitted to membership: Haddington, Hamilton Academicals, Marr, Old Aloysians and Queens Park FP. The Old Spierians club were permitted to change their name to Garnock. The Jordanhill School FP and Jordanhill College clubs were permitted to amalgamate under the name of Jordanhill RFC.

At the AGM, a Committee motion to set up a form of League system failed only because the Committee had insisted that a two-thirds majority must be met for such a fundamental change. Throughout the season the Committee continued to consider the formulation of an alternative system.

It was decided that the XV could meet at Murrayfield for a session on the Thursday before flying to Wales or Ireland and that training could take place on the Sunday before the English match. It was also agreed that W. Dickinson should again assist at these sessions on the same terms as the previous season.

The Laws Sub-committee was widened to be the Laws and Referees Sub-committee. The B Internationals with France were begun. It was confirmed that no capped players would be selected.

The Irish match in Dublin was cancelled after considerable debate, because of the political situation. London Scottish were given permission to play certain fixtures on Sundays in England. A request from the Rugby Union Writers Club to be allowed to interview the two captains and the referee after a match was refused.

It was agreed to be represented on the new Sports Council for Scotland. The subject of mini-rugby was referred to for the first time. A grant was made from the Benevolent Fund to provide a car for a badly hurt Falkirk schoolboy.

The knock-on Law was amended to permit the so-called 'cricket catch'. R. W. Shaw was awarded the CBE and Dr D. W. C. Smith the OBE.

The death was noted of Dr C. A. Hepburn.

143

President: A.W.Wilson (Dunfermline)
Vice-President: Dr J.R.S.Innes (Aberdeen Grammar School FP)

The following clubs were admitted to membership; Dalziel HSFP and White-craigs. There were three changes of club names: Hillhead High School FP and Royal High School FP became Hillhead and Royal High, respectively, whilst amalgamation saw Stewart's-Melville College FP replace Stewart's FP and Melville College FP.

At the AGM, a Committee motion to establish a system of competitive Rugby in Scotland was faced by two amendments but was eventually passed. The Committee was given powers to arrange the composition of the League Divisions and the fixtures involved.

A new style of presenting the Annual Accounts revealed that 33 member clubs were receiving loans totalling £90,650. It was minuted that the Benevolent Fund had been replaced by a properly constituted Murrayfield Centenary Fund.

This being the Centenary season, the Committee was deeply involved in the successful organisation of many functions and matches. One innovation was the International Seven-a-side Tournament played at Murrayfield. The interval between the semi-final and final was filled in by an exhibition of old-style Rugby played by the Edinburgh Academicals and Royal High clubs, both Founder Members of the Union. A design produced by the Lord Lyon was accepted for the SRU Armorial Bearings. The Irish RFU presented the Union with a beautiful Waterford Glass Chandelier which was placed in the Committee Room.

The question of advertising and sponsorship was discussed and, eventually, Gala were given permission to set up banners at matches not being televised.

It was decided that the Committee would invite members of the Press to attend the International Match Dinners and that the pressmen attached to the New Zealand party should attend functions. The BBC was given permission to interview the Scottish captain for a radio broadcast after the French match. W.Dickinson was re-appointed as Advisor to the Captain.

There was considerable discussion on the playing of National Anthems at International matches, but it was decided that no change should be made in the arrangements. At the request of the FFR it was agreed that the 1974 B International with France at Bayonne should be played on a Sunday.

A Five Nations scheme for the nomination of International referees came into operation. A tremendous amount of work continued to be done by the Schools' Liaison and Coaching Sub-committees.

« 1973–74 »

President: Dr J.R.S.Innes (Aberdeen Grammar School FP)
Vice-President: C.W.Drummond (Melrose)

The following clubs were admitted to membership: Corstorphine, Grangemouth, Hyndland School FP, Lanark, Preston Lodge, St Mungo's Academicals and Uddingston.

The centenaries of the Hawick and Melville College FP (formerly Edinburgh Institution FP) club were noted.

During the season nine persons, being regarded as professional broadcasters or journalists, were permitted to become members of clubs but advised that, although they would be allowed to play, they must not comment on any game in which they took part nor could they hold office in the club. Bye-Law 23, referring to writing and broadcasting, was rewritten. W.Dickinson was again appointed as Advisor to the Captain.

The North and Midlands v Anglo-Scots match was designated as a Trial so that replacements might be nominated if needed, but a suggestion that replacements should be permitted in the forthcoming Championship matches was turned down. The Championship fixtures were registered with Stationers' Hall to ensure their copyright. The Committee issued a statement that they '. . . have agreed in principle to advertising at Murrayfield and will investigate what other forms of controlled financial assistance would be acceptable and of benefit to the game in Scotland'.

A group of former International referees was set up to observe and report on the referees in the pools for Divisions I and II in the Championship. The Committee decided to provide Trophies to the Division winners.

It was agreed to assist the growth of mini-rugby. It was decided to advertise for a Technical Administrator for coaching—J.H.Roxburgh (Jordanhill) was appointed in 1975–76. The home Touch Judge at an International game was henceforth to be an International Panel referee and therefore capable of taking over should the referee be incapacitated.

The Netherlands RB accepted the offer of a match in Scotland, and later, the Belgian Union suggested that in the event of Scotland paying a return visit to the Netherlands, then a second fixture could be played in Belgium. It was agreed that a match in Scotland should be arranged for the Tongan tourists in 1974.

The deaths were noted of W.M.Simmers, M.A.Allan and A.Wemyss.

« 1974–75 »

President: C.W.Drummond (Melrose)
Vice-President: J.H.Orr (Heriot's FP)

The following clubs were admitted to membership: Cumnock, Dalkeith, Drumpellier, Dunbar, Irvine, Lismore, Portobello FP and Strathmore.

At the AGM, a motion allowing play on Sundays was passed, in an amended form, which left the Committee in full control. A separate Referees' Sub-committee was re-established. The Sunday squad sessions were continued. W.Dickinson was appointed as Advisor to the Captain, whilst J.W.Telfer was asked to look after the B International sessions. The Committee, however, was concerned about the increasing demands on the time of the players.

Invitations from Fiji, and later, Canada, for Scotland to visit these countries when returning from the short tour in New Zealand, were regretfully turned down. However, a team was sent to take part in the Sevens Tournament arranged for the Ulster Centenary.

The extraordinary attendance at the Welsh match (over 102,000) raised problems, and eventually the SRU accepted the policy that all matches at Murrayfield should, in future be all-ticket, with a maximum in the region of 70,000. It was observed that the metric system of field markings would come into use the following season.

The Orkney Club were granted permission to play Aberdeen GSFP on a Sunday whilst returning from watching the International match. The conferment of the OBE on A.W.Wilson was noted and the deaths of R.F.Kelly and A.R.Smith were recorded.

« 1975–76 »

President: J.H.Orr (Heriot's FP)
Vice-President: H.S.P.Monro, MP (Langholm)

The Edinburgh Northern, Moray and North Berwick clubs were admitted to membership.

The England match at Murrayfield, in February 1976, was honoured by the presence of HM The Queen, accompanied by the Duke of Edinburgh and The Prince Edward.

Consideration was given to proposals made by the Union's Engineer regarding long-term development at Murrayfield, but, in view of the implications of the Safety of Sports Grounds Act, it was resolved to take no immediate action. The match against France in January 1976 was the first all-ticket game at Murrayfield.

Approval was given to a recommendation by the Finance Sub-committee that, in future, loans to clubs would be restricted to requests for acquisition of land for playing-pitches and that additional loans would not be granted to clubs with outstanding balances of previous loans. A sub-committee, which involved the Vice-President and Special Representatives, was appointed to review the Bye-laws of the Union including the structure of the Committee. During the season the position of the District Unions was considered. It was eventually decided that they should be retained in their existing format.

The Netherlands Rugby Board asked if it might become an Associate Member of the SRU, but, as the Union Bye-Laws did not cover such a possibility, the request was, with regret, turned down. A sincere hope was expressed, however, that cordial links between the two bodies could be maintained. There was discussion on the possibility of repeating the very successful 1973 International Seven-a-side Tournament—the proposed date being April 1978. The proposal came to nothing because of lack of support from the other Unions.

The Australian tour in the UK, which included three fixtures in Scotland, was noted. A fixture for a Scottish XV v Japan was accepted for September 1976. With the approval of the Union, a Scottish Schools' Under-18 XV met an Irish Schools' XV for the first time. The game was played in Dublin.

G.Burrell was nominated (and later accepted) as the Honorary Manager of the British Isles tour to New Zealand in 1977.

« 1976–77 »

President: H.S.P.Monro, MP (Langholm)
Vice-President: Brigadier F.H.Coutts (Melrose)

It was decided that a more flexible policy with regard to loans to clubs should be adopted but that a ceiling of £250,000 should be imposed. Consequent to the lack of support from the other Unions, the plan to stage another International Sevens tournament was abandoned. Possible future development of the Leagues was covered in a paper issued to the clubs, but following reports received by the Committee from meetings held by the clubs, it was agreed to adhere to the existing format of twelve clubs per division.

It was agreed that Scottish players could accept invitations as members of a Select team to play three matches in South Africa to mark the opening of a new ground in Pretoria for the Northern Transvaal RU. The Committee accepted an invitation from the Rugby Union of Japan to undertake a short tour in Japan during the summer of 1977. T.Pearson was appointed Hon. Manager with G.W.Thomson as Hon. Assistant Manager. N.A.MacEwan was appointed as Player/Coach.

It was agreed that Scotland would join with England to receive New Zealand on a short tour in 1979–80. W.Dickinson was appointed as Adviser to the Captain. J.W.Telfer was appointed in a similar capacity to the Captains of the Scottish B xvs and Select xvs.

« 1977—78 »

President: Brigadier F.H.Coutts (Melrose)
Vice-President: A.D.Govan (Stewart's-Melville FP)

The Falkirk and Glenrothes clubs were admitted to the Union.

To ease the work-load on the Secretary-Treasurer, it was decided to appoint a Treasurer in the latter part of the season and also to provide additional offices at Murrayfield for the use of the Coaching Office. The BBC agreed to meet the cost of renewal of the camera platform attached to the stand.

A fresh agreement, covering a three-year period, was entered into with Arena Sports Advertising Ltd for advertising at Murrayfield and at club matches covered by television. An agreement was also reached with the Schweppes Company for a three-year sponsorship of the Club Championship. It was subsequently decided that the monies received would be paid directly to the clubs in such amounts as would be decided from time-to-time.

The question of replacements in Championship and other matches was discussed, but the general view of the Committee was against the use of replacements beyond representative matches—as matters stood at the time. A B International against Ireland was played at Murrayfield in December 1978. N.A.MacEwan was appointed as Adviser to the Captain; J.W.Telfer continued as such for the B xv, whilst D.Grant was appointed for the Under 21 and Select xvs.

It was noted that a tour of the British Isles, by New Zealand in 1978–79, had been arranged in place of the scheduled tour to South Africa, which had been cancelled. An invitation from the Argentine Union to tour here in 1986 was accepted in principle. The Union agreed to the establishment of a Summer Rugby Camp for Schoolboys run in conjunction with the Scottish Schoolboys' Club.

The death of J.A.Beattie was recorded.

« 1978—79 »

President: A.D.Govan (Stewart's-Melville FP)
Vice-President: J.Ross (Heriot's FP)

I.A.L.Hogg, CA (Watsonians) was appointed Treasurer of the Union with effect from 1 December 1978. The appointment of a Public Relations Officer was considered but not taken further.

During the season, works in terms of the Safety of Sports Ground Act, requested by Lothian Region were carried out. Perimeter fences were erected behind the Schoolboys' enclosure seating, opposite the stand, and behind the dead-ball areas. On 8 June 1979, the Field Convener reported that Lothian Region had granted the necessary Safety Certificate to Murrayfield.

New office premises for the Coaching Office were completed. Part of the Car Park area was made available to Murrayfield Ice Rink to permit the erection of a curling rink.

Following on last season's decision not to visit South Africa in 1978, the Committee considered an invitation from the South African Board's President for Scotland to visit, which was declined, it being kept in mind that a British Isles tour was scheduled there during 1980. It was agreed to receive a visit, involving two matches in Scotland, by the South Africa Barbarians, who were due to make a short tour to the UK. The South African Board stated that the touring party would be made up of equal numbers of black, coloured and white players. The Committee opposed the proposed introduction by the Rugby Union Writers Club of a 'Man-of-the-Match' award for players in Five Nations matches. The other Unions took a similar view. At the Annual Meeting of the IB in March 1979, France, following their election to membership at the 1978 meeting, attended for the first time.

« 1979—80 »

President: J. Ross (Heriot's FP)
Vice-President: C. W. Wilton (London Scottish)

It was agreed to propose at the 1980 AGM that in future there should be two Vice-Presidents.

However, a proposal that there should be two District Representatives from the Midlands was not approved.

It was decided to appoint an Assistant Technical Administrator.

The Committee were happy to accept an offer by Messrs Schweppes to continue for a further three seasons, after 1979—80, their financial assistance to Scottish Rugby.

A new advertising contract between the Union and Arena Sports Advertising Ltd was signed to cover three seasons up to 1982—83.

It was agreed to establish during the following season after the approval of the clubs a compulsory club Accident Insurance Scheme which would cover death, loss of limbs and permanent total disablement and include all club players and in any match the referee and touch judges, coaches, doctors, physios, and up to 6 ball boys. Optional schemes would be available for temporary total disablement, mini/midi teams, committee members, team annual travel and individual travel.

The Committee studied a presentation by Messrs Thorburn and Partners, Consulting Engineers, relative to possible developments at Murrayfield, which included the erection of a new stand. The Field Convener was instructed to enter into discussion with the Engineers on this subject.

Representations were made by the Committee that the provisions in the Criminal Justice (Scotland) Bill regarding the consumption of alcohol at certain Soccer grounds in Scotland, should also apply to Murrayfield. The Government accepted this request and so the Act included Murrayfield.

It was agreed that the Anglo-Scots should be introduced into the Inter-District Championship during the 1981—82 season. It was also agreed that the Anglo-Scots should now have their own Selection Committee and Secretary.

It was decided to provide a flag for presentation to the winners of the Inter-District Championship.

N. A. MacEwan was re-appointed as Coach to the National XV and to continue as a member of the Selection Committee. J. W. Telfer was re-appointed as the B XV coach and to become a member of the Selection Committee.

During the season a second B International v Ireland was played at Lansdowne Road.

The South African Barbarians completed a successful tour, which included two games in Scotland.

It was decided that Scotland should undertake a short tour in France in the spring of 1980 in the course of which three matches would be played against French Regional selections.

It was agreed to accept a visit by a Fiji team to England and Scotland in the autumn of 1981 (in the event this visit was postponed until 1982).

An invitation was received from the New Zealand RFU for Scotland to tour in New Zealand during May/June 1981.

An invitation from the Australian Union for Scotland to undertake a nine-match tour in July 1982 was accepted.

The Committee of Home Unions decided that a British Isles tour to South Africa would take place in July 1980.

A motion proposing the use of replacements in the Club Championship matches was brought forward at the 1980 AGM, but it failed to receive the necessary support.

The death of R.W.Shaw was recorded.

Note was made of the award of CBE, in the New Year's Honours List, to H.Waddell.

« 1980–81 »

President: C.W.Wilton (London Scottish)
Vice-President: F.MacAllister (Clarkston and Shawlands Academicals)

The Stobswell (Dundee) club were admitted to membership. The amalgamation of Bellahouston Academicals with the Cartha Queen's Park club was accepted.

The retiral date for the Secretary was fixed for June 1983, and preliminary steps were taken for the appointment of a successor. D.W.Arneil (Dunfermline) was appointed Assistant Technical Administrator. The Technical Administrator was authorised to go to New Zealand to study the structure and coaching techniques in that country.

A paper from the Committee on the structure of Rugby in Scotland was circulated to the clubs and the format of the Championship was discussed at the AGM. There, motions to increase the number of clubs in each division from 12 to 14 and creating a new division VII were passed, but a motion to permit the use of replacements in Championship matches again failed to receive the necessary majority. A motion was approved that the Committee should review the Constitution of the Union and the District Unions with particular regard to the position of the Full Member clubs. As proposed at the previous AGM, the Minute of the previous AGM was circulated with the notice calling the Meeting. A Ground Development Sub-committee was formed to process the scheme put forward by Thorburn and Partners for a new stand or stands at Murrayfield.

It was decided to install floodlights on the main pitch at the back of the stand, at present used by Edinburgh Wanderers. A Medical Services Advisory Committee was established.

A request from Zimbabwe for a short tour by a Scotland B team was declined because of the impending tour to New Zealand. It was agreed to receive a three-match tour of Scotland by a Romanian Rugby Federation team. This would include an International match, for which caps would be awarded. Later, an invitation to visit Romania in May 1984 was accepted. Arrangements

149

were put in hand for a short tour to Scotland and England by a Fiji Rugby Union team in the autumn of 1982.

It was noted that a report by the French Rugby Federation to the Five Nations Committee revealed that the International Rugby Federation (FIRA) had 25 member Unions. The Melrose club were given permission to arrange a number of special events during March–April 1983 to mark the Centenary of the first Seven-a-side Tournament.

« 1981–82 »

President: F.MacAllister (Clarkston and Shawlands Academicals)
Vice-Presidents:
G. W. Thomson (Watsonians), A. Robson (Hawick)

Various Bye-laws were altered to cover the introduction of two Vice-Presidents and the change of designation of the London District Representatives to that of Anglo-Scots Representative.

The following clubs were admitted to membership of the Union: East Kilbride and Livingston. The amalgamation of Paisley Grammarians and Craigielea clubs with the new name of Paisley RFC was accepted as was the amalgamation of the Glasgow High and Kelvinside Academicals clubs with the new name of Glasgow High/Kelvinside.

The Union Treasurer, I.A.L.Hogg, CA, was appointed as Secretary-Designate from 1 April 1982. Later, I.A.Forbes, BA, was appointed to succeed as Union Treasurer from 1 July 1982. The changes in the Championship passed at the last AGM were studied and it was agreed that these would be effective from season 1982–83. A special sub-committee was appointed to study the future of Scottish rugby with a remit to consider not only the Championship but also the Inter-District Championship and any other aspect of the game in Scotland.

The Committee was totally against a proposal by Sports Sponsorship International Ltd to introduce a Rugby Union World Cup to be contested at four-yearly intervals beginning in 1985. This proposal was also rejected by the IB. A Scotland Under-18 XV played an International match against West Germany in Berlin in March 1982. A match was also played against a Scottish Schools' XV.

It was agreed that Scottish players could be invited through the Union to take part in special matches arranged by the Transvaal Union to mark the opening of the new Ellis Park ground at Johannesburg. It had been decided that, in future, National Anthems would not be played at Murrayfield prior to the start of an International match except when Royalty was present. Strong representations were voiced by some delegates at the next AGM on this decision and a show of hands indicated that most of those present wished the matter to be reconsidered by the Committee.

The use of Murrayfield was granted to the Roman Catholic Church for a Youth Rally to be attended by His Holiness the Pope during his visit in 1982. The President and Secretary of the Union welcomed the Pope on his arrival at Murrayfield, against a background of the construction of the new East Stand by Norwest Holst Scotland Ltd.

The Clubs again rejected a motion for the introduction of replacements in Championship matches.

The 1982 AGM was brought forward a week to permit the President and Secretary to join the Scottish party on their Australian tour. The Press were

150

admitted to the AGM. J.W.Telfer had been nominated by the Union for the post of Assistant Manager and Coach to the British Isles touring team to New Zealand in 1983. He was subsequently appointed to that post by the Tours Committee of the four Home Rugby Unions.

During the year, the deaths of D.A.Thom, J.B.Nelson and G.P.S. Macpherson were recorded.

« 1982–83 »

President: G.W.Thomson (Watsonians)
Vice-Presidents:
A.Robson (Hawick), J.W.Y.Kemp (Glasgow High/Kelvinside)

The designation of the Assistant Secretary (J.D.Cock' urn) was amended to that of Administrative Secretary. Because of his appoin ment with the British Isles touring team, J.W.Telfer did not act as a Scottish s. 'ector, his place being taken by D.F.Madsen. C.M.Telfer was appointed Coach for the season with D.Grant assisting as Coach to the forwards.

The Union's Honorary Medical Adviser, Mr D.A.D.Macleod, FRSCE) was appointed as Honorary Medical Officer to the British Isles touring team for which eight Scottish players were subsequently selected. The new East Stand was in use for the first time on the occasion of the International match *v* Ireland in January 1983. However, it was officially opened by HRH The Princess Anne in March 1983 prior to the match between Scotland and the Barbarians. Preceding the opening ceremony there was a presentation of Youth Rugby, including mini-rugby, midi-rugby and a match between a Scottish Under-18 xv and a Scottish Schools' xv.

The Marketing Consultants to the Union erected a large marquee in the tennis court car park at Murrayfield which could be booked by commercial concerns who wished to entertain their guests at International matches. A Laws Advisory Panel was established. The first members were D.C.J. McMahon, A.M.Hosie, I.N.Cosgrove and D.W.Morgan, the Technical Administrator acting as Secretary.

Approval was given to a suggestion that the Secretaries of the four Home Unions should meet to discuss matters of mutual interest. The first meeting took place in June 1983. It was agreed that three or four Scottish players could be invited by the Western Province Union of Cape Town as members of their Overseas Invitation xv to take part in three matches in July 1983 in celebration of that Union's Centenary. In the event, only one player (D.G.Leslie, Gala) took part.

Discussion took place on allegations by the media of monetary gifts made to International players who wore boots of a named manufacture, but, in the absence of any specific details, including the naming of players, the Committee decided not to take any action in the case of Scottish players until such names were available. However, it was agreed to approach various boot manufacturers with a view to entering into a contract for the supply to the Scottish squad of boots which did not bear any distinguishing marks of their manufacturer.

Some concern was expressed at the growing practice of marketing replicas of various International jerseys (including Scottish jerseys), but it was felt that nothing could be done to stop this unless a new jersey badge was designed and copyright registered. A new agreement with Schweppes was entered into for the sponsorship of the Union Championship for a further three seasons com-

151

mencing season 1983–84.

Following the representations made at the last AGM it was decided to rescind the decision not to play the National Anthem at Internationals.

A request by the Netherlands Rugby Board for a Scottish Select XV to play in the Netherlands in April 1983 was considered, but it was felt that it would be more beneficial for an Under-21 XV to undertake the fixture, possibly in 1984. It was agreed to participate in a UK tour by Zimbabwe schools in 1983, when two or three games would be played in Scotland. Fiji played a Scottish XV at Murrayfield in September 1982.

It was agreed that caps would be awarded for the match against Romania in Bucharest in 1984. It was reported that while France would continue to play Romania annually, in rotation the Home Unions would play one further match with Romania in each season.

Consideration was again given to the possibility of staging another International Seven-a-side tournament at Murrayfield in the near future. Murrayfield was made available for a performance by the pop music star, David Bowie.

The Committee report on 'The Future of Scottish Rugby', outlining proposed alterations in the Championship and suggesting the possibility of a Scottish Cup, was presented at the AGM in 1983. This produced a lengthy discussion, but, as arranged, no vote was taken on the report. A report on District Union Constitutions prepared under the remit at the 1981 AGM was also submitted and approved.

For the fourth time a motion to allow the use of replacements in the Championship matches, this time in Divisions I–III, was not passed. Authorisation to attend the Western Province celebrations was given to the President for 1984 and the retiring Secretary, whose retirement was marked at the AGM by presentations from the Union and from the clubs, there having previously been presentations from the Murrayfield stewards at a Stewards Supper at Murrayfield and from the Committee members and the Past Presidents at a function at Murrayfield.

« 1983–84 »

President: A. Robson (Hawick)
Vice-Presidents:
J. W. Y. Kemp (Glasgow High/Kelvinside), G. Burrell (Gala)

The Currie (Edinburgh), Hillfoots (Tillicoultry), Cumbernauld, Helensburgh and Linlithgow clubs were admitted to the Union. The Minutes recorded the deaths of W. E. Bryce, D. D. Curr, R. J. Henderson and A. B. Kinnear. Also noted at the end of the season at the AGM were the deaths of Past President R. K. Cutherbertson and Championship Committee member D. M. Hogg (Melrose)

The professional rugby circus, proposed by Mr D. Lord, was discussed. The sister associations of the Scottish Football Association and the Scottish Football League indicated their support for the Union in that neither body intended to lease their grounds for professional rugby matches. It was agreed to replace the floodlighting system at Kelso so that adequate systems were available there and also at Hillhead, Howe of Fife and at Murrayfield.

There was preliminary discussion on a Scottish National Representative side to British Columbia and Alberta in May 1985 and also on the Australian tour to the British Isles in season 1984–85. A New Zealand tour to Scotland and England was, at short notice, arranged to compensate for the cancellation of the New Zealand tour to Argentina. A Zimbabwe Schools' tour took place in England and Scotland.

The regulations relating to amateurism were reviewed. This involved the proposals to come before the IB on daily allowances to tourists and on the status of players who wrote books. The participation in the Hong Kong Sevens Tournament was examined and it was agreed that a composite club could accept an invitation to appear.

A start was made with Under-21 International matches, the Netherlands being played at Hilversum. The second and third Under-18 Internationals (the first was against West Germany in Berlin in 1982) were played against West Germany at Meggetland and against Belgium in Brussels.

A greater financial commitment was agreed to be made available for Schools' International and District matches and for the Schools' Cup. The first Scottish Schools' cup final was played at Bridgehaugh, Stirling, where North Berwick High School beat Marr College by 6–0.

D.C.J.McMahon, Chairman of the Referees Advisory Panel, was co-opted as a member of the Referees Sub-committee and A.M.Hosie was co-opted as Advisor to the Laws Sub-committee. Four advisory bodies now exist— Referees Advisory Panel, Coaching Advisory Panel, Laws Advisory Panel, Medical Service Advisory Committee.

The general subject of club rating was discussed at length and in depth with various other bodies—The Scottish Office, the Association of Assessors, Members of Parliament, Scottish Sports Council, other national sporting bodies.

As part of the celebrations of the 100th Scotland v England match in February 1984, a special postal cover was issued, while various other souvenirs were made available for sale to the public. Before the game, an exhibition of mini-rugby was staged. A special Dinner Dance was arranged to celebrate the Grand Slam and Triple Crown successes.

Equipment for the International match players, especially boots, was discussed at several meetings, while another matter of concern was the reporting of injuries, on which it was agreed to invite the co-operation of all clubs and all schools so that a full record was obtained of all serious injuries. Various medical matters were discussed on several occasions, while the Laws Committee also discussed Law changes, including the IB directive on the Flying Wedge and possible experimentation on grounds of safety in schools and youth rugby.

At the AGM in June 1984, J.W.Y.Kemp (Glasgow High/Kelvinside) was elected President and G.Burrell (Gala) and Dr D.W.C.Smith (Aberdeen Grammar School FP and London Scottish) as Vice-Presidents.

The retiring President in his 'State-of-the-Union' remarks referred to the 1984 Triple Crown/Grand Slam successes, paying tribute to the Captain, J.Aitken, and Coach, J.W.Telfer, MBE. He also made reference to the May tour to Romania in which three matches were played including an International which Romania had won by 28 points to 22; and also to an alarming increase in indiscipline, with 150 players sent off in the season. Comment was also made on there currently being 42 clubs with loans from the Union totalling £211,894; and to the astonishing numbers of games now played by Scottish clubs overseas and by overseas clubs in Scotland.

The question of Sunday play was raised, on which the President intimated that a letter giving guide-lines was shortly being sent to clubs.

153

The Field Convener advised of a proposed Office, Committee Room and Hospitality areas and International Dressing-rooms development to be carried out in the summer of 1985 at an estimated cost of £720,000.

A proposal by the Committee, arising out of the second Committee report on 'The Future of Scottish Rugby', to have three Divisions of eight teams at the top of the Club Championship playing home and away games within each Division and with the remaining five Divisions continuing to contain fourteen teams playing each other once per season, attracted a lengthy discussion but was not passed.

The Finance Convener presented the accounts for season 1983–84 which showed the following figures which make a striking contrast with the accounts detailed earlier for season 1873–74:

	£	£
Surplus on Home International and Tour matches		893,961
Costs of Away International matches		(57,736)
Deficit on other Representative matches		(53,873)
Cost of Match Equipment		(18,715)
Match Account Balance		763,637
Club Subscriptions		550
Interest on Loans to Clubs		7,725
Interests and Dividends		22,168
Rents received		23,267
		817,347
Administration Expenses	113,646	
Coaching Account	52,471	
Repairs and upkeep of Murrayfield	103,379	
Expenses of Committees and District Unions	41,614	
Scottish Schools' Rugby Unions Grants and Expenditure	20,917	
Contribution to Club Accident Insurance Scheme	9,952	
Rates, Insurances and Services	52,363	
Depreciation	26,169	
	420,511	
Covenant to Murrayfield Centenary Fund	10,000	
Safety of Sports Ground Act Additional Provision	40,000	
Taxation	55,000	
Transfer to Ground Development Fund (towards cost of East Stand)	250,000	
		775,511
Revenue Account Balance carried to Balance Sheet		41,836

154

Appendix 2

The year of admission to the Union is appended after each name. An asterisk indicates that a club is a founder member.

Aberdeen Grammar School FP, 1893
Aberdeenshire, 1892
Aberdeen University, 1882
Aberdeen Wanderers/Academicals, 1950
Allan Glen's, 1920
Alloa, 1967
Ardrossan Academicals, 1922
Ayr, 1898
Boroughmuir, 1939
Broughton FP, 1963
Cambuslang, 1921
Cartha Queen's Park, 1908
Clarkston, 1958
Corstorphine, 1973
Cumnock, 1974
Currie, 1983
Dalkeith, 1974
Dalziel High School FP, 1972
Drumpellier, 1974
Dumfries, 1970
Dunbar, 1974
Dundee High School FP, 1920
Dundee University, 1967
Dunfermline, 1920
Earlston, 1921
East Kilbride, 1981
Edinburgh Academicals, 1873*
Edinburgh Borderers, 1922
Edinburgh Northern, 1975
Edinburgh University, 1873*
Edinburgh Wanderers, 1873
Falkirk, 1977
Fettesian-Lorettonians, 1882
Gala, 1879
Garnock, 1911

Glasgow Academicals, 1873*
Glasgow High/Kelvinside, 1888
Glasgow University, 1873*
Glenrothes, 1977
Gordonians, 1911
Grangemouth, 1973
Greenock Wanderers, 1879
Haddington, 1971
Hamilton Academicals, 1971
Harris Academy FP, 1951
Hawick, 1886
Heriot's FP, 1891
Highland, 1922
Hillfoots, 1983
Hillhead, 1905
Howe of Fife, 1921
Hutchesons', 1937
Hyndland School FP, 1973
Irvine, 1974
Jed-Forest, 1889
Jordanhill, 1955
Kelso, 1912
Kilmarnock, 1911
Kirkcaldy, 1895
Lanark, 1973
Langholm, 1887
Lasswade, 1973
Leith Academicals, 1952
Lenzie, 1920
Linlithgow, 1983
Lismore, 1974
Livingston, 1981
London Scottish, 1879
Madras College FP, 1960
Marr, 1971
Melrose, 1880
Merchistonians, 1873*
Moray, 1975
Morgan Academy FP, 1956
Musselburgh, 1948
North Berwick, 1975
Old Aloysians, 1971
Paisley, 1952
Panmure, 1884
Peebles, 1922
Penicuik, 1973
Perthshire, 1937
Portobello FP, 1974
Preston Lodge FP, 1973
RAF Leuchars, 1921
Royal (Dick) Veterinary College, 1951
Royal High, 1873*

St Andrews University, 1873*
St Mungo's, 1973
Selkirk, 1908
Stewart's Melville College FP, 1874
Stirling County, 1904
Stobswell, 1980
Strathclyde University, 1922
Strathmore, 1974
Trinity Academicals, 1950
Uddingston, 1973
Walkerburn, 1920
Watsonians, 1877
West of Scotland, 1873*
Whitecraigs, 1972
Wigtownshire, 1922

District Unions
Edinburgh and District Rugby Union, 1924
Glasgow and District Rugby Union, 1924
Midlands District Rugby Union, 1924
North District Rugby Union, 1924
South District Rugby Union, 1924

A full list of all clubs who have been members has not been given as this would be of considerable length. Many clubs have gone out of existence for varying reasons; some clubs ceased to be members and were then re-admitted; while there have also been several amalgamations.

Note the areas of the District Unions as stated in 1924 (as follows), although it will be appreciated that there have been changes since that date due to regionalisation and other reasons, while there have always been variations:

Edinburgh: The counties of the City of Edinburgh and the Lothians.

Glasgow: The counties of the City of Glasgow, Lanark, Renfrew, Dumbarton, Stirling and Ayr.

Midlands: The counties of Forfar, Perth, Fife, Clackmannan and Kinross.

North: The counties of Kincardine and all those to the North thereof.

South: The counties of Peebles, Roxburgh, Selkirk, Berwick, Dumfries, Kirkcudbright and Wigtown.

Appendix 3

THE STRUCTURE OF THE COMMITTEE
1873–1984

	President	Vice-Presidents	Club Captains	Special Representatives	East/Edinburgh	West/Glasgow	South	North	London/Anglo-Scots	Midlands	Hon. Secretary	Hon. Treasurer	Secretary	Treasurer	Asst./Admin. Secretary	Tech. Administrator	Asst. Tech. Administrator
1873–74	1	1	10	.	.	.	.	.	.	.	1 -	1	.	.	.	.	.
1874–75	1	1	13	.	.	.	.	.	.	.	1 -	1	.	.	.	.	.
1875–76	1	1	14	.	.	.	.	.	.	.	1 -	1	.	.	.	.	.
1876–80	1	1	.	.	2	2	.	.	.	.	1 -	1	.	.	.	.	.
1880–89	1	1	.	.	3	3	.	.	.	.	1 -	1	.	.	.	.	.
1889–94	1	1	.	.	3	3	1	1	.	.	1 -	1	.	.	.	.	.
1894–96	1	1	.	.	3	2	2	1	.	.	1 -	1	.	.	.	.	.
1896–1908	1	1	.	.	3	2	2	1	1	.	1 -	1	.	.	.	.	.
1908–10	1	1	.	.	2	2	1	1	1	.	1 -	1	.	.	.	.	.
1910–14	1	1	.	.	2	2	1	1	1	.	1	.	.	1	.	.	.
1914–24	1	1	.	5	2	2	1	1	1	.	.	.	1 -	1	.	.	.
1924–38	1	1	.	6	2	2	1	1	1	.	.	.	1 -	1	.	.	.
1938–48	1	1	.	6	2	2	1	1	1	1	.	.	1 -	1	.	.	.
1948–50	1	1	.	6	2	2	1	1	1	1	.	.	1	1 -	1	.	.
1950–51	1	1	.	6	2	2	2	1	1	1	.	.	1	1 -	1	.	.
1951–72	1	1	.	6	2	2	2	1	1	1	.	.	1 -	1	.	.	.
1972–75	1	1	.	6	2	2	2	1	1	1	.	.	1 -	1	1	.	.
1975–81	1	1	.	6	2	2	2	1	1	1	.	.	1 -	1	1	1	.
1981–	1	2	.	6	2	2	2	1	1	1	.	.	1	1	1	1	1

114. Waterford Crystal Chandelier, 1973. Centenary gift presented by the Irish RFU. The chandelier hangs in the SRU Museum area.

115. Murrayfield, 1984. An aerial view showing the original Centre West Stand and its two later wing stands faced by the new East Stand.

116. The SRU Arms and Bearings granted in 1973.
Per saltire Azure and Argent in chief and in base a thistle slipped of the Second and in each flank a garland of laurel proper riboned Murrey: all within a bordure counter—company of the First and Second, and in an Escrol beneath the same this Motto 'NON SINE GLORIA'.

117. Centenary of the SRU, 1973. Gifts from other Rugby Unions.
At front, l. to r.:
Figure of an Eskimo, presented by the Canadian RU.
Gavel and Stand, presented by the South African RB.
Plaque, presented by the Australian RFU.
Rare Rock Crystals, presented by the French RF.
At back, l. to r.:
Pennant, presented by the Belgian RF.
Two Candelabra, presented by the RFU (England).
Two Drinking Horns, presented by the Welsh RU.
Touch Judge's Flag, Crystal Decanter and Glasses—SRU mementos.
These gifts rest on one of a set of Travelling Rugs presented by the New Zealand RFU. There is missing a cigar box, presented by the Rhodesian RFU, which was in use when the picture was taken.

118. The First Trophy Cap, 1871. This International cap (and jersey badge) belonged to J. W. Arthur (Glasgow Acads.). The players bought their own trophy caps and kept them dated. The Union eventually decided that for the 1891–92 season, and in the future, these International caps would be presented by the Union.

119. Scottish Jersey and Trophy Cap, 1879. These were worn by H. M. Napier (1877–79) and have been loaned to the SRU Museum by the family. In 1877 H. M. Napier was recorded as being 13st. 3lb., and only J. Reid at 13st. 10lb. was heavier (see photograph of 1879 Scottish XV).

120. Programmes 1880–1984.

1880 Scotland v Ireland. This is one of the early type of single sheet programmes and it is interesting to note that the price has risen by one penny since 1877. This was the second International Match to be played at Hamilton Crescent and it was the first to be played on a Saturday instead of a Monday. Note the disposition of one full-back, two half-backs, two quarter-backs and ten forwards. The Scottish half-backs were a great club pair who were famed for their continual breaking away from the mauls as an interpassing and scoring partnership. The Irish x v are described as wearing white jerseys with a shamrock badge.

1891 Scotland v Wales. The Welsh x v are shown as using the recently adopted formation of four half-backs with two quarter-backs playing behind eight forwards, whereas Scotland have retained the older formation of three half-backs with two quarter-backs playing behind nine forwards. The famous cricket Test wicket-keeper, Gregor McGregor, is named as playing centre to the two wingers. In this match the referee was in full charge for the umpires have now left the field of play and are designated as touch judges.

1905 Scotland v Ireland. The venue is now Inverleith which was the first ground to be owned and used by any Rugby Union. Both teams are now using the four threequarters formation; the term 'quarter-back' has gone and we find two half-backs working behind a pack of eight forwards.

1905 Scotland v New Zealand. This was the first tour in the u k by a recognised colonial Union. The n z team are numbered 1–15 and their set-out is interesting: one full-back, five threequarter-backs, two half-backs and seven forwards (who packed down as 2-3-2). The Scottish team is set out in the same manner, but includes an A. N. Other. A. N. Fell, a New Zealander, declined his place and a late decision saw L. L. Greig come in as a third half-back to nullify the unorthodox n z strategy.

1906 Scotland v South Africa. The second recognised colonial Union tour. This programme was apparently printed in Cardiff and adjusted for each match and venue. This was the game played at New Hampden Park in which the young K. G. MacLeod scored his historic try. The s a players are each given their tour numbers, but the Scots remain unnumbered.

1908 Scotland v England. A new style of official programme, perhaps because, as also happened in later years, there were too many unofficial team sheets being offered for sale outside the ground. Dr Guthrie's two School bands, as usual since the opening of Inverleith in 1899, played the teams on to the field but there is no sign of the National Anthem being played, as had happened at the English game in 1900.

1909 Scotland v Ireland. Another style and size of official programme. The half-backs are named for the right or left of the scrum.

1912 Scotland v France. Again a distinctive change to a style which will be familiar to older readers for it was to last until season 1952–53. The half-backs are now labelled as 'scrum half' and 'stand-off half' but this distinction was actually made in the Welsh programme in 1911.

1954 Scotland v France. The programmes are now produced by a commercial concern. They carry articles and biographical notes on the players. The style was started at least for the Calcutta Cup game of 1953 at Twickenham.

1984 Scotland v France. The last match of the Grand Slam season.

The s r u Library carries a nearly complete set of programmes for all matches from 1909 to date. A few earlier programmes are also held.

121. Grand Slam Season 1984 and The 100th Match s v E.
At back: Painting commissioned by The Royal Bank of Scotland from Ronnie Browne.
l. to r.: SRU Grand Slam Commemorative Plaque: 100th Match s v E Tankard; Quaich presented by The Royal Bank of Scotland; Grand Slam Tankard; Silver Salver presented by the City of Edinburgh.
Ties, l. to r.: Grand Slam tie; SRU Committee tie; SRU Tour tie; Scottish Player's tie; 100th Match s v E tie; SRU Centenary tie.

TO · ALL · AND · SUNDRY · WHOM · THESE · PRESENTS · DO · OR · MAY · CONCERN

WE, Sir James Monteith Grant, Knight Commander of the Royal Victorian Order, Write to Her Majesty's Signet, Lord Lyon King of Arms, send Greeting: Whereas, John Law, Secretary of THE SCOTTISH RUGBY UNION, having by Petition unto Us of date 21 December 1971, for and on behalf of the said The Scottish Rugby Union, Shewn; THAT the Scottish Football Union was founded on 3 March 1873 at a meeting in Glasgow Academy attended by representatives of Edinburgh Academicals, Glasgow Academicals, West of Scotland, Royal High School F.P., Merchistonians, Edinburgh University, St. Andrews University and Glasgow University; THAT the name of The Scottish Football Union was changed to The Scottish Rugby Union at the Annual General Meeting on 2 May 1924; THAT in 1925 the said Union acquired from Sir Archibald Spencer Lindsey Campbell of Succoth, Bart, part of the lands of Murrayfield at Drumsheah; THAT the first International match was played at Murrayfield in March 1925, England being the first visiting country; THAT the President of The Scottish Rugby Union for 1971/72 is Alexander H. Brown, L.D.S., F.R.C.S.E, of 80 Great King Street, Edinburgh, and the Vice-President is Alfred William Wilson, D.S.O, T.D, D.L, of 39 Townhill Road, Dunfermline, Fife; THAT the Committee of the said Union, in addition to the President and Vice-President, comprises six Special Representative Members; AND the Petitioner having prayed that there might be granted as for the said The Scottish Rugby Union such Ensigns Armorial as might be found suitable and according to the Laws of Arms, KNOW YE THEREFORE that We have Devised, and Do by These Presents Assign, Ratify and Confirm unto the Petitioner for and on behalf of The Scottish Rugby Union, Murrayfield, Edinburgh, the following Ensigns Armorial, as depicted upon the margin hereof, and matriculate of even date with these Presents upon the 50th page of the 55th Volume of Our Public Register of All Arms and Bearings in Scotland, videlicet: Per saltier Azure and Argent in chief and in base a thistle slipped of the Second and in each flank a garland of laurel proper ribboned Murray; all within a bordure counter-company of the First and Second, and in an Escrol (over the same) this Motto NON-SINE-GLORIA, by demonstration of which Ensigns Armorial the said Union is amongst all Nobles and in all Places of Honour to be taken, numbered, accounted and received as an Incorporation Noble in the Noblesse of Scotland; IN TESTIMONY WHEREOF We have Subscribed These Presents and the Seal of Our Office is appended hereto at Edinburgh this 28th day of February in the Twenty-second Year of the Reign of Our Sovereign Lady Elizabeth the Second, by the Grace of God, of the United Kingdom of Great Britain and Northern Ireland, and of Her Other Realms and Territories, Queen, Head of the Commonwealth, Defender of the Faith, and in the Year of Our Lord One Thousand, Nine Hundred and Seventy-three.

J Monteith Grant
Lyon

NON · SINE · GLORIA

119

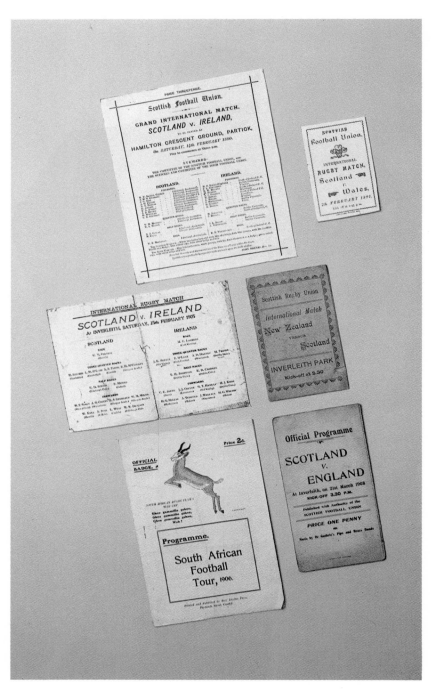

Appendix 4

OFFICE-BEARERS, COMMITTEE MEMBERS
AND OFFICIALS

« 1873–74 »
President: J. Chiene (Edin. Acads.).
Vice-President: H. Gibson (Merchistonians).
Hon. Sec./Treas.: J. Wallace (Edin. Acads.).
East and West: The captains of the ten member clubs.

« 1874–75 »
President: A. Harvey (Glas. Acads.).
Vice-President: H. Cheyne (Edin. Acads.).
Hon. Sec./Treas.: J. Wallace.
East and West: The captains of the thirteen member clubs.

« 1875–76 »
President: B. Hall Blyth (Merchistonians).
Vice-President: R. McClure (West of Scot.).
Hon. Sec./Treas.: A. R. Stewart (Edin. Wanderers).
East and West: The captains of the fourteen member clubs.

« 1876–77 »
President: W. H. Kidston (West of Scot.).
Vice-President: A. Buchanan (RHSFP).
Hon. Sec./Treas.: A. R. Stewart.
East: J. Reid (Edin. Wanderers), J. H. S. Graham (Edin. Acads.).
West: G. R. Fleming (Glas. Acads.), W. B. Russell (West of Scot.).

« 1877–78 »
President: J. Chiene (Edin. Acads.).
Vice-President: G. R. Fleming (Glas. Acads.).
Hon. Sec./Treas.: A. R. Stewart.
East: J. H. S. Graham, A. G. Petrie (RHSFP).
West: D. H. Watson (Glas. Acads.), H. W. Little (West of Scot.).

« 1878–79 »
President: G. R. Fleming (Glas. Acads.).
Vice-President: Hon. J. W. Moncreiff (Edin. Acads.).
Hon. Sec./Treas.: A. R. Stewart.
East: J. H. S. Graham, A. G. Petrie.
West: H. W. Little, M. Cross (Glas. Acads.).

159

« 1879–80 »
President: A. Buchanan (RHSFP).
Vice-President: H. W. Little (West of Scot.).
Hon. Sec./Treas.: J. Brewis (RHSFP).
East: J. H. S. Graham, N. T. Brewis (Edin. Inst. FP).
West: M. Cross, W. Colville (West of Scot.).

« 1880–81 »
President: D. H. Watson (Glas. Acads.).
Vice-President: J. Reid (Edin. Wanderers).
Hon. Sec./Treas.: J. Brewis.
East: N. T. Brewis, J. H. S. Graham, A. G. Petrie (RHSFP).
West: R. C. Mackenzie (Glas. Acads.), D. Y. Cassels (West of Scot.), R. B. Young (Glas. Univ.).

« 1881–82 »
President: A. G. Petrie (RHSFP).
Vice-President: W. Cross (Glas. Acads.).
Hon. Sec./Treas.: A. S. Paterson (Edin. Univ.).
East: R. Ainslie (Edin. Inst. FP), F. Hunter (Edin. Univ.), T. A. Begbie (Edin. Wanderers).
West: D. Y. Cassels, J. M. Sim (Southern), J. A. D. McKean (Paisley).

« 1882–83 »
President: W. Cross (Glas. Acads.).
Vice-President: J. H. S. Graham (Edin. Acads.).
Hon. Sec./Treas.: A. S. Paterson.
East: T. Ainslie (Edin. Inst. FP), J. A. Gardner (Edin. Acads.), G. C. Alexander (Edin. Wanderers).
West: D. Y. Cassels, J. B. Brown (Glas. Acads.), R. R. Beveridge (Glas. Univ.).

« 1883–84 »
President: J. H. S. Graham (Edin. Acads.).
Vice-President: M. Cross (Glas. Acads.).
Hon. Sec./Treas.: J. A. Gardner (Edin. Acads.).
East: T. Ainslie, A. R. Don Wauchope (Fet.-Lor.), W. A. Peterkin (Edin. Univ.).
West: J. B. Brown, J. Jamieson (West of Scot.), J. S. Laing (Glas. Univ.).

« 1884–85 »
President: M. Cross (Glas. Acads.).
Vice-President: N. T. Brewis (Edin. Inst. FP).
Hon. Sec./Treas.: J. A. Gardner.
East: T. Ainslie, A. R. Don Wauchope, C. Reid (Edin. Acads.).
West: J. B. Brown, J. Jamieson, R. B. Young (Glas. Univ.).

« 1885–86 »
President: N. T. Brewis (Edin. Inst. FP).
Vice-President: J. S. Carrick (Glas. Acads.).
Hon. Sec./Treas.: J. A. Gardner.
East: A. R. Don Wauchope, C. Reid, J. P. Veitch (RHSFP).
West: J. B. Brown, W. H. Kidston (West of Scot.), R. Hutcheson (Glas. Univ.).

160

« 1886–87 »

President: J. S. Carrick (Glas. Acads.).
Vice-President: W. S. Brown (Edin. Inst FP).
Hon. Sec./Treas.: J. A. Gardner.
East: J. P. Veitch, A. R. Don Wauchope, C. Reid.
West: J. B. Brown, R. Hutcheson, W. A. Macdonald (1st LRV).

« 1887–88 »

President: W. S. Brown (Edin. Inst. FP).
Vice-President: Dr R. B. Young (Glas. Univ.).
Hon. Sec./Treas.: A. S. Blair (Fet.-Lor.).
East: C. Reid, J. A. Smith (RHSFP), W. A. Peterkin (Edin. Univ.).
West: W. A. Macdonald, H. W. Edmiston (Clydesdale), D. S. Morton (West of Scot.).

« 1888–89 »

President: Dr R. B. Young (Glas. Univ.).
Vice-President: A. R. Don Wauchope (Fet.-Lor.).
Hon. Sec./Treas.: A. S. Blair.
East: C. Reid, J. A. Smith, Dr Wilson (Watsonians).
West: D. S. Morton, W. A. Macdonald, J. S. Carrick (Glas. Acads.).

« 1889–90 »

President: A. R. Don Wauchope (Fet.-Lor.).
Vice-President: J. G. Mitchell (West of Scot.).
Hon. Sec./Treas.: A. S. Blair.
East: J. A. Smith, T. Ainslie (Edin. Inst FP), H. F. T. Chambers (Edin. Univ.).
West: J. S. Carrick, D. G. Findlay (West of Scot.), R. Hutcheson (Glas. Univ.).
South: J. K. Brown (Gala).
North: A. E. Pullar (Perthshire).

« 1890–91 »

President: J. G. Mitchell (West of Scot.).
Vice-President: T. Ainslie (Edin. Inst. FP).
Hon. Sec./Treas.: J. A. Smith (RHSFP).
East: M. C. McEwan (Edin. Acads.), A. T. Clay (Edin. Acads.), A. G. G. Asher (Fet.-Lor.), R. D. Rainie (Edin. Wanderers).
West: D. G. Findlay, R. Hutcheson, J. S. Carrick.
South: J. K. Brown.
North: J. D. Campbell (Aberdeen).

« 1891–92 »

President: T. Ainslie (Edin. Inst. FP).
Vice-President: D. S. Morton (West of Scot.).
Hon. Sec./Treas.: J. A. Smith.
East: M. C. McEwan, R. D. Rainie, J. Tod (Watsonians).
West: D. G. Findlay, R. Hutcheson, J. B. Brown (Glas. Acads.).
South: G. Wilson (Hawick).
North: A. J. Shepherd (Panmure).

« 1892–93 »

President: D. S. Morton (West of Scot.).
Vice-President: L. M. Balfour-Melville (Edin. Acads.).
Hon. Sec./Treas.: J. A. Smith.
East: M. C. McEwan, R. D. Rainie, T. Ainslie (Edin. Inst. FP).
West: D. G. Findlay, W. A. Macdonald (Glas. Univ.), J. S. Carrick (Glas. Acads.).
South: G. Wilson.
North: A. J. Shepherd.

« 1893–94 »

President: L. M. Balfour-Melville (Edin. Acads.).
Vice-President: W. E. Maclagan (London Scot.).
Hon. Sec./Treas.: J. A. Smith.
East: T. Ainslie, R. D. Rainie, R. M. M. Roddick (Watsonians).
West: D. G. Findlay, J. S. Carrick, W. C. Thomson (Kelvinside Acads.).
South: G. Wilson.
North: A. J. Shepherd.

« 1894–95 »

President: W. E. Maclagan (London Scot.).
Vice-President: M. C. McEwan (Edin. Acads.).
Hon. Sec./Treas.: J. A. Smith.
East: R. M. M. Roddick, T. Ainslie, R. D. Rainie.
West: D. G. Findlay, Lockhart (Clydesdale).
South: G. Wilson, G. Cochrane (Gala).
North: R. S. Davidson (Aberdeen).

« 1895–96 »

President: W. E. Maclagan (London Scot.).
Vice-President: D. G. Findlay (West of Scot.).
Hon. Sec./Treas.: J. A. Smith.
East: R. M. M. Roddick, I. MacIntyre (Fet.-Lor.) R. D. Rainie.
West: C. J. P. Fraser (Glas. Univ.), W. C. Thomson (Kelvinside Acads.).
South: G. Cochrane, A. Turnbull (Hawick).
North: R. S. Davidson.

« 1896–97 »

President: D. G. Findlay (West of Scot.).
Vice-President: R. D. Rainie (Edin. Wanderers).
Hon. Sec./Treas.: J. A. Smith.
East: R. M. M. Roddick, I. MacIntyre, H. N. Boyd (Edin. Acads.).
West: C. J. P. Fraser, J. D. Boswell (West of Scot.).
South: A. Turnbull, G. Cochrane.
North: R. S. Davidson.
London: W. E. Maclagan (London Scot.).

« 1897–98 »

President: R. D. Rainie (Edin. Wanderers).
Vice-President: J. D. Boswell (West of Scot.).
Hon. Sec./Treas.: J. A. Smith.
East: I. MacIntyre, H. N. Boyd, R. B. Laird (Edin. Inst. FP).

162

West: C. J. P. Fraser, W. M. Dykes (Clydesdale).
South: A. Turnbull, G. Cochrane.
North: R. S. Davidson.
London: W. E. Maclagan.

« 1898–99 »
President: J. D. Boswell (West of Scot.).
Vice-President: I. MacIntyre (Fet.-Lor.).
Hon. Sec./Treas.: J. A. Smith.
East: H. N. Boyd, R. Welsh (Watsonians), C. J. N. Fleming (Edin. Wanderers).
West: W. M. Dykes, R. C. Greig (Glas. Acads.).
South: A. Turnbull, G. Cochrane.
North: R. S. Davidson.
London: W. E. Maclagan.

« 1899–1900 »
President: I. MacIntyre (Fet.-Lor.).
Vice-President: R. G. MacMillan (Merchistonians).
Hon. Sec./Treas.: J. A. Smith.
East: R. Welsh, C. J. N. Fleming, H. N. Boyd.
West: R. C. Greig, W. M. Dykes.
South: A. Turnbull, G. Cochrane.
North: R. B. Lockhart (Panmure).
London: W. E. Maclagan.

« 1900–01 »
President: R. G. MacMillan (Merchistonians).
Vice-President: G. T. Neilson (West of Scot.).
Hon. Sec./Treas.: J. A. Smith.
East: R. Welsh, H. N. Boyd, J. W. Simpson (RHSFP).
West: W. M. Dykes, G. Wingate (Kelvinside Acads.).
South: A. Turnbull, G. Cochrane.
North: R. B. Lockhart.
London: D. Macgregor (London Scot.).

« 1901–02 »
President: G. T. Neilson (West of Scot.).
Vice-President: Rev. R. S. Davidson (Perthshire).
Hon. Sec./Treas.: J. A. Smith.
East: R. Welsh, J. W. Simpson, H. N. Boyd.
West: W. M. Dykes, J. C. Findlay (West of Scot.).
South: A. Jardine (Hawick), W. Mabon (Jed-Forest).
North: R. B. Lockhart.
London: D. Macgregor.

« 1902–03 »
President: R. S. Davidson (Perthshire).
Vice-President: R. C. Greig (Glas. Acads.).
Hon. Sec./Treas.: J. A. Smith.
East: R. Welsh, J. W. Simpson, A. B. Flett (Edin. Univ.).
West: J. C. Findlay, J. T. Tulloch (Kelvinside Acads.).
South: A. Jardine, W. Mabon.

163

North: R. B. Lockhart.
London: D. Macgregor.

« 1903—04 »
President: R. C. Greig (Glas. Acads.).
Vice-President: J. W. Simpson (RHSFP).
Hon. Sec./Treas.: J. A. Smith.
East: R. Welsh, A. B. Flett, A. S. Pringle (Edin. Acads.).
West: J. C. Findlay, J. T. Tulloch.
South: A. Jardine, T. M. Scott (Melrose).
North: R. B. Lockhart.
London: D. Macgregor.

« 1904—05 »
President: J. W. Simpson (RHSFP).
Vice-President: W. Neilson (London Scot.).
Hon. Sec./Treas.: J. A. Smith.
East: R. Welsh, A. S. Pringle, A. B. Flett.
West: J. C. Findlay, J. T. Tulloch.
South: A. Jardine, T. M. Scott.
North: I. MacLennan (Panmure), R. M. Mitchell (Perthshire).
London: D. Macgregor.

« 1905—06 »
President: W. Neilson (London Scot.).
Vice-President: J. T. Tulloch (Kelvinside Acads.).
Hon. Sec./Treas.: J. A. Smith.
East: J. D. Dallas (Watsonians), J. W. Simpson (RHSFP), J. I. Gillespie (Edin. Acads.).
West: J. C. Findlay, I. Maclennan (Clydesdale).
South: A. Jardine, T. M. Scott.
North: R. M. Mitchell.
London: J. N. Morrison (London Scot.).

« 1906—07 »
President: J. T. Tulloch (Kelvinside Acads.).
Vice-President: A. B. Flett (Edin. Univ.).
Hon. Sec./Treas.: J. A. Smith.
East: J. D. Dallas, J. W. Simpson, J. I. Gillespie.
West: J. C. Findlay, I. Maclennan.
South: T. M. Scott, C. W. Brown (Gala).
North: W. G. Falconer (Aberdeen Nomads).
London: J. N. Morrison.

« 1907—08 »
President: A. B. Flett (Edin. Univ.).
Vice-President: D. Y. Cassels (West of Scot.).
Hon. Sec./Treas.: J. A. Smith.
East: J. D. Dallas, J. W. Simpson, J. I. Gillespie.
West: J. C. Findlay, J. T. Tulloch (Kelvinside Acads.).

164

South: C. W. Brown, T. M. Scott.
North: W. G. Falconer.
London: J. N. Morrison.

« 1908–09 »
President: D. Y. Cassels (West of Scot.).
Vice-President: A. S. Blair (Fet.-Lor.).
Hon. Sec./Treas.: J. A. Smith.
East: J. D. Dallas, A. B. Flett (Edin. Univ.).
West: J. C. Findlay, A. C. Frame (Glas. Acads.).
South: A. Dalgleish (Gala.).
North: W. G. Falconer.
London: J. N. Morrison.

« 1909–10 »
President: A. S. Blair (Fet.-Lor.).
Vice-President: C. J. N. Fleming (Melrose).
Hon. Sec./Treas.: J. A. Smith.
East: J. D. Dallas, A. B. Flett.
West: A. C. Frame, J. M. Dykes (Glas. HSFP).
South: A. Dalgleish.
North: W. F. Wilkie (Midland Cos.).
London: I. C. Geddes (London Scot.).

« 1910–11 »
President: C. J. N. Fleming (Melrose).
Vice-President: W. A. Walls (Glas. Acads.).
Hon. Sec.: J. A. Smith.
East: J. D. Dallas, A. G. Ramage (Edin. Acads.).
West: J. M. Dykes, J. R. C. Greenlees (Kelvinside Acads.).
South: A. Dalgleish.
North: W. F. Wilkie.
London: H. S. Dixon (London Scot.).
Treas.: A. D. Flett (Edin. Wanderers).

« 1911–12 »
President: W. A. Walls (Glas. Acads.).
Vice-President: J. D. Dallas (Watsonians).
Hon. Sec.: J. A. Smith.
East: A. G. Ramage, J. G. Cunningham (Watsonians).
West: J. M. Dykes, J. R. C. Greenlees.
South: G. S. Scott (Selkirk).
North: W. F. Wilkie.
London: H. S. Dixon.
Treas.: A. D. Flett.

« 1912–13 »
President: J. D. Dallas (Watsonians).
Vice-President: J. R. C. Greenlees (Kelvinside Acads. and Fet.-Lor.).
Hon. Sec.: J. A. Smith.
East: J. G. Cunningham, J. H. Lindsay (Edin. Inst. FP).
West: R. T. Neilson (West of Scot.), W. C. Church (Glas. Acads.).

165

South: G. S. Scott.
North: D. Nicoll (Panmure).
London: H. S. Dixon.
Treas.: A. D. Flett.

« 1913–14 »
President: J. R. C. Greenlees (Kelvinside Acads. and Fet.-Lor.).
Vice-President: T. Scott (Langholm).
Hon. Sec.: J. A. Smith.
East: J. G. Cunningham, J. M. Usher (Edin. Wanderers), J. M. B. Scott (Edin. Acads.), J. H. Lindsay (Edin. Inst. FP).
West: R. T. Neilson, W. C. Church.
South: G. S. Scott.
North: D. Nicholl.
London: H. S. Dixon.
Treas.: A. D. Flett.

« 1914–15 »
President: T. Scott (Langholm).
Vice-President: J. M. Dykes (Glas. HSFP).
Special Representatives: J. D. Dallas, C. J. N. Fleming, W. W. Mabon, W. A. Walls, J. A. Smith.
East: J. M. Usher, J. C. Sturrock (RHSFP), J. H. Lindsay, J. M. B. Scott (Edin. Acads.).
West: W. Russell (Glas. Acads.), D. M. Hutchison (Glas. HSFP).
South: G. S. Scott.
North: D. Nicholl.
London: H. S. Dixon.
Sec./Treas.: A. D. Flett (Edin. Wanderers).
Hon. Sec./Treas.: J. A. Smith.

J. M. Usher d. 1915, J. H. Lindsay d. 1915, A. D. Flett d. 1917

« 1919–20 »
President: T. Scott.
Vice-President: J. M. Dykes.
Special Representatives: J. A. Smith, J. D. Dallas, C. J. N. Fleming, W. W. Mabon, W. A. Walls.
East: J. C. Sturrock, J. M. B. Scott.
West: W. Russell, J. Macgill (Glas. Acads.), D. M. Hutchison.
South: G. S. Scott.
North: D. Nicholl.
London: H. S. Dixon.
Sec./Treas.: H. M. Simson (Watsonians).

166

« 1920–21 »
President: J. M. Dykes (Glas. HSFP).
Vice-President: T. Anderson (Glas. Acads.).
Special Representatives: J. D. Dallas, J. A. Smith, T. Scott, R. T. Neilson,
　　W. W. Mabon.
East: J. C. Sturrock, J. M. B. Scott.
West: J. Macgill, J. M. Tennent (West of Scot.).
South: R. L. Scott (Hawick).
North: W. G. Falconer (Queen's Cross).
London: H. S. Dixon.
Sec./Treas.: H. M. Simson.

« 1921–22 »
President: J. M. Dykes.
Vice-President: H. S. Dixon (London Scot.).
Special Representatives: J. D. Dallas, J. A. Smith, T. Scott, R. T. Neilson, W. W.
　　Mabon, J. Macgill.
East: J. C. Sturrock, J. M. B Scott.
West: J. M. Tennent, T. H. H. Warren (Kelvinside Acads.).
South: R. L. Scott.
North: W. G. Falconer.
London: J. M. Mackenzie (London Scot.).
Sec./Treas.: H. M. Simson.

« 1922–23 »
President: H. S. Dixon (London Scot.).
Vice-President: R. T. Neilson (West of Scot.).
Special Representatives: J. D. Dallas, J. Macgill, J. M. Dykes, J. C. Sturrock,
　　J. A. Smith.
East: J. M. B. Scott, A. W. Angus (Watsonians).
West: T. H. H. Warren, J. M. Tennent.
South: R. L. Scott.
North: W. G. Falconer.
London: J. M. Mackenzie.
Sec./Treas.: H. M. Simson.

« 1923–24 »
President: R. T. Neilson (West of Scot.).
Vice-President: Sir R. C. Mackenzie (Glas. Acads.)
Special Representatives: J. D. Dallas, J. Macgill, J. M. Dykes, J. C. Sturrock,
　　J. A. Smith.
East: A. W. Angus, A. A. Lawrie (Fet.-Lor.).
West: T. H. H. Warren, J. M. Tennent, W. L. Russell (Glas. Acads.).
South: R. L. Scott.
North: W. G. Falconer.
London: J. M. Mackenzie.
Sec./Treas.: H. M. Simson.

« 1924–25 »
President: Sir R. C. Mackenzie (Glas. Acads.).
Vice-President: R. Welsh (Watsonians).

167

Special Representatives: J. D. Dallas, R. T. Neilson, J. M. Dykes, J. Macgill,
  J. A. Smith, J. C. Sturrock.
East: A. W. Angus, A. A. Lawrie.
West: T. H. H. Warren, W. L. Russell.
South: R. L. Scott.
North: W. G. Falconer.
London: J. M. Mackenzie.
Sec./Treas.: H. M. Simson.

« 1925—26 »

President: R. Welsh (Watsonians).
Vice-President: J. A. Smith (RHSFP).
Special Representatives: J. D. Dallas, J. Macgill, J. M. Dykes, J. C. Sturrock,
  R. T. Neilson, Sir R. C. Mackenzie.
East: A. W. Angus, A. A. Lawrie.
West: T. H. H. Warren, J. Anderson (Glas. HSFP).
South: R. L. Scott.
North: G. Aitken (Kirkcaldy).
London: J. M. Mackenzie.
Sec./Treas.: H. M. Simson.

« 1926—27 »

President: J. A. Smith (RHSFP).
Vice-President: Col. M. M. Duncan (Fet.-Lor.).
Special Representatives: J. D. Dallas, J. Macgill, J. M. Dykes, J. C. Sturrock,
  R. T. Neilson, Sir R. C. Mackenzie.
East: A. W. Angus, A. A. Lawrie.
West: T. H. H. Warren, J. Anderson.
South: R. L. Scott.
North: R. M. Ledingham (Aber. GSFP).
London: J. M. Mackenzie.
Sec./Treas.: H. M. Simson.

« 1927—28 »

President: Col. M. M. Duncan (Fet.-Lor.).
Vice-President: D. McCowan (West of Scot.).
Special Representatives: J. D. Dallas, J. Macgill, J. A. Smith, J. C. Sturrock,
  R. T. Neilson, Sir R. C. Mackenzie.
East: A. W. Angus, A. A. Lawrie.
West: T. H. H. Warren, J. Anderson.
South: R. L. Scott.
North: R. M. Ledingham.
London: J. M. Mackenzie.
Sec./Treas.: H. M. Simson.

« 1928—29 »

President: Sir D. McCowan (West of Scot.).
Vice-President: Sir A. G. G. Asher (Fet.-Lor.).
Special Representatives: J. D. Dallas, J. Macgill, J. A. Smith, J. C. Sturrock,
  R. T. Neilson, T. H. H. Warren.
East: A. A. Lawrie, G. W. Simpson (Heriot's FP).
West: J. Anderson, R. B. Waddell (Glas. Acads.).

168

South: R. L. Scott.
North: R. Howie (Kirkcaldy).
London: J. M. Mackenzie.
Sec./Treas.: H. M. Simson.

« 1929–30 »

President: Sir A. G. G. Asher (Fet.-Lor.).
Vice-President: Dr A. Balfour (Watsonians./London Scot.).
Special Representatives: J. D. Dallas, J. Macgill, J. A. Smith, J. C. Sturrock,
    R. T. Neilson, T. H. H. Warren.
East: G. W. Simpson, A. A. Lawrie.
West: R. B. Waddell, J. Anderson.
South: R. L. Scott.
North: R. Howie.
London: J. M. Mackenzie.
Sec./Treas.: H. M. Simson.

« 1930–31 »

President: Sir A. Balfour (London Scot.)/J. C. Sturrock (RHSFP).
Vice-President: J. C. Sturrock (RHSFP)/J. D. Dallas (Watsonians).
Special Representatives: J. D. Dallas, J. Macgill, J. A. Smith, T. H. H. Warren,
    R. T. Neilson, R. L. Scott.
East: G. W. Simpson, A. A. Lawrie.
West: R. B. Waddell, J. Anderson.
South: W. Laidlaw (Jed-Forest).
North: R. M. Ledingham (Aber. GSFP).
London: D. Drysdale (London Scot.).
Sec./Treas.: H. M. Simson.

« 1931–32 »

President: J. C. Sturrock (RHSFP).
Vice-President: J. C. Findlay (West of Scot./London Scot.).
Special Representatives: J. D. Dallas, T. H. H. Warren, R. T. Neilson,
    R. L. Scott, J. Macgill, A. A. Lawrie.
East: G. W. Simpson, F. J. C. Moffat (Watsonians).
West: M. A. Allan (Glas. Acads.), J. Anderson.
South: W. Laidlaw.
North: R. M. Ledingham.
London: J. M. Mackenzie (London Scot.).
Sec./Treas.: H. M. Simson.

« 1932–33 »

President: J. C. Findlay (West of Scot./London Scot.).
Vice-President: J. Macgill (Glas. Acads.).
Special Representatives: J. D. Dallas, R. L. Scott, R. T. Neilson, A. A. Lawrie,
    J. C. Sturrock, J. Anderson.
East: G. W. Simpson, F. J. C. Moffat.
West: M. A. Allan, R. L. H. Donald (Glas. HSFP).
South: W. Laidlaw.
North: R. M. Ledingham.
London: D. Drysdale (London Scot.).
Sec./Treas.: H. M. Simson.

« 1933–34 »

President: J. Macgill (Glas. Acads.).
Vice-President: M. C. Morrison (RHSFP).
Special Representatives: J. D. Dallas, R. L. Scott, R. T. Neilson, A. A. Lawrie,
J. C. Sturrock, J. Anderson.
East: G. W. Simpson, F. J. C. Moffat.
West: M. A. Allan, J. B. Nelson (Glas. Acads.).
South: W. Laidlaw.
North: R. M. Ledingham.
London: D. Drysdale.
Sec./Treas.: H. M. Simson.

« 1934–35 »

President: M. C. Morrison (RHSFP).
Vice-President: W. P. Scott (West of Scot.).
Special Representatives: J. D. Dallas, R. L. Scott, R. T. Neilson, A. A. Lawrie,
J. C. Sturrock, J. Anderson.
East: F. J. C. Moffat, G. P. S. Macpherson (Edin. Acads.).
West: M. A. Allan, J. B. Nelson.
South: W. Laidlaw.
North: R. M. Ledingham.
London: D. Drysdale.
Sec./Treas.: H. M. Simson.

« 1935–36 »

President: W. P. Scott (West of Scot.).
Vice-President: A. A. Lawrie (Edin. Wanderers/Fet.-Lor.).
Special Representatives: J. D. Dallas, R. L. Scott, R. T. Neilson, M. C. Morrison,
J. C. Sturrock, F. J. C. Moffat.
East: G. P. S. Macpherson, R. M. Meldrum (RHSFP).
West: M. A. Allan, J. B. Nelson.
South: W. Laidlaw.
North: R. M. Ledingham.
London: D. Drysdale.
Sec./Treas.: H. M. Simson.

« 1936–37 »

President: A. A. Lawrie (Edin. Wanderers/Fet.-Lor.).
Vice-President: W. H. Welsh (Merchistonians).
Special Representatives: J. D. Dallas, R. L. Scott, R. T. Neilson, M. C. Morrison,
J. C. Sturrock, F. J. C. Moffat.
East: R. M. Meldrum, R. K. Cuthbertson (Edin. Acads.).
West: M. A. Allan, J. C. H. Ireland (Glas. HSFP).
South: W. Laidlaw.
North: R. M. Ledingham.
London: D. Drysdale.
Sec./Treas.: H. M. Simson.

« 1937–38 »

President: A. A. Lawrie.
Vice-President: W. H. Welsh.

170

Special Representatives: J. D. Dallas, R. L. Scott, R. T. Neilson, M. C. Morrison,
    J. C. Sturrock, F. J. C. Moffat.
East: R. K. Cuthbertson, R. M. Meldrum.
West: M. A. Allan, J. C. H. Ireland.
South: W. Laidlaw.
North: R. M. Ledingham.
London: D. Drysdale.
Sec./Treas.: H. M. Simson.

« 1938–39 »

President: W. H. Welsh (Merchistonians).
Vice-President: P. Munro, MP (London Scot.).
Special Representatives: J. D. Dallas, R. L. Scott, R. T. Neilson, A. A. Lawrie,
    J. C. Sturrock, F. J. C. Moffat.
East: R. K. Cuthbertson, R. M. Meldrum.
West: M. A. Allan, J. C. H. Ireland.
South: W. Laidlaw. *North:* R. M. Ledingham. *London:* D. Drysdale.
Midlands: J. S. C. Sharp (Panmure). *Sec./Treas.:* H. M. Simson.

« 1939–40 »

President: P. Munro, MP (London Scot.).
Vice-President: H. O. Smith (Watsonians).
Special Representatives: J. D. Dallas, R. L. Scott, R. T. Neilson, A. A. Lawrie,
    J. C. Sturrock, F. J. C. Moffat.
East: R. K. Cuthbertson, R. M. Meldrum.
West: J. C. H. Ireland, G. C. Muir (Kelvinside Acads.).
South: W. Laidlaw. *North:* R. M. Ledingham. *London:* D. Drysdale.
Midlands: J. S. C. Sharp. *Sec./Treas.:* H. M. Simson.

« 1940–41 »

President: P. Munro, MP.
Vice-President: H. O. Smith.
Special Representatives: J. D. Dallas, R. L. Scott, R. T. Neilson,
    J. M. Mackenzie, A. A. Lawrie, J. C. Sturrock, F. J. C. Moffat.
East: R. K. Cuthbertson, R. M. Meldrum.
West: J. C. H. Ireland, G. C. Muir, W. A. Mackinnon (Hillhead HSFP).
South: W. Laidlaw, R. J. Hogg (Gala). *North:* R. M. Ledingham.
London: D. Drysdale. *Midlands:* J. S. C. Sharp. *Sec./Treas.:* H. M. Simson.

P. Munro d. 1942, J. D. Dallas d. 1942, R. T. Neilson d. 1945, A. A. Lawrie d.
1942, J. C. Sturrock d. 1940, G. C. Muir d. 1943, W. Laidlaw d. 1943.

« 1946–47 »

President: H. O. Smith (Watsonians).
Vice-President: R. L. Scott (Hawick).
Special Representatives: F. J. C. Moffat, J. C. H. Ireland, M. A. Allan,
    R. M. Meldrum, W. H. Welsh, R. K. Cuthbertson.
East: R. J. Henderson (Edin. Acads.), D. S. Kerr (Heriot's FP).
West: W. A. Mackinnon, H. Waddell (Glas. Acads.).
South: R. J. Hogg. *North:* R. M. Ledingham.

171

London: D. Drysdale.
Midlands: J. S. C. Sharp.
Sec./Treas.: H. M. Simson.

« 1947—48 »

President: R. L. Scott (Hawick).
Vice-President: J. M. Mackenzie (Fet.-Lor.).
Special Representatives: F. J. C. Moffat, J. C. H. Ireland, M. A. Allan,
    W. H. Welsh, R. K. Cuthbertson, R. M. Meldrum.
East: D. S. Kerr, A. B. Kinnear (Stewart's FP).
West: W. A. Mackinnon, H. Waddell.
South: R. J. Hogg.
North: R. M. Ledingham.
London: D. Drysdale.
Midlands: J. S. C. Sharp.
Sec.: H. M. Simson.
Treas./Assist. Sec.: F. A. Wright (Edin. Acads.).

« 1948—49 »

President: J. M. Mackenzie (Fet.-Lor.).
Vice-President: J. N. Shaw (Edin. Acads.).
Special Representatives: M. A. Allan, R. M. Meldrum, W. H. Welsh,
    R. K. Cuthbertson, J. C. H. Ireland, D. Drysdale.
East: A. B. Kinnear, D. S. Kerr.
West: W. A. Mackinnon, H. Waddell.
South: R. J. Hogg.
North: R. M. Ledingham.
London: D. A. Thom (London Scot.).
Midlands: J. S. C. Sharp.
Sec.: H. M. Simson.
Treas./Assist. Sec.: F. A. Wright.

« 1949—50 »

President: J. N. Shaw (Edin. Acads.).
Vice-President: J. C. H. Ireland (Glas. HSFP).
Special Representatives: M. A. Allan, R. K. Cuthbertson, W. H. Welsh,
    D. Drysdale, R. M. Meldrum R. M. Ledingham.
East: A. B. Kinnear, D. S. Kerr.
West: H. Waddell, R. W. Shaw (Glas. HSFP).
South: R. J. Hogg.
North: Dr J. R. S. Innes (Aber. GSFP).
London: D. A. Thom.
Midlands: J. S. C. Sharp.
Sec.: H. M. Simson.
Treas./Assist. Sec.: F. A. Wright.

« 1950—51 »

President: J. C. H. Ireland (Glas. HSFP).
Vice-President: D. Drysdale (London Scot.).
Special Representatives: M. A. Allan, R. K. Cuthbertson, W. H. Welsh,
    R. M. Ledingham, R. M. Meldrum, H. Waddell.
East: A. B. Kinnear, D. S. Kerr.

172

West: R. W. Shaw, W. A. Mackinnon (Hillhead HSFP).
South: R. J. Hogg, W. E. Bryce (Selkirk).
North: Dr J. R. S. Innes.
London: D. A. Thom.
Midlands: J. S. C. Sharp.
Sec.: H. M. Simson.
Treas./Assist. Sec.: F. A. Wright.

« 1951—52 »

President: D. Drysdale (London Scot.).
Vice-President: F. J. C. Moffat (Watsonians).
Special Representatives: M. A. Allan, R. M. Ledingham, R. M. Meldrum,
   H. Waddell, R. K. Cuthbertson, D. S. Kerr.
East: A. B. Kinnear, D. D. Curr (Edin. Inst. FP).
West: R. W. Shaw, J. M. Anderson (Allan Glen's).
South: R. J. Hogg, W. E. Bryce.
North: Dr J. R. S. Innes.
London: D. A. Thom.
Midlands: J. S. C. Sharp.
Sec./Treas.: F. A. Wright.

« 1952—53 »

President: F. J. C. Moffat (Watsonians).
Vice-President: M. A. Allan (Glas. Acads.).
Special Representatives: R. M. Meldrum, H. Waddell, R. K. Cuthbertson,
   D. S. Kerr, R. M. Ledingham, R. J. Hogg.
East: A. B. Kinnear, D. D. Curr.
West: R. W. Shaw, J. M. Anderson.
South: W. E. Bryce, J. Graham (Kelso).
North: Dr J. R. S. Innes.
London: D. A. Thom.
Midlands: J. S. C. Sharp.
Sec./Treas.: F. A. Wright.

« 1953—54 »

President: M. A. Allan (Glas. Acads.).
Vice-President: J. M. Bannerman (Glas. HSFP).
Special Representatives: R. M. Meldrum, H. Waddell, R. K. Cuthbertson,
   D. S. Kerr, R. M. Ledingham, R. J. Hogg.
East: D. D. Curr, A. H. Brown (Heriot's FP).
West: R. W. Shaw, J. M. Anderson.
South: J. Graham, W. E. Bryce.
North: Dr J. R. S. Innes.
London: D. A. Thom.
Midlands: J. S. C. Sharp.
Sec./Treas.: F. A. Wright.

« 1954—55 »

President: J. M. Bannerman (Glas. HSFP).
Vice-President: R. M. Meldrum (RHSFP).
Special Representatives: R. K. Cuthbertson, D. S. Kerr, R. M. Ledingham,
   R. J. Hogg, H. Waddell, R. W. Shaw.

East: A. H. Brown, D. D. Curr.
West: J. M. Anderson, G. G. Crerar (Glas. Acads.).
South: C. W. Drummond (Melrose), A. R. Stewart (Jed-Forest).
North: Dr J. R. S. Innes.
London: D. A. Thom.
Midlands: A. W. Wilson (Dunfermline).
Sec./Treas.: J. Law (Kelvinside Acads.).

« 1955–56 »

President: R. M. Meldrum (RHSFP).
Vice-President: W. M. Simmers (Glas. Acads.).
Special Representatives: R. K. Cuthbertson, D. S. Kerr, R. M. Ledingham,
     R. J. Hogg, H. Waddell, R. W. Shaw.
East: A. H. Brown, R. F. Kelly (Watsonians).
West: G. G. Crerar, J. M. Anderson.
South: C. W. Drummond, A. R. Stewart.
North: Dr J. R. S. Innes.
London: D. A. Thom.
Midlands: A. W. Wilson.
Sec./Treas.: J. Law.

« 1956–57 »

President: W. M. Simmers (Glas. Acads.).
Vice-President: R. J. Hogg (Gala.).
Special Representatives: H. Waddell, J. M. Anderson, D. S. Kerr, A. H. Brown,
     R. W. Shaw, Dr J. R. S. Innes.
East: R. F. Kelly, R. Tod (Edin. Acads.).
West: G. G. Crerar, W. C. W. Murdoch (Hillhead HSFP).
South: C. W. Drummond, A. R. Stewart.
North: R. F. Tully (Gordonians).
London: D. A. Thom.
Midlands: A. W. Wilson.
Sec./Treas.: J. Law.

« 1957–58 »

President: R. J. Hogg (Gala.).
Vice-President: Dr D. J. MacMyn (London Scot.).
Special Representatives: H. Waddell, J. M. Anderson, D. S. Kerr, A. H. Brown,
     R. W. Shaw, Dr J. R. S. Innes.
East: R. Tod, R. F. Kelly.
West: G. G. Crerar, W. C. W. Murdoch.
South: C. W. Drummond, A. R. Stewart.
North: R. F. Tully.
London: D. A. Thom.
Midlands: A. W. Wilson.
Sec./Treas.: J. Law.

« 1958–59 »

President: Dr D. J. MacMyn (London Scot.).
Vice-President: R. K. Cuthbertson (Edin. Acads.).
Special Representatives: H. Waddell, Dr J. R. S. Innes, D. S. Kerr,
     A. W. Wilson, R. W. Shaw, C. W. Drummond.

174

East: R. Tod, G. H. Topp (E&DRU).
West: G. G. Crerar, W. C. W. Murdoch.
South: A. R. Stewart, H. S. P. Monro (Langholm).
North: R. F. Tully.
London: D. A. Thom.
Midlands: I. W. Kilgour (Kirkcaldy).
Sec./Treas.: J. Law.

« 1959–60 »
President: R. K. Cuthbertson (Edin. Acads.).
Vice-President: D. S. Kerr (Heriot's FP).
Special Representatives: H. Waddell, A. W. Wilson, R. W. Shaw,
     C. W. Drummond, Dr J. R. S. Innes, G. G. Crerar.
East: R. Tod, G. H. Topp.
West: W. C. W. Murdoch, R. P. Johnston (G&DRU).
South: H. S. P. Monro, A. R. Stewart, R. P. Johnston (Whitehill FP).
North: R. F. Tully.
London: D. A. Thom.
Midlands: I. W. Kilgour.
Sec./Treas.: J. Law.

« 1960–61 »
President: D. S. Kerr (Heriot's FP).
Vice-President: R. M. Ledingham (Aber. GSFP).
Special Representatives: H. Waddell, A. W. Wilson, R. W. Shaw,
     C. W. Drummond, Dr J. R. S. Innes, G. G. Crerar.
East: R. Tod, J. H. Orr (Heriot's FP).
West: R. P. Johnston, W. C. W. Murdoch.
South: H. S. P. Monro, A. R. Stewart.
North: R. F. Tully.
London: D. A. Thom.
Midlands: H. Lind (Dunfermline).
Sec./Treas.: J. Law.

« 1961–62 »
President: R. M. Ledingham (Aber. GSFP).
Vice-President: A. R. Stewart, (Jed-Forest).
Special Representatives: H. Waddell, A. W. Wilson, R. W. Shaw,
     W. Drummond, Dr J. R. S. Innes, G. G. Crerar.
East: R. Tod, A. D. Govan (Stewart's FP).
West: R. P. Johnston, W. C. W. Murdoch.
South: H. S. P. Monro, A. Bowie (Hawick).
North: R. F. Tully.
London: D. A. Thom.
Midlands: H. Lind.
Sec./Treas.: J. Law.

« 1962–63 »
President: A. R. Stewart (Jed-Forest).
Vice-President: H. Waddell (Glas. Acads.).
Special Representatives: R. W. Shaw, G. G. Crerar, A. W. Wilson, R. Tod,
     C. W. Drummond, R. F. Tully.

East: A. D. Govan, A. Watson (Edin. Wanderers).
West: R. P. Johnston, A. Cameron (Glas. HSFP).
South: H. S. P. Monro, A. Bowie.
North: J. M. Milne (Aber. GSFP).
London: D. A. Thom.
Midlands: H. Lind.
Sec./Treas.: J. Law.

« 1963—64 »

President: H. Waddell (Glas. Acads.).
Vice-President: W. R. Logan (Edin. Wanderers).
Special Representatives: R. W. Shaw, G. G. Crerar, A. W. Wilson, R. Tod,
    C. W. Drummond, H. S. P. Monro.
East: A. Watson, A. D. Govan.
West: R. P. Johnston, W. C. W. Murdoch (Hillhead HSFP).
South: A. E. Bunyan (Selkirk), A. Bowie.
North: J. M. Milne.
London: D. A. Thom.
Midlands: H. Lind.
Sec./Treas.: J. Law.

« 1964—65 »

President: W. R. Logan (Edin. Wanderers).
Vice-President: D. A. Thom (London Scot.).
Special Representatives: R. W. Shaw, G. G. Crerar, A. W. Wilson, R. Tod,
    C. W. Drummond, H. S. P. Monro.
East: A. Watson, A. D. Govan.
West: R. P. Johnston, W. C. W. Murdoch.
South: A. E. Bunyan, A. Bowie.
North: J. M. Milne.
London: C. W. Wilton (London Scot.).
Midlands: H. Lind.
Sec./Treas.: J. Law.

« 1965—66 »

President: D. A. Thom (London Scot.).
Vice-President: M. S. Stewart (Stewart's FP).
Special Representatives: R. W. Shaw, G. G. Crerar, A. W. Wilson, R. Tod,
    C. W. Drummond, H. S. P. Monro.
East: A. Watson, A. D. Govan.
West: R. P. Johnston, W. C. W. Murdoch.
South: A. E. Bunyan, A. Bowie.
North: J. M. Milne.
London: C. W. Wilton.
Midlands: H. Lind.
Sec./Treas.: J. Law.

« 1966—67 »

President: M. S. Stewart (Stewart's FP).
Vice-President: R. Tod (Edin. Acads.).
Special Representatives: R. W. Shaw, G. G. Crerar, A. W. Wilson,
    H. S. P. Monro, C. W. Drummond, A. D. Govan.

176

East: A. Watson, G. W. Thomson (Watsonians).
West: W. C. W. Murdoch, J. W. Y. Kemp (Glas. HSFP).
South: A. E. Bunyan, A. Bowie.
North: J. M. Milne.
London: C. W. Wilton.
Midlands: H. Lind.
Sec./Treas.: J. Law.

« 1967–68 »

President: R. Tod (Edin. Acads.).
Vice-President: W. Nicholson (West of Scot.).
Special Representatives: R. W. Shaw, G. G. Crerar, A. W. Wilson,
    H. S. P. Monro, C. W. Drummond, A. D. Govan.
East: A. Watson, G. W. Thomson.
West: J. W. Y. Kemp, F. MacAllister (G & D RU).
South: A. E. Bunyan, A. Bowie.
North: J. M. Milne.
London: C. W. Wilton.
Midlands: H. Lind.
Sec./Treas.: J. Law.

« 1968–69 »

President: W. Nicholson (West of Scot.).
Vice-President: G. G. Crerar (Glas. Acads.).
Special Representatives: R. W. Shaw, H. S. P. Monro, A. W. Wilson,
    A. D. Govan, C. W. Drummond, A. Bowie.
East: A. Watson, G. W. Thomson.
West: J. W. Y. Kemp, F. MacAllister.
South: J. R. B. Wilson (Jed-Forest), G. Burrell (Gala.).
North: W. L. Connon (Aber. GSFP).
London: C. W. Wilton.
Midlands: H. Lind.
Sec./Treas.: J. Law.

« 1969–70 »

President: G. G. Crerar (Glas. Acads.).
Vice-President: R. W. Shaw (Glas. HSFP).
Special Representatives: A. W. Wilson, A. D. Govan, C. W. Drummond,
    A. Bowie, H. S. P. Monro, H. Lind.
East: A. Watson, G. W. Thomson.
West: J. W. Y. Kemp, F. MacAllister.
South: J. R. B. Wilson, G. Burrell.
North: W. L. Connon.
London: C. W. Wilton.
Midlands: T. Pearson (Howe of Fife).
Sec./Treas.: J. Law.

« 1970–71 »

President: R. W. Shaw (Glas. HSFP).
Vice-President: A. H. Brown (Heriot's FP).
Special Representatives: A. W. Wilson, A. D. Govan, C. W. Drummond,
    A. Bowie, H. S. P. Monro, H. Lind.

East: A. Watson, G. W. Thomson.
West: J. W. Y. Kemp, F. MacAllister.
South: J. R. B. Wilson, G. Burrell.
North: W. L. Connon.
London: C. W. Wilton.
Midlands: T. Pearson.
Sec./Treas.: J. Law.

« 1971–72 »

President: A. H. Brown (Heriot's FP).
Vice-President: A. W. Wilson (Dunfermline).
Special Representatives: C. W. Drummond, A. Bowie, H. S. P. Monro, H. Lind,
    A. D. Govan, F. MacAllister.
East: G. W. Thomson, A. W. Harper (RHSFP).
West: J. W. Y. Kemp, J. T. McNeil (Hutchesons' FP).
South: J. R. B. Wilson, G. Burrell.
North: W. L. Connon.
London: C. W. Wilton.
Midlands: T. Pearson.
Sec./Treas.: J. Law.

« 1972–73 »

President: A. W. Wilson (Dunfermline).
Vice-President: Dr J. R. S. Innes (Aber. GSFP).
Special Representatives: C. W. Drummond, A. Bowie, H. S. P. Monro, H. Lind,
    A. D. Govan, F. MacAllister.
East: A. W. Harper, G. W. Thomson.
West: J. W. Y. Kemp, J. T. McNeil.
South: J. R. B. Wilson, G. Burrell.
North: W. L. Connon.
London: C. W. Wilton.
Midlands: T. Pearson.
Sec./Treas.: J. Law.
Assist. Sec.: J. D. Cockburn.

« 1973–74 »

President: Dr J. R. S. Innes (Aber. GSFP).
Vice-President: C. W. Drummond (Melrose).
Special Representatives: H. S. P. Monro, F. MacAllister, A. D. Govan,
    G. W. Thomson, H. Lind, W. L. Connon.
East: A. W. Harper, R. Brown (Boroughmuir).
West: J. W. Y. Kemp, J. T. McNeil.
South: J. R. B. Wilson, G. Burrell.
North: G. B. Masson (Gordonians).
London: C. W. Wilton.
Midlands: T. Pearson.
Sec./Treas.: J. Law.
Assist. Sec.: J. D. Cockburn.

« 1974–75 »

President: C. W. Drummond (Melrose).
Vice-President: J. H. Orr (Heriot's FP).

Special Representatives: H. S. P. Monro, F. MacAllister, A. D. Govan,
G. W. Thomson, H. Lind, W. L. Connon.
East: A. W. Harper, R. Brown.
West: J. W. Y. Kemp, J. T. McNeil.
South: J. R. B. Wilson, G. Burrell.
North: G. B. Masson.
London: C. W. Wilton.
Midlands: T. Pearson.
Sec./Treas.: J. Law.
Assist. Sec.: J. D. Cockburn.

« 1975—76 »

President: J. H. Orr (Heriot's FP).
Vice-President: H. S. P. Monro, MP (Langholm).
Special Representatives: A. D. Govan, G. W. Thomson, H. Lind, W. L. Connon,
F. MacAllister, J. W. Y. Kemp.
East: A. W. Harper, R. Brown.
West: J. T. McNeil, I. A. A. MacGregor (Glas. Acads.).
South: J. R. B. Wilson, G. Burrell.
North: G. B. Masson.
London: C. W. Wilton.
Midlands: T. Pearson.
Sec./Treas.: J. Law.
Assist. Sec.: J. D. Cockburn.
Tech. Admin.: J. H. Roxburgh (Jordanhill).

« 1976—77 »

President: H. S. P. Monro, MP (Langholm).
Vice-President: Brig. F. H. Coutts (Melrose).
Special Representatives: A. D. Govan, G. W. Thomson, H. Lind, W. L. Connon,
F. MacAllister, J. W. Y. Kemp.
East: A. W. Harper, R. Brown.
West: I. A. A. MacGregor, J. T. McNeil.
South: J. R. B. Wilson, G. Burrell.
North: G. B. Masson.
London: C. W. Wilton.
Midlands: T. Pearson.
Sec./Treas.: J. Law.
Assist. Sec.: J. D. Cockburn.
Tech. Admin.: J. H. Roxburgh.

« 1977—78 »

President: Brig. F. H. Coutts (Melrose).
Vice-President: A. D. Govan (Stew.-Mel. FP).
Special Representatives: F. MacAllister, J. W. Y. Kemp, G. W. Thomson,
G. Burrell, W. L. Connon, T. Pearson.
East: A. W. Harper, R. Brown.
West: I. A. A. MacGregor, J. T. McNeil.
South: J. R. B. Wilson, R. G. Charters (Hawick).
North: G. B. Masson.
London: C. W. Wilton.
Midlands: J. B. Steven (Madras Coll. FP).

Sec./Treas.: J. Law.
Assist. Sec.: J. D. Cockburn.
Tech. Admin.: J. H. Roxburgh.

« 1978–79 »

President: A. D. Govan (Stew.-Mel. FP).
Vice-President: J. Ross (Heriot's FP).
Special Representatives: F. MacAllister, J. W. Y. Kemp, G. W. Thomson,
    G. Burrell, W. L. Connon, T. Pearson.
East: A. W. Harper, R. Brown.
West: I. A. A. MacGregor, J. T. McNeil.
South: G. K. Smith (Kelso), R. G. Charters.
North: G. B. Masson.
London: C. W. Wilton.
Midlands: J. B. Steven.
Sec.: J. Law.
Treas.: J. Law/I. A. L. Hogg (Watsonians).
Assist. Sec.: J. D. Cockburn.
Tech. Admin.: J. H. Roxburgh.

« 1979–80 »

President: J. Ross (Heriot's FP).
Vice-President: C. W. Wilton (London Scot.).
Special Representatives: F. MacAllister, J. W. Y. Kemp, G. W. Thomson,
    G. Burrell, W. L. Connon, T. Pearson.
East: R. Brown, R. D. S. Munro (Leith Acads.).
West: I. A. A. MacGregor, J. T. McNeil.
South: G. K. Smith, R. G. Charters.
North: G. B. Masson.
London: A. C. W. Boyle (London Scot.).
Midlands: J. B. Steven.
Sec.: J. Law.
Treas.: I. A. L. Hogg.
Assist. Sec.: J. D. Cockburn.
Tech. Admin.: J. H. Roxburgh.

« 1980–81 »

President: C. W. Wilton (London Scot.).
Vice-President: F. MacAllister (Clarkston and Shawlands).
Special Representatives: G. W. Thomson, G. Burrell, W. L. Connon,
    T. Pearson, J. W. Y. Kemp, J. T. McNeil.
East: R. D. S. Munro, R. Brown.
West: I. A. A. MacGregor, I. M. Todd (Hillhead).
South: G. K. Smith, R. G. Charters.
North: G. B. Masson.
London: A. C. W. Boyle.
Midlands: J. B. Steven.
Sec.: J. Law.
Treas.: I. A. L. Hogg.
Assist. Sec.: J. D. Cockburn.
Tech. Admin.: J. H. Roxburgh.

180

« 1981—82 »
President: F. MacAllister (Clarkston and Shawlands).
Vice-Presidents: G. W. Thomson (Watsonians), A. Robson (Hawick).
Special Representatives: W. L. Connon, T. Pearson, J. W. Y. Kemp,
    J. T. McNeil, G. Burrell, R. Brown.
East: R. D. S. Munro, F. C. H. McLeod (Stew.-Mel. FP).
West: I. A. A. MacGregor, I. M. Todd.
South: G. K. Smith, R. G. Charters.
North: G. B. Masson.
London: A. C. W. Boyle.
Midlands: J. B. Steven.
Sec.: J. Law.
Treas.: I. A. L. Hogg.
Admin. Sec.: J. D. Cockburn.
Tech. Admin.: J. H. Roxburgh.
Assist. Tech. Admin.: D. W. Arneil.

« 1982—83 »
President: G. W. Thomson (Watsonians).
Vice-Presidents: A. Robson (Hawick), J. W. Y. Kemp (Glas. High/Kelv.).
Special Representatives: W. L. Connon, J. T. McNeil, G. Burrell, R. Brown,
    T. Pearson, G. B. Masson.
East: R. D. S. Munro, F. C. H. McLeod.
West: I. A. A. MacGregor, I. M. Todd.
South: G. K. Smith, R. G. Charters.
North: C. Ritchie (Aber. GSFP).
London: A. C. W. Boyle.
Midlands: J. B. Steven.
Sec.: J. Law, I. A. L. Hogg (*Des.*).
Treas.: I. A. Forbes.
Admin. Sec.: J. D. Cockburn.
Tech. Admin.: J. H. Roxburgh.
Assist. Tech. Admin.: D. W. Arneil.

« 1983—84 »
President: A. Robson (Hawick).
Vice-Presidents: J. W. Y. Kemp (Glas. High/Kelv.), G. Burrell (Gala.).
Special Representatives: W. L. Connon, R. Brown/R. G. Charters, T. Pearson,
    G. B. Masson, J. T. McNeil, I. A. A. MacGregor.
East: R. D. S. Munro, F. C. H. McLeod.
West: I. M. Todd, F. M. McDougall (G & D RU).
South: G. K. Smith, R. G. Charters/G. D. M. Brown (Melrose).
North: C. Ritchie.
London: A. C. W. Boyle.
Midlands: J. B. Steven.
Sec.: I. A. L. Hogg (Watsonians).
Treas.: I. A. Forbes.
Admin. Sec.: J. D. Cockburn.
Tech. Admin.: J. H. Roxburgh.
Assist. Tech. Admin.: D. W. Arneil.

Appendix 5

1984–85

OFFICE-BEARERS, COMMITTEE MEMBERS, OFFICIALS, ETC.

President: J. W. Y. Kemp (Glasgow High/Kelvinside)
Vice-Presidents: G. Burrell (Gala), Dr D. W. C. Smith (Aberdeen Grammar School FP and London Scottish)
Committee:
  Special Representatives: W. L. Connon, T. Pearson, J. T. McNeil, G. B. Masson, I. A. A. MacGregor, R. G. Charters
  District Representatives: R. D. S. Munro, F. C. H. McLeod, Dr I. M. Todd, F. M. McDougall, G. K. Smith, G. D. M. Brown, J. B. Steven, C. Ritchie, A. C. W. Boyle
Trustees: J. N. Shaw, J. C. H. Ireland, Sir J. H. Orr, Brig. F. H. Coutts
Officials: I. A. L. Hogg, I. A. Forbes, J. D. Cockburn, J. H. Roxburgh, D. W. Arneil, J. Thain (Head Groundsman)
Office Staff: R. L. Scott (Ticket Officer), Mrs L. M. Moffat, Mrs M. M. Reid, Miss L. McLeod, Miss H. Rayner, Miss R. Montgomery
Ground Staff: D. Cant, I. Stewart, D. Mathie, R. McLean, D. Copland
Selection Committee: R. G. Charters, I. A. A. MacGregor, R. D. S. Munro, C. M. Telfer, D. Grant
Coaches:
  National XV: C. M. Telfer, D. Grant (assistant)
  B XV: D. Grant, D. W. Morgan (assistant)
Medics:
  Doctors: D. A. D. Macleod, Dr J. C. M. Sharp, Dr K. B. Slawson
  Physiotherapists: D. A. McLean, R. C. McNaught
  Dentist: T. P. L. McGlashan
Chief Steward: G. McN. Reid
Historian and Librarian: A. M. C. Thorburn
Referees Advisory Panel Chairman: D. C. J. McMahon
Laws Advisory Panel Chairman: A. M. Hosie
District Union Secretaries: D. G. Mieras, J. M. R. Butters, J. F. McCaffer, A. G. Morgan, J. C. Robertson, D. F. Madsen
Auditors: Deloitte, Haskins and Sells
Solicitors: Strathern and Blair
Stockbrokers: Speirs and Jeffrey
Insurance Brokers: Sedgwick UK Ltd
Bankers: Royal Bank of Scotland
Architects: T. M. Miller and Partners
Surveyors: Peter S. Shearer
Home International Match Sponsors: The Royal Bank of Scotland plc

182

Club Championship Sponsors: Schweppes Ltd
Youth Leagues Sponsors: The Royal Bank of Scotland plc
Ground Advertising Agents: Arena Sports Advertising Ltd
Programmes Agents: Programme Publications Ltd
Hospitality Area Agents: Ring and Brymer Ltd
Home International Match Television and Radio: British Broadcasting
   Corporation
Sub-Committees: Selection, Amateur Status, Coaching and Youth Develop-
   ment, Emergency, Equipment, Field, Finance, Future of Scottish Rugby,
   Hospitality, Laws, Referees, Schools' Liaison, Ticket Allocation, Tours,
   Travel and Hotel Accommodation for Away Matches, *Ad hoc*, SRU
   Championship
Advisory Panels: Referees' Advisory Panel (and National Referee Observers),
   Coaching Advisory Panel (and Advisory Coaches), Laws Advisory Panel,
   Medical Services Advisory Committee

Appendix 6

THE SELECTION COMMITTEE

The first Constitution of 1873 stated that one object of the Union was the selection of the International teams and this function was indeed carried out by the entire Committee up to the 1913–14 season. A motion to have a Selection Committee consisting of the President, Vice-President with two past players, one each from the East and West Districts, was defeated at the 1887 AGM.

After the First World War, the 1919–20 Committee did nominate a separate Selection Committee of five which included four co-opted from non-Union Committee members. A similar Committee, containing, however, only one co-opted member, operated for the next two seasons, whereafter control reverted to the entire elected Union Committee.

With the acquisition of Murrayfield the burden on the Committee increased so much that, year after year, various sub-committees had to be set-up. In 1928 and 1930 there were two attempts within the Committee and another at the 1931 AGM to set-up a Selection Sub-Committee, but these failed and it was not until after the 1932 AGM that the Committee implemented a motion and established a five-man sub-committee drawn from its own elected members. However, in 1955–56 J.M. Bannerman came in as a co-opted member and others have been co-opted at intervals since then.

Selection Committee 1919–20
C.J.N. Fleming (Melrose); J.E. Crabbie* (Edin. Acads.); J.G. Cunningham* (Watsonians); J.T. Tulloch* (Kelvinside Acads.); G.T. Campbell* (London Scot.).

Selection Committee 1920–21 / 1921–22
J.M. Dykes (Glas. HSFP); J. Macgill (Glas. Acads.); J.M. Tennent (West of Scot.); T. Scott (Langholm); J.E. Crabbie* (Edin. Acads.).

Selection Committees 1932–84

R. L. Scott (Hawick)	1932–39	1945–48		10
D. Drysdale (London Scot.)	1932–39	1945–46	1947–50	11
M. A. Allan (Glas. Acads.)	1932–39	1948–53		12
F. J. C. Moffat (Watsonians)	1932–39	1945–46		8
R. L. H. Donald (Glas. HSFP)	1932–33			1
J. B. Nelson (Glas. Acads.)	1933–36			3
J. C. H. Ireland (Glas. HSFP)	1936–39	1945–48		6
R. M. Meldrum (RHSFP)	1945–46			1
H. Waddell (Glas. Acads.)	1946–52			6
R. J. Henderson (Edin. Acads.)	1946–47			1
D. S. Kerr (Heriot's FP)	1946–50	1951–52	1953–56	8
R. J. Hogg (Gala)	1948–52			4
R. W. Shaw (Glas. HSFP)	1950–55			5
D. A. Thom (London Scot.)	1950–51	1952–54		3
D. D. Curr (Mel. Coll. FP)	1952–55			3
W. E. Bryce (Selkirk)	1952–54			2
A. H. Brown (Heriot's FP)	1952–53	1954–56		3
C. W. Drummond (Melrose)	1954–69			15
J. M. Bannerman* (Glas. HSFP)	1955–58			3
A. W. Wilson (Dunfermline)	1955–63			8
G. G. Crerar (Glas. Acads.)	1956–60	1962–68		10
R. F. Kelly (Watsonians)	1956–58			2
D. E. Muir* (Heriot's FP)	1958–62			4
W. C. W. Murdoch (Hillhead HSFP)	1958–62	1963–67		8
H. S. P. Monro (Langholm)	1959–67			8
A. D. Govan (Stewart's Coll. FP)	1962–73			11
J. W. Y. Kemp (Glas. HSFP)	1967–78			11
G. W. Thomson (Watsonians)	1967–77			10
G. Burrell (Gala)	1968–76			8
T. Pearson (Howe of Fife)	1969–80			11
I. H. P. Laughland* (London Scot.)	1969–72			3
A. W. Harper (RHSFP)	1973–79			6
I. A. A. MacGregor (Glas. Acads.)	1976–			8
R. G. Charters (Hawick)	1977–			7
N. A. McEwan* (Highland)	1978–80			2
J. W. Telfer* (Melrose)	1979–82	1983–84		4
R. D. S. Munro (Leith Acads.)	1980–			4
C. M. Telfer* (Hawick)	1980–			4
D. F. Madsen* (Gosforth)	1982–83			1

* Co-opted Member

Coaching at International Level
Prior to 1971 it fell to the Selectors to assist the Scotland Captain to organise his team. In 1971 an Adviser to the Captain was appointed and in 1977 a Coach was appointed.

	National xv	B xv
W. Dickinson (Jordanhill)	Adviser to Captain 1971–77	
N. A. McEwan (Highland)	Coach 1977–80	
J. W. Telfer (Melrose)	Coach 1980–82; 1983–84	Coach 1974–81
C. M. Telfer (Hawick)	Asst. Coach 1980–82; 1983–84 Coach 1982–83	Coach 1981–82; 1983–84
D. Grant (Hawick)	Asst. Coach 1982–83	Asst. Coach 1983–84
I. R. McGeechan (Headingley)		Coach 1982–83
A. C. McNish (Watsonians)		Asst. Coach 1981–82
J. R. Dixon (Jordanhill)		Asst. Coach 1982–83

Appendix 7

INTERNATIONAL MATCH RESULTS, 1871–1984

Prior to the 1876 season, matches were won by the majority of goals scored. This included converted tries, dropped goals, goals from a mark and the seldom-found field goal. There was no points scoring scheme and tries had no scoring value. At their AGM in 1875, the RFU discussed a points scoring system which would have given 10 points for each goal scored, 5 points for a try and 1 point for a touch down or a touch in goal. The scheme as proposed was not adopted.

A revised scheme was suggested in November 1875, thus:

> A match shall be decided by a majority of goals but if the number of goals be equal, or no goal be kicked, by a majority of tries; if no goal be kicked or try obtained, the match shall be drawn.

The following month, December 1875, the SFU Committee voted to adopt this new ruling and announced that it should operate from the start of the new season.

In 1882, a penalty kick for offside was introduced into the rules but no goal could be dropped or placed from such an award. In 1888, the RFU decided that a goal could be scored from a penalty kick but it was not until 1891 that this new rule was adopted by the IB.

A points scoring scheme in international matches was introduced in season 1890–91 when the IB system was adopted. Prior to that time, various experiments had been tried but confusion over different scoring values in the Home Countries caused difficulties. The following table shows the scoring values since season 1890–91. In season 1977–78, the goal from a mark was discontinued with the introduction of the free kick.

	Goal from mark	Conversion	Dropped goal	Penalty goal	Try
1889–90	3	2	3	2	2
1890–91	3	2	3	2	1
1891–92 to 1892–93	4	3	4	3	2
1893–94 to 1904–05	4	2	4	3	3
1905–06 to 1947–48	3	2	4	3	3
1948–49 to 1970–71	3	2	3	3	3
1971–72 to 1976–77	3	2	3	3	4
1977–78 to present	void	2	3	3	4

The 1878 Scotland v Ireland match, scheduled to be played in Glasgow, did not take place owing to disagreements between the two Irish Unions.

In 1885, the match against Ireland, in Belfast, was abandoned after 20 minutes play because of the appalling weather conditions—gale force winds and heavy rain. It was agreed to play a second match at Raeburn Place a month later.

Scheduled matches against England, in 1885, 1888 and 1889, were not played because of the dispute over the 1884 game. The resultant discussions led to the firm establishment of the new IB early in 1890.

The games v Wales in 1897 and 1898 were not played because Wales had withdrawn from the IB between February 1897 and February 1898.

Games were not played against France between 1914 and 1919, and between 1932 and 1939 due to broken relationships.

During the Second World War, 'Services' matches were played against England: 1941–42, H, W 21–6; A, W 8–5. 1942–43, H, L 6–29; A, L 19–24. 1943–44, H, L 13–23; A, L 15–27. 1944–45, A, W 18–11; H, L 5–16.

The political situation in 1972 prevented the playing of the match v Ireland.

For fuller details and reports of Scotland's international matches, 1870–71 to 1979–80, see A.M.C.Thorburn, *The History of Scottish Rugby* (Johnston & Bacon, 1980).

Games in a summer tour after a season end are shown in the following season.

Key to the table:

H – home	mg – goal from a mark	J – Japan
A – Away	NG – No game	NSW – New South Wales
W – Won	A – Australia	NZ – New Zealand
L – Lost	Arg – Argentina	P – President's XV (SRU Centenary)
D – Drawn	Bar – Barbarians	R – Romania
g – Goal	C – Canada	SA – South Africa
t – Try	F – France	T – Tonga
d – Drop goal	Fj – Fiji	* – No caps awarded

INTERNATIONAL MATCHES

	England	Ireland	Wales	France	Other
1870–71	H–W g1,t1–t1				
1871–72	A–L d1,–g1,d1,t2				
1872–73	H–D 0–0				
1873–74	A–L t1–d1				
1874–75	H–D 0–0				
1875–76	A–L 0–g1,t1				
1876–77	H–W d1–0	A–W g4,d2,t2–0			
1877–78	A–D 0–0	NG			
1878–79	H–D d1–g1	A–W g1,d1,t1–0			
1879–80	A–L g1–g2,t3	H–W g1,d2,t2–0			
1880–81	H–D g1,t1–d1,t1	A–L t1–d1			
1881–82	A–W t2–0	H–W t2–0			

188

	England	Ireland	Wales	France	Other
1882–83	H–L t1–t2	A–W g1,t1–0	H–W g3–g1		
1883–84	A–L t1–g1	H–W g2,t2–t1	A–W d1,t1–0		
1884–85	N G	A–Aban. t1–0 H–W g1,t2–0	H–D 0–0		
1885–86	H–D 0–0	H–W g3,d1,t2–0	A–W g2,t1–0		
1886–87	A–D t1–t1	A–W g1,mg1,t2–0	H–W g4,t8–0		
1887–88	N G	H–W g1–0	A–L 0–t1		
1888–89	N G	A–W d1–0	H–W t2–0		
1889–90	H–L 0–6	H–W 5–0	A–W 8–2		
1890–91	A–W 9–3	A–W 14–0	H–W 15–0		
1891–92	H–L 0–5	H–W 2–0	A–W 7–2		
1892–93	A–W 8–0	A–D 0–0	H–L 0–9		
1893–94	H–W 6–0	A–L 0–5	A–L 0–7		
1894–95	A–W 6–3	H–W 6–0	H–W 5–4		
1895–96	H–W 11–0	A–D 0–0	A–L 0–6		
1896–97	A–L 3–12	H–W 8–3	N G		
1897–98	H–D 3–3	A–W 8–0	N G		
1898–99	A–W 5–0	H–L 3–9	H–W 21–10		
1899–00	H–D 0–0	A–D 0–0	A–L 3–12		
1900–01	A–W 18–3	H–W 9–5	H–W 18–8		
1901–02	H–L 3–6	A–L 0–5	A–L 5–14		
1902–03	A–W 10–6	H–W 3–0	H–W 6–0		
1903–04	H–W 6–3	A–W 19–3	A–L 3–21		
1904–05	A–W 8–0	H–L 5–11	H–L 3–6		
1905–06	H–L 3–9	A–W 13–6	A–L 3–9		NZ: H–L 7–12
1906–07	A–W 8–3	H–W 15–3	H–W 6–3		SA: H–W 6–0
1907–08	H–W 16–10	A–L 11–16	A–L 5–6		
1908–09	A–W 18–8	H–W 9–3	H–L 3–5		
1909–10	H–L 5–14	A–W 14–0	A–L 0–14	H–W 27–0	
1910–11	A–L 8–13	H–L 10–16	H–L 10–32	A–L 15–16	
1911–12	H–W 8–3	A–L 8–10	A–L 6–21	H–W 31–3	

	England	Ireland	Wales	France	Other
1912–13	A–L 0–3	H–W 29–14	H–L 0–8	A–W 21–3	SA: H–L 0–16
1913–14	H–L 15–16	A–L 0–6	A–L 5–24	NG	
1919–20	A–L 4–13	H–W 19–0	H–W 9–5	A–W 5–0	
1920–21	H–L 0–18	A–L 8–9	A–W 14–8	H–L 0–3	
1921–22	A–L 5–11	H–W 6–3	H–D 9–9	A–D 3–3	
1922–23	H–L 6–8	A–W 13–3	A–W 11–8	H–W 16–3	
1923–24	A–L 0–19	H–W 13–8	H–W 35–10	A–L 10–12	
1924–25	H–W 14–11	A–W 14–8	A–W 24–14	H–W 25–4	
1925–26	A–W 17–9	H–L 0–3	H–W 8–5	A–W 20–6	
1926–27	H–W 21–13	A–L 0–6	A–W 5–0	H–W 23–6	
1927–28	A–L 0–6	H–L 5–13	H–L 0–13	A–W 15–6	NSW: H–W 10–8
1928–29	H–W 12–6	A–W 16–7	A–L 7–14	H–W 6–3	
1929–30	A–D 0–0	H–L 11–14	H–W 12–9	A–L 3–7	
1930–31	H–W 28–19	A–L 5–8	A–L 8–13	H–W 6–4	
1931–32	A–L 3–16	H–L 8–20	H–L 0–6	NG	SA: H–L 3–6
1932–33	H–W 3–0	A–W 8–6	A–W 11–3	NG	
1933–34	A–L 3–6	H–W 16–9	H–L 6–13	NG	
1934–35	H–W 10–7	A–L 5–12	A–L 6–10	NG	
1935–36	A–L 8–9	H–L 4–10	H–L 3–13	NG	NZ: H–L 8–18
1936–37	H–L 3–6	A–L 4–11	A–W 13–6	NG	
1937–38	A–W 21–16	H–W 23–14	H–W 8–6	NG	
1938–39	H–L 6–9	A–L 3–12	A–L 3–11	NG	
1945–46 (unofficial)	A–L 8–12* H–W 27–0*	H–W 9–0*	A–W 25–6* H–W 13–11*		NZ Army: H–W 11–6*
1946–47	A–L 5–24	H–L 0–3	H–L 8–22	A–L 3–8	
1947–48	H–W 6–3	A–L 0–6	A–L 0–14	H–W 9–8	A: H–L 7–16
1948–49	A–L 3–19	H–L 3–13	H–W 6–5	A–W 8–0	
1949–50	H–W 13–11	A–L 0–21	A–L 0–12	H–W 8–5	
1950–51	A–L 3–5	H–L 5–6	H–W 19–0	A–L 12–14	
1951–52	H–L 3–19	A–L 8–12	A–L 0–11	H–L 11–13	SA: H–L 0–44
1952–53	A–L 8–26	H–L 8–26	H–L 0–12	A–L 5–11	

	England	Ireland	Wales	France	Other
1953–54	H–L 3–13	A–L 0–6	A–L 3–15	H–L 0–3	NZ: H–L 0–3
1954–55	A–L 6–9	H–W 12–3	H–W 14–8	A–L 0–15	
1955–56	H–L 6–11	A–L 10–14	A–L 3–9	H–W 12–0	
1956–57	A–L 3–16	H–L 3–5	H–W 9–6	A–W 6–0	
1957–58	H–D 3–3	A–L 6–12	A–L 3–8	H–W 11–9	A: H–W 12–8
1958–59	A–D 3–3	H–L 3–8	H–W 6–5	A–L 0–9	
1959–60	H–L 12–21	A–W 6–5	A–L 0–8	H–L 11–13	
1960–61	A–L 0–6	H–W 16–8	H–W 3–0	A–L 0–11	SA: A–L 10–18 SA: H–L 5–12
1961–62	H–D 3–3	A–W 20–6	A–W 8–3	H–L 3–11	
1962–63	A–L 8–10	H–W 3–0	H–L 0–6	A–W 11–6	
1963–64	H–W 15–6	A–W 6–3	A–L 3–11	H–W 10–0	NZ: H–D 0–0
1964–65	A–D 3–3	H–L 6–16	H–L 12–14	A–L 8–16	C: A– SA: H–W 8–5
1965–66	H–W 6–3	A–W 11–3	A–L 3–8	H–D 3–3	
1966–67	A–L 14–27	H–L 3–5	H–W 11–5	A–W 9–8	A: H–W 11–5
1967–68	H–L 6–8	A–L 6–14	A–L 0–5	H–L 6–8	NZ: H–L 3–14
1968–69	A–L 3–8	H–L 0–16	H–L 3–17	A–W 6–3	A: H–W 9–3
1969–70	H–W 14–5	A–L 11–16	A–L 9–18	H–L 9–11	Arg: A–L 3–20* Arg: A–W 6–3* SA: H–W 6–3 Bar: H–L 17–33*
1970–71	A–W 16–15 H–W 26–6	H–L 5–17	H–L 18–19	A–L 8–13	A: A–L 3–23
1971–72	H–W 23–9	NG	A–L 12–35	H–W 20–9	
1972–73	A–L 13–20	H–W 19–14	H–W 10–9	A–L 13–16	NZ: H–L 9–14 P: H–W 27–16
1973–74	H–W 16–14	A–L 6–9	A–L 0–6	H–W 19–6	Arg: H–W 12–11*
1974–75	A–L 6–7	H–W 20–13	H–W 12–10	A–L 9–10	T: H–W 44–8*
1975–76	H–W 22–12	A–W 15–6	A–L 6–28	H–L 6–13	NZ: A–L 0–24 A: H–W 10–3
1976–77	A–L 6–26	H–W 21–18	H–L 9–18	A–L 3–23	J: H–W 34–9*
1977–78	H–L 0–15	A–L 9–12	A–L 14–22	H–L 16–19	J: A–W 74–9*
1978–79	A–D 7–7	H–D 11–11	H–L 13–19	A–L 17–21	NZ: H–L 9–18
1979–80	H–L 18–30	A–L 15–22	A–L 6–17	H–W 22–14	NZ: H–L 6–20

INTERNATIONAL MATCHES

	England	Ireland	Wales	France	Other
1980–81	A–L 17–23	H–W 10–9	H–W 15–6	A–L 9–16	F: A–
1981–82	H–D 9–9	A–L 12–21	A–W 34–18	H–W 16–7	NZ: A–L 4–11 NZ: A–L 15–40 R: H–W 12–6 A: H–W 24–15
1982–83	A–W 22–12	H–L 13–15	H–L 15–19	A–L 15–19	A: A–W 12–7 A: A–L 9–33 Fj: H–W 32–12* Bar: H–L 13–26*
1983–84	H–W 18–6	A–W 32–9	A–W 15–9	H–W 21–12	NZ: H–D 25–25

	England					Ireland					Wales					France					Other				
	P	W	D	L	O	P	W	D	L	O	P	W	D	L	O	P	W	D	L	O		P	W	D	L	O
Totals	100	37	16	47	3	95	47	5	43	2	88	37	2	49	2	54	26	2	26	9	NZ	12	0	2	10	0
																					SA	8	3	0	5	0
																					A	9	6	0	3	0

B INTERNATIONALS   OTHER INTERNATIONALS

	France	Ireland	OTHER INTERNATIONALS
1971–72	A–L 9–23		
1972–73	H–L 15–17		
1973–74	A–L 9–13		
1974–75	H–W 19–6		
1975–76	A–L 6–14		
1976–77	H–L 16–19		
1977–78	A–L 3–11	H–L 3–7	
1978–79	H–cancelled (snow)		
1979–80	A–W 6–0	A–W 20–13	
1980–81	H–W 18–4		
1981–82	A–L 4–44		West Germany U-18: A–L 12–15
1982–83	H–L 12–26		
1983–84	A–W 13–10	H–W 22–13	West Germany U-18: H–W 9–7 Belgium U-18: A–W 35–10 Netherlands U-21: A–W 24–9

Appendix 8

INTERNATIONAL REFEREES

In the early International encounters between Scotland and England the umpire and, eventually, the referee supported by two umpires (one from each country), was invariably a senior member of the Home Union Committee. Following the Calcutta Cup match at Raeburn Place in 1881, which Scotland drew by a late score and conversion, the President of the RFU made some scathing remarks about the Scottish refereeing which were not appreciated. The official concerned was D.H.Watson, President of the SFU, while J.Reid, the Vice-President, was the Scottish umpire.

However, a positive step was taken by England, who asked an Irishman, H.L.Robinson, to referee the next Calcutta Cup game at Manchester in 1882, and this use of a neutral referee was continued in all later International games. Two years later at Blackheath in 1884, the referee was again an Irishman and an even greater crisis arose over the famous 'knock-forward' decision from which England scored their much-disputed winning score. The controversy over the legality of the score led to the formation of the IB and was not settled until the arbitration decision in 1890.

Scottish Referees (and Umpires)

H. H. Almond (Loretto)	1	1871 S V E	
B. Hall Blyth (Merchistonians)	2	1872 E V S	1873 S V E
Name(s) not known	2	1874 E V S and 1875 S V E	
A. Buchanan (RHSFP)	2	1877 I V S	1880 S V I
W. Cross (Glas. Acads.)	1	1877 S V E	
J. Chiene (Edin. Acads.)	1	1879 I V S	
G. R. Fleming (Glas. Acads.)	1	1879 S V E	
D. H. Watson (Glas. Acads.)	1	1881 S V E	
A. G. Petrie (RHSFP)	1	1882 S V I	
A. S. Pattison	1	1883 E V I	
J. S. Lang (Glas. Univ.)	1	1884 I V E	
J. A. Gardner (Edin. Acads.)	2	1884 E V W	1887 W V I
A. R. Don Wauchope (Fet.-Lor.)	3	1889 W V I	1890 E V I 1893 I V E
R. D. Rainie (Edin. Wands.)	3	1890 E V W	1891 W V E
		1894 I V W	
M. C. McEwan (Edin. Acads.)	1	1892 E V W	
D. S. Morton (West of Scot.)	1	1893 W V E	
J. A. Smith (RHSFP)	3	1892 E V I	1894 E V W
		1895 W V E	

D. G. Findlay (West of Scot.)	7	1895 I V E	1896 E V I, E V W		
		1897 I V E	1398 E V I	1899 I V E	
		1900 E V I			
A. Turnbull (Hawick)	7	1898 I V W	1899 W V E, W V I		
		1900 E V W, I V W	1901 I V E, W V E		
R. Welsh (Watsonians)	3	1902 E V I	1903 W V E		
		1905 I V E			
J. C. Findlay (West of Scot.)	6	1902 I V W	1903 I V E		
		1904 E V W, I V W	1906 I V NZ		
		1911 I V F			
J. D. Dallas (Watsonians)	8	1906 W V NZ	1908 I V W		
		1909 I V E, W V E	1910 E V W, I V W		
		1911 I V E	1912 I V W		
A. Jardine (Hawick)	1	1906 E V W			
J. W. Simpson (RHSFP)	1	1906 I V W			
J. T. Tulloch (Kelvin Acads.)	9	1907 E V SA, I V SA, I V E			
		1908 E V W	1912 E V W		
		1913 E V SA	1914 I V W		
		1920 W V E	1924 W V I		
J. I. Gillespie (Edin. Acads.)	2	1907 W V E	1911 W V E		
G. Bowden	1	1910 F V E			
J. R. C. Greenlees (Kelvin. Acads.)	2	1913 I V E	1914 E V W		
J. G. Cunningham (Watsonians)	2	1913 W V I	1921 F V I		
W. A. Robertson (Watsonians)	2	1920 I V E, E V F			
J. M. Tennent (West of Scot.)	7	1920 I V F	1921 I V W		
		1922 I V E, W V E, E V F, I V F			
		1923 I V W			
J. C. Sturrock (RHSFP)	3	1921 E V W, F V E	1922 W V I		
J. M. B. Scott (Edin. Acads.)	1	1923 E V W			
A. W. Angus (Watsonians)	2	1924 W V E	1928 I V NSW		
A. A. Lawrie (Edin. Wands.)	3	1924 I V F	1925 E V W		
		1926 I V F			
J. Macgill (Glas. Acads.)	2	1925 F V I	1929 I V W		
R. L. Scott (Hawick)	2	1927 E V W, F V I			
T. H. H. Warren (Kelvin. Acads.)	1	1928 W V I			
C. Anderson	1	1928 I V F			
M. A. Allan (Glas. Acads.)	11	1931 I V W	1932 I V SA		
		1933 E V I, I V W	1934 I V E		
		1935 E V I, I V W	1936 I V E		
		1937 I V W	1947 I V E		
		1948 I V W			
W. Burnet (Hawick)	2	1932 I V E	1934 W V I		
F. J. C. Moffat (Watsonians)	1	1932 W V E			
R. A. Beattie (Watsonians)	8	1937 E V W	1938 W V E		
		1947 W V E	1948 I V A, E V W		
		1949 I V E	1950 E V I, I V W		
J. C. H. Ireland (Glas. HSFP)	5	1938 I V E, W V I	1939 E V I, E V W, I V W		
W. C. W. Murdoch (Hillhead HSFP)	4	1951 W V I	1952 F V E, E V SA, I V SA		

A. W. C. Austin (Glas. HSFP)   3   1952 W v F   1953 I v E
1954 I v W

A. I. Dickie (Gala)   11   1954 E v I, F v I, W v F
1955 I v E, W v I   1956 E v I,
I v W   1957 I v E, W v E
1958 W v A, W v F

J. A. S. Taylor (Musselburgh)   7   1957 W v I   1960 E v W, F v E,
W v SA   1962 E v W, F v I, I v W

G. Burrell (Gala)   2   1958 E v I   1959 W v I

D. C. J. McMahon (Heriot's FP)   6   1961 W v I   1963 E v F
1964 E v NZ
1967 E v NZ, W v E
1969 W v I

H. B. Laidlaw (Hawick)   5   1963 I v E   1964 W v F
1965 I v E   1968 F v E, W v F

R. P. Burrell (Gala)   5   1966 I v W   1967 I v F, F v NZ
1969 I v E, F v W

T. F. E. Grierson (Hawick)   4   1970 I v SA   1972 F v E
1973 W v I   1975 E v F

J. Young (Heriot's FP)   3   1971 F v W   1972 E v W
1973 E v NZ

A. M. Hosie (Hillhead)   21   1973 I v E   1974 F v I
1975 W v E   1976 E v I,
F v A   1977 F v W, I v F
1978 Canada v F   1979 W v I, I v E
1980 W v F, F v I   1981 E v F,
R v NZ   1982 E v I, NZ v A(2),
R v F   1983 I v F
1984 E v NZ, F v E

N. R. Sanson (Marr & Lond. Scot.)   18   1974 W v F, F v SA   1975 I v P XV,
SA v F(2), Japan v W(2), F v R
1976 I v A, I v W, W v Arg.
1977 W v I, Bar. v Br.Lions
1978 F v E, E v W, E v NZ, Bar. v NZ
1979 E v NZ

J. A. Short (Hawick)   3   1980 F v R   1981 F v Japan
1982 I v W

J. B. Anderson (Corstorphine)   7   1981 W v E, I v A   1982 Ru. v F,
E v Fiji   1983 I v E, A v NZ
1984 E v W

Appendix 9

ROLL OF HONOUR

The names recorded are of those who played rugby for Scotland at international level.

The Boer War 1899–1902
  1900   D. B. Monypenny (London Scottish)

The 1914–1918 War
  1914   R. F. Simson (London Scottish)
         J. L. Huggan (London Scottish and Jed-Forest)
         J. Ross (London Scottish)
         L. Robertson (London Scottish and United Services)
  1915   F. H. Turner (Oxford University and Liverpool)
         J. Pearson (Watsonians)
         D. M. Bain (Oxford University)
         W. C. Church (Glasgow Academicals)
         E. T. Young (Glasgow Academicals)
         P. C. B. Blair (Cambridge University)
         W. M. Wallace (Cambridge University)
         D. R. Bedell-Sivright (Cambridge Univ. and Edinburgh Univ.)
         W. M. Dickson (Blackheath and Oxford University)
  1916   D. D. Howie (Kirkcaldy)
         A. Ross (Royal High School FP)
         C. H. Abercrombie (United Services)
         J. S. Wilson (United Services and London Scottish)
         R. Fraser (Cambridge University)
         E. Milroy (Watsonians)
  1917   J. G. Will (Cambridge University)
         T. A. Nelson (Oxford University)
         W. T. Forrest (Hawick)
         A. L. Wade (London Scottish)
         J. Y. M. Henderson (Watsonians)
         J. A. Campbell (Cambridge University)
         S. S. L. Steyn (Oxford University)
  1918   G. A. W. Lamond (Kelvinside Academicals)
         W. R. Hutchison (Glasgow High School FP)
         R. E. Gordon (Royal Artillery)
         W. R. Sutherland (Hawick)

The 1939–1945 War
- 1940 D. K. A. Mackenzie (Edinburgh Wanderers)
- 1941 T. F. Dorward (Gala)
  - A. W. Symington (Cambridge University)
- 1942 P. Munro (Oxford University and London Scottish)
  - J. M. Ritchie (Watsonians)
  - R. M. Kinnear (Geo. Heriot's School FP)
  - W. A. Ross (Hillhead High School FP)
  - J. G. S. Forrest (Cambridge University)
  - D. St C. Ford (United Services)
- 1943 G. Roberts (Watsonians)
  - W. M. Penman (Royal Air Force)
- 1944 A. S. B. McNeil (Watsonians)
  - W. N. Renwick (London Scottish and Edinburgh Wanderers)
  - G. H. Gallie (Edinburgh Academicals)
- 1945 E. H. Liddell (Edinburgh University)

Appendix 10

INTERNATIONAL DINNER MENU
Glasgow, 3 March 1873

Chairman: Hon. F. J. Moncreiff   *Croupier*: J. W. Arthur, Esq.

POTAGES

Mock Turtle   Oxtail   Cockie Leekie
Misa's Oloroso Sherry

POISSONS

Salmon, with Cucumber   Fillet of Whiting, à la Maître d'Hotel
Chablis, Steinberg 1857

ENTREES

Scotch Haggis   Sweetbreads, à la Financier   Lobster cutlets, à la Cardinal
Supreme de Volaille aux Truffles   Fricandeau of Veal Sauce Tomato
Sparkling Hock, Creme de Marcobrun

RELEVES

Sirloin of Beef, Horse Radish   Saddle of Mutton, with Jelly
Roast Quarter Lamb, Mint Sauce   Boiled Turkeys, Macaroni Sauce
Brunswick Ham   Ox Tongues
Pollinger's Extra Dry Champagne 1865

ENTREMETS

Meringue Neapolitaine   Compote of Apricot   Cabinet Pudding
Gooseberry Tart   Blancmange   Maraschino Jelly

GLACES

Vanilla   Raspberry

DESSERT

Ch. Leoville 1862   Port 1851   Royal Pale Amontillado   Liquers

The Queen	*The Chair*
The Prince and Princess of Wales and other Members of the Royal Family	*The Chair*
The Army, Navy and Reserve Forces	*The Chair*
The English Twenty	*The Chair*
	F. Stokes
The Scotch Twenty	F. Stokes
	F. J. Moncreiff
Rugby Football	J. W. Arthur
	D. F. Turner
The Rugby Football Unions	B. Hall Blyth
	A. G. Guillemard
	Dr J. Chiene
The Match Committee	A. G. Guillemard
	B. Hall Blyth
The Chairman	A. St G. Hamersley
	F. J. Moncreiff
The Ladies	Mr Forrester
	Mr Luscombe

R. J. Phillips: STORY OF SCOTTISH RUGBY

'He (Arthur Budd) does full credit to Scottish hospitality, with the reservation that it might have ended seriously for an English forward, who was picked up by some of his companions at midnight driving one of Her Majesty's mail carts round the town.'

It is interesting that the Scottish Football Union and its President, Dr John Chiene, appear on the Toast List, because the Union was only constituted at a meeting held after the match that same afternoon.

Appendix 11

THE NEW ZEALAND AFFAIR

From *The Scotsman*, Monday, 5 May 1924:

'The Annual Meeting was held in private . . . an official report was supplied to the Press. . . .

No mention is made of anything being said regarding the reason why the New Zealand Rugby team are not to come to Scotland, but a statement was made by the Chairman on the subject and it was pointed out that there was no quarrel between the Scottish Union and that of New Zealand. It was shown that it was the English Union that Scotland had a grievance against in that they had taken upon themselves the making of all arrangements for the New Zealanders' visit, which was against an agreement come to some years ago when it was decided by all the countries, England, Scotland, Wales, and Ireland . . . that in future all tours, either from Britain or to Britain, shall be under the auspices and control of the Rugby International Board. Obviously there had been a break in that agreement and because of that the Scottish Union had decided to decline the two matches with the New Zealanders offered to them by the English Union.'

A similar statement appeared in the *Glasgow Herald*.

Appendix 12

The Committee has from time to time at the Annual Meetings of the Union given detailed statements of their actings and policy in regard to Dominion Football, but recent events have decided them that the Clubs are entitled to a more permanent record of their views, as with new elements emerging in Clubs from day to day it is hardly fair to tax their loyalty unduly, in view of the fact that younger Members may not be aware of what older Members have heard.

Recently there have been in certain organs of the English Press attacks upon this Union in regard to their conduct of the recent visit of the New South Wales team, without a reply to which the Committee feel that their Clubs may be under some misapprehension.

In the first place the Committee would point out a fact which is either not generally known, or if known is sometimes conveniently forgotten, viz., that the International Board consists of ten Members – four from England and two from each of the other three Countries – and that the Board exists for two purposes:

1. For framing the Laws of the Game for International Matches.
2. For settling International disputes.

Accordingly, the Board, as such, has nothing whatever to do with the arrangements connected with the visit of a British team to the Dominions or vice versa, these being undertaken by a committee appointed by the four Countries with equal representation, and no one Country is bound to participate in such tours. It was, therefore, quite wrong and misleading, that the New South Wales team were even published as being the guests of the International Board, as the invitation asked for by New South Wales was sent in name of the four Countries, and was so accepted.

Further, all arrangements for this tour were made by a committee of two from each Country, along with an Honorary Treasurer and a Secretary, and those arrangements were on the same lines as obtained when the last South African team visited this Country, and the tour was similarly managed. The same arrangements applied when British teams toured abroad, and the Committee were most careful, as they were of opinion that all such tours should be conducted on the same lines.

In March 1927 a request was made by the New South Wales Union that, in addition to the travelling expenses of their team back to Australia, they should be given a grant to enable them to return via Canada and Vancouver, as it appeared had been done in the case of the last New Zealand team. The Tour Committee, after careful consideration, decided that as the New South Wales team were guaranteed £500 at the Vancouver end, they would grant the sum of £600 towards this purpose, but no more. Most unfortunately the matter did not end there, as, after the arrival of the New South Wales team, the request for an additional £400 was made, notwithstanding the above decision of the Committee. After correspondence, it was agreed that the Committee of the four Countries should meet and discuss this renewed request, and accordingly a meeting was held at Chester on 10 December 1927, when after discussion and careful consideration, the following Resolution was unanimously passed:

The New South Wales Tour Committee met at the Queen's Hotel, Chester, on the 10th December 1927, to consider the application from Dr L.G. Brown, on behalf of the New South Wales team, for an additional grant of £400 (over the £600 already allowed) towards the expenses of returning to New South Wales via Vancouver, when it was decided that this application could not be entertained. When the arrangements for the visit to France were left in the hands of the New South Wales Union it was not contemplated by this Committee that these would be on any lines other than those laid down by the International Board and accepted by the four Home Counties, viz.: 'That the visiting team should be the guests of the countries visited'. If this Committee had had any idea that a profit (which it is now informed by Dr Brown amounts to £1,600) was to have been made out of the visit to France, it (the Committee) would not have allowed the arrangements to have left their hands. This Committee strongly deprecates the financial arrangements made with France, as in its opinion it is contrary to the spirit in which these tours are arranged.

It has been deliberately stated that your Committee alone were responsible for this refusal to make a further grant, which is a very poor compliment to the representatives of the other countries. Following upon this, the above Resolution was reported to the International Board at their Meeting on 16 March 1928 and unanimously approved, and the Board at the same meeting unanimously passed the following additional Resolution, which has been adopted by your Committee:

That in the opinion of this Board, it be a condition of all invitations to visiting Unions and teams that such Unions or teams be the guests of the Unions or Clubs visited, and are not entitled to make any arrangements with either the home or other Unions or clubs under which payments or allowances in cash or otherwise above the actual travelling and hotel expenses incurred, be made to them or for their benefit or the benefit of their Unions or clubs.

From these facts it can be seen whether or not your Committee are out of sympathy in any way with the other countries on this matter, and what cause there can be for attaching any special onus to your Committee for any failure in the arrangements, of which they are certainly not aware, though it appears to exist in the imagination of certain critics. The Committee, while on this subject, desire to say that they were highly pleased to welcome such a sporting side as the New South Wales Team, who have, of course, no responsibility in the above matter, and while they did all they could to make their visit agreeable, they wish to thank those Clubs and private Members who assisted so materially to make the Tour in Scotland the success it was.

The Committee think it advisable to take this opportunity of saying a few words on their position in regard to Dominion Football generally, which has been constantly misrepresented in certain quarters.

When the first New Zealand and first South African Teams visited this country they came at their own risk, and not as guests of the Home Countries. In these circumstances, your Committee decided to hand over to the visitors the whole gate, so that the Union made no profit, and this was done in both cases. The propriety of this action, which might presumably enable Tourists to take home cash in their pockets, was discussed by the four countries, and the following extract from a Memorandum detailing the method of conduct of future Dominion Tours placed before the Committees of the four countries under date 18 May 1911 may be referred to: '1. That all Dominion Teams must come as guests, no division of profits to be considered'.

Then followed the details of how the tour was to be conducted and what travelling expenses were to be allowed. This was believed to be a binding agreement between the four countries as to the future conduct of Dominion Tours in this country. Accordingly, when the second South African Team visited this country in 1912, the tour was conducted on the lines thus laid down, without difficulty and without friction.

In March 1923 the four countries agreed by request that a British Team should visit South Africa in 1924 (summer), and that touring team contained numerous Scottish players. At the same time a cable from New Zealand was intimated to the effect that they considered they had a preference if England were touring, but would prefer to receive an invitation to tour England in 1924. Upon this no decision was taken.

In July 1923 your Committee were more than surprised to be advised that the Rugby Union were bringing over a New Zealand Team in 1924, and were asked if they wished fixtures. This arrangement was so absolutely opposed to the agreement formerly come to, under which the last South African Team visited this country, and would naturally open the way to any of the four countries having a right to entertain a Touring Team for their own profit, that they promptly declined to entertain the proposal, and, in any case, no fixtures would have been arranged by your Union, even if willing, under the financial arrangements which they understood were laid down by the Rugby Union. In addition, the visit almost overlapped the South African Tour, players in which could not be expected to do themselves justice in November and December after their return.

Your Committee have every sympathy with the encouragement of Dominion Football, but it must always be second in importance to Home Football, which is their first consideration, and they cannot be parties to any arrangement whereby any Dominion is to have a say in the government of the game at home, particularly as the matches between the Home Countries and the Dominions are only intermittent. The original request from the Dominion end was that a Conference might be held at stated times at which the Dominion views as to alterations in the Laws of the Game might be discussed, and this request was acceded to. Now, however, the demand is for a place on the International Board, and that a percentage of the gates taken at International Matches should be set aside to pay the travelling and other expenses of those meetings, and that those meetings should be held alternately, here and in the Dominions. Your Committee quite appreciate why a particular Dominion should find it necessary to adopt a particular Law of the Game not acceptable to the Home Unions, but they do not see why the Home Unions should be called upon to accept such Law, when such case could be met by any British team touring in a particular Dominion agreeing to accept the Laws played there, and vice versa. It is obvious that climatic and other reasons may prevent the use of such Laws at home, just as it is necessary for touring cricket teams to play on matting in some Countries, though not at home. Early in their negotiations it was evident that the main desire of the Dominion representatives was to make the Game faster, and, indeed, one Dominion representative, in pressing forward a suggested alteration, frankly stated that it had been adopted by his own Union as making the Game faster, more interesting to spectators, and had increased the gates. These reasons have not the sympathy of your Committee, who are satisfied from the public interest at present taken in our Game, that the Game is both sufficiently fast and interesting enough. It must not be forgotten that Rugby Football originated as a School Game, and your Committee will never consent to it being made so fast that schoolboys will be unable to play it without undue strain, and in this they are satisfied that they have the support of the Schools themselves, whose views should surely be considered, since for years the Game was practically maintained by them.

At the International Board Meeting in March 1928 the above referred-to consideration was given to a request from New Zealand that a British Team should tour there in season 1930. The feeling was definitely expressed that in view of past experience, it is useless now to send a British Team abroad unless it is absolutely a first-class team, failing which it does more harm than good, and in view of this the four countries regretfully had to decline the invitation. As it means a period of 6–7 months to undertake the tour, it does not seem fair to induce a young man engaged either in business or at a University, at a critical time in his career, to undertake such a mission, in addition to having to provide a certain amount of cash for his out-of-pocket expenses during that period.

H. M. Simson
Secy. SRU

204

Index

209

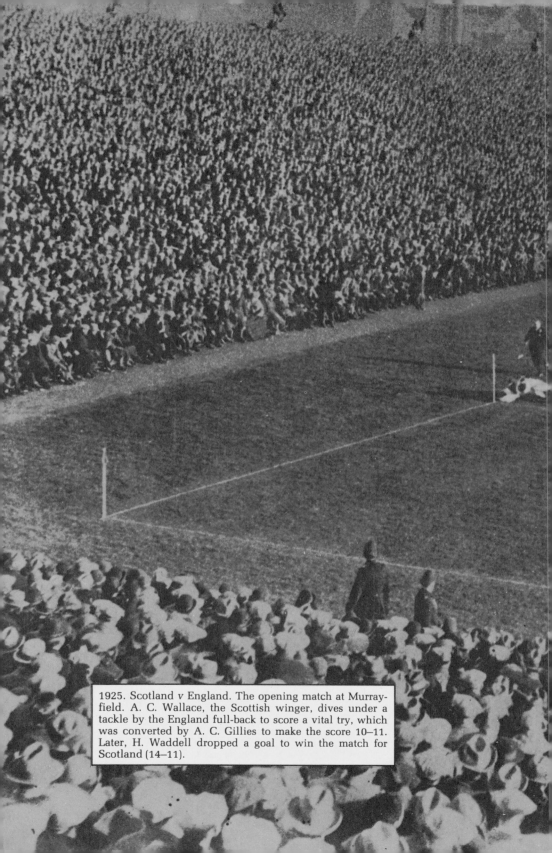

1925. Scotland v England. The opening match at Murray-field. A. C. Wallace, the Scottish winger, dives under a tackle by the England full-back to score a vital try, which was converted by A. C. Gillies to make the score 10–11. Later, H. Waddell dropped a goal to win the match for Scotland (14–11).